COMPARATIVE MENTAL HEALTH POLICY

From Institutional to Community Care

SIMON GOODWIN

SAGE Publications
London • Thousand Oaks • New Delhi

First published 1997

SAGE Publications Ltd
6 Bonhill Street
London EC2A 4PU

SAGE Publications Inc
2455 Teller Road
Thousand Oaks, California 91320

SAGE Publications India Pvt Ltd
32, M-Block Market
Greater Kailash - I
New Delhi 110 048

British Library Cataloguing in Publication data

A catalogue record for this book is available from the British Library

ISBN 0 8039 7728 X
ISBN 0 8039 7729 8 (pbk)

Library of Congress catalog record available

Typeset by Photoprint, Torquay, Devon
Printed in Great Britain by Biddles Ltd, Guildford, Surrey

COMPARATIVE MENTAL HEALTH POLICY

Contents

Introduction

Over the postwar period, in much of Western Europe and North America, it has generally come to be accepted that people experiencing mental health problems are, for the most part, better provided for in community rather than institutional settings (Jones, 1988; Walker, 1989). Accordingly, there has been a massive shift in emphasis from the provision of in-patient treatment in mental hospitals, towards the provision of a more varied and community-based set of services.

Support for this policy shift has, however, proven to be very much for the general principles underlying community care, of reintegration and normalization. In contrast, its practice has been fiercely criticized. The lack of funds for new community-based facilities (Aviram, 1990), the lack of imagination given to their development (Mechanic & Rochefort, 1990), and the lack of coordination between institutional and community services (Hafner et al., 1989) have all been frequent targets of criticism. The result for some service users has been homelessness (Schnabel, 1992), declining physical and mental health (Tessler & Dennis, 1992), and failure to integrate with the local community (Taylor, 1988).

A question that arises, therefore, is why are we doing this? Why, despite long-term, serious, and common failings in the mental health policies of many of the Western industrialized countries, do we continue to run down institutional care in favour of community care? There are, as we review later, numerous answers to these questions. Some writers maintain support for community care, some argue that the policy has a been a sham since its inception, and others that it has become so over the course of its development. Reflecting these different viewpoints, some writers argue that the policy, while problematic, remains the most appropriate means of providing for service users, while others argue that we should halt or even reverse its progress.

The intention of this book is to review the development of the postwar shift towards community care in Western Europe and North America, and to examine the main policy debates that have accompanied it. Chapter 1 offers a review of the policy development in a number of countries, and Chapters 2, 3 and 4 review the theoretical arguments that have been developed to explain the policy upheavals of the last 40 years. Chapter 5 develops an argument intended to build upon our existing knowledge and understanding of the nature and development of mental health policy. Chapter 6 develops a review of some of the main problems and issues that have arisen as a result of the policy shift, and Chapter 7 reviews the main debates concerning how these problems might be best overcome. The overall intention of the book is to offer an analytical review of the transition for institutional to community care for people with mental health problems: to identify the process of change, to offer explanation for why it has occurred, and to reach an assessment of its value.

Issues in comparative social policy analysis

Before proceeding with this, we should note the context within which the current vogue for comparative social policy analysis has arisen. Through the 1970s and 1980s, as the postwar consensus broke down, much attention was focused upon the issue of how to understand the nature and development of welfare states within the advanced capitalist countries. The New Right argued that the welfare state was inefficient, ineffective, and sapped the ability of private enterprise to produce goods and services. Substantial reductions in the scale and scope of state welfare activity were therefore considered inevitable (Stockman, 1986; King, 1987). Social democrats maintained that, despite recent setbacks, the welfare state could and would retain its central functions of compensating for injuries and adversity resulting from the operation of market economies, together with ensuring the maintenance of social cohesion (Donnison, 1979; Room, 1979). Marxists argued that the functions of the welfare state, to help sustain continued capital accumulation, social reproduction and legitimation of the social formation, were becoming increasingly contradictory; the crisis of capitalism was, in part, making itself apparent as a crisis of the welfare state (Gough, 1979; Offe, 1984).

Yet, by the mid-1980s, it was becoming apparent that none of these theoretical frameworks could describe and analyse adequately the pattern of development of welfare states in the advanced capitalist countries. In part, this derived from their failure to accurately predict developments in the relationship of economic, political and social affairs. In particular, recent change and development within the welfare arrangements of capitalist societies has been diverse. Rather than see a certain few discrete forces determine the nature and pattern of welfare service provision, what we have witnessed is a variety of developments that could not in the mid-1980s easily be accommodated within existing welfare theory (Heidenheimer et al., 1990). As Mishra noted, 'The variations, the choices and the options available, even within limits, have on the whole been played down. ... What the breakdown of the Keynesian welfare state paradigm has underlined above all is the possibility of variations' (1990, 4–5).

A key issue that has arisen concerns the relationship between general theories about the development of welfare states in the advanced capitalist countries, and the specific experience of each country. Central to this debate is the relationship between social structure and social agency; for example, to what extent is the class structure of capitalist societies a determining influence, and of what importance is the nature of the political system or the character of particular individuals in determining the nature of policy development? Furthermore, there has in recent years been increasing recognition of the analytical importance of the concepts of race and gender, in addition to class, in the study of policy development (Williams, 1989; Ginsburg, 1992). Reflecting these concerns, Ashford suggests a synthetic approach is required; that the growth of the welfare state was 'a gradual and often uninformed process propelled as much by ambitious politicians and rather visionary civil servants as by an abstract notion of a crumbling social order or of fears of major social unrest' (1986, 3–4).

It is in this context that a comparative approach has in recent years received growing interest and gained greater popularity as a method for taking social policy analysis forward. Such an approach allows for the identification of broad and general developments such as the tendency in the twentieth century for state welfare expenditure to increase, while at the same time allowing for attention to be paid to the fact that the welfare arrangements of countries vary widely. Hence, comparative social policy analysis may offer a means of addressing problems that have tended to hinder attempts to develop analytical models of the nature and development of welfare states in the advanced capitalist countries.

This is not, however, to suggest that a comparative approach is without difficulty. A central issue has been the lack of agreement over what is to be considered an appropriate methodology. One approach has been to concentrate upon the analysis of aggregate data, seeking to reduce the variety and depth of social reality to a number of quantifiable and comparable variables (e.g. Hicks, 1988; Griffin et al., 1989). This method has been criticized for paying insufficient regard to qualitative issues, and for concentrating attention only upon issues for which data are readily available (Castles, 1989, 5). At the other extreme are historical studies of individual countries, that pay far more attention to the detail of social arrangements (e.g. Flora, 1986). This approach is open to the criticism that it results in a lack of generalizable data, and hence an inability to generate comparisons between countries. There have been efforts made to synthesize these approaches (e.g. Cochrane & Clarke, 1993), but problems certainly remain. It is, as Esping-Anderson notes, 'analytically difficult to confront detailed historiography with a table of regression coefficients' (1990, 106).

More specific difficulties also arise. Perhaps the most immediate and most obvious is the lack of readily available, and comparable, data in many countries and in many areas of welfare provision. International agencies such as the United Nations and the Organization for Economic

Cooperation and Development (OECD) provide aggregated data on a number of economic and social indicators. This is certainly of some use, particularly in relation to economic issues such as levels of employment, taxation, and so on. But the specific detail of welfare policy development in many countries often remains difficult to acquire or is simply not available.

These issues are as pertinent to the study of mental health policy as to other areas of welfare provision. With policy and practice in a state of flux, there is considerable difficulty in collecting data which accurately describe existing situations. When mental hospitals were virtually the only form of provision, it was relatively easy to maintain records. With the shift towards community-based services, some of which are provided outside of the state sector, there is an increasingly differentiated range of services that make data gathering far more difficult. Many countries do not collect information on a range of important indicators. This often includes out-patient services and homes and hostels, especially where these are provided in the private and voluntary sectors. Equally, with the large numbers of office psychiatrists who practise in the private sector in some countries, together with the growing number of clinical psychologists, it is possible for people to be in receipt of services without necessarily registering on psychiatric statistics (Freeman et al., 1985, 85).

Countries with federal structures pose additional problems of data collection, where health services are generally provided regionally and national governments do not always collate and provide information. Furthermore, even where data are available considerable problems of interpretation can arise. In some countries such as Germany 'neurology' is as large a medical specialism as 'psychiatry', and may provide services to many people with mental health problems who would be provided for by psychiatric services in other countries. The meaning given to terminology employed can vary considerably, even so far as making the comparison of basic terms such as 'psychiatrist, 'hospital bed', and 'patient' problematic (Freeman et al., 1985; Mangen, 1985).

It is worth making clear at this point that the analysis offered in this book is subject to these difficulties. Lack of available data means that some countries have been omitted from the study, while others are perhaps insufficiently detailed. While the book attempts to tread a path between overly relying upon aggregate statistical data or specific country-based studies, the dearth of material concerning certain aspects of some countries' services makes this balance difficult to sustain consistently.

There are also two points of clarification to make in relation to the countries being considered. Firstly, where reference is made to England, it specifically excludes the services of Scotland and Northern Ireland, which are administered separately, and demonstrate very different patterns of development. Wales, however, is included within the description of English services, but because of its relatively small size and for the sake of brevity is not mentioned in relation to every reference to these services. Secondly, in 1990 the two parts of Germany were reunited. The mental health services of what was East Germany, like much of the old Eastern bloc, were provided mainly within old institutions and changed little in the postwar period. The influences upon their development have clearly been very different from those in the old West Germany and other Western European countries (Breemer ter Stege, 1992). As a result of the reunification of Germany we might expect dramatic change in the mental health services of the old East Germany, but for this study the available literature is insufficient to include these recent changes within the overall review and analysis that is presented. As such, reference to Germany throughout this book should be taken to mean the services as they have developed in the old West Germany.

Despite such difficulties as these, it is in the comparative study of social policies that some of the most interesting and productive analyses have been conducted in recent years. Such study may provide a means of taking understanding forward concerning issues such as the relationship between agency and structure in the development and organization of welfare provision (Ginsburg, 1992, 18). It may also provide a means of identifying the forces involved in the origins of social policies, and of analysing the motive forces that underlie welfare provision (Esping-Anderson, 1990). Specifically within the field of mental health policy, it is suggested that this approach offers a means of achieving greater understanding of the nature and development of services:

> Comparative analysis is an antidote to the generally highly localised implications of results of research of service settings: by testing the equivalent relevance of the concept in a sample of countries, cross-national treatment sharpens the parameters of the problematic, critically refining assessments of generalizability and identifying specificities peculiar to location. The ultimate scientific purpose, of course, is to generate robust explanatory models that hold over space. (Mangen, 1994, 235)

It is within this context that this study seeks to provide a fairly detailed overview of the main postwar developments in mental health policy in Western Europe and North America, and to offer explanation and assessment of these. The extent to which it achieves this is of course open to interpretation.

Note to the reader

Lunacy and lunatics are terms used in the book where reference is being made to historical events when such terms were current. These terms are now considered – quite rightly – to be offensive to people with mental health problems, but they are used here in order to help represent accurately how such issues and problems were perceived and responded to during the periods of time we are considering.

PART 1: THE ORIGINS AND DEVELOPMENT OF MENTAL HEALTH SERVICES

1

Postwar Mental Health Policy

The rise of the asylum

Mental health services in the countries of Western Europe and North America have developed over a number of centuries. This began with the creation of secure provision for lunatics: the asylum. In Europe the Bethlem hospital in London, England, was the first to be opened in 1403, and the Casa de Orates opened in 1408 in Valencia, Spain, was the second (World Health Organization, 1955, 4). In France, the 'great confinement' began in the seventeenth century, with the incarceration of the poor, the sick and the mentally disabled in general hospitals, the first of which opened in Paris in 1657 (Foucault, 1973). In North America an asylum was built by religious orders of New France (Quebec) in 1639 'for the care of indigent patients, the crippled and idiots' (Dear et al., 1979, 45), and an asylum for lunatics was opened in Virginia in 1773 (World Health Organization, 1955, 5). An 1833 Act that allowed for relief to be made available to 'destitute lunatics' was passed in Ontario, and in 1841 its first asylum was opened (Dear et al., 1979, 45).

During the early to mid-nineteenth century the pace of development increased, with a policy of building asylums for the containment of lunatics being established across most of Western Europe and North America. In the 1820s, parliamentary inquiries and plans for service development were operative in France, England and Denmark. By the middle of the nineteenth century, legislation was introduced allowing for the building of asylums in France in 1838, in the Netherlands in 1841, England in 1845 and Belgium in 1850 (Mangen, 1985, 6).

Incarceration of lunatics proved to be an effective nineteenth-century solution to the problem of madness. The numbers afflicted were relatively small, and their condition was generally recognized to be severe. With an emphasis upon protecting society from the lunatic, the regulation of admission and discharge was left largely in judicial hands, and for the most part involved compulsion. Reflecting these concerns, the vast majority of the newly created asylums resembled prisons. Their main purpose was to remove the insane from society, and hold them. Inmates were often chained, and conditions were harsh.

Efforts to reform the conditions in which lunatics were held took place as early as the late eighteenth century. In 1792 at the Bicêtre hospital in Paris, Philippe Pinel had chains, which had been worn by some for 30 years, removed from 50 of the inmates and a regime based on moral treatment was introduced. A number of further reforms, such as the creation of a farm, were subsequently introduced by Ferrus at Bicêtre, while others, such as Esquirol, sought to introduce a more humanitarian approach to lunatics more widely in France. In England similar ideas were introduced in a Quaker-led initiative by William Tuke and Lindley Murray, who founded the York Retreat in 1796. The use of chains was prohibited, and therapy based on work and exercise and the encouragement of moral behaviour was introduced. These ideas were also of influence in America, with the Friends' Asylum being opened in 1817 in Pennsylvania. Subsequently, Dorothea Dix attempted to take forward the cause of reform in America by campaigning extensively for an improvement in asylum conditions.

Overall, however, these attempts at improving the quality of care and treatment within the asylums had limited effect. In the second half of the nineteenth century, because of fiscal constraints and overcrowding, conditions tended to deteriorate, becoming more custodial than therapeutic in character (Grob, 1991). Nevertheless, over the next several decades the institutional system grew rapidly. In the United States in 1860 there were 8,500 psychiatric in-patients, and less than a century later there were 535,500 (Thornicroft & Bebbington, 1989, 740). In the mid-1860s there were 11 asylums in Canada and by 1920 there were 20 asylums, most of them being large, with anything up to 6,000 beds (Williams & Luterbach, 1976, 15). In Spain there were very few mental hospitals in 1860, yet by 1975 there were 116 (Comelles & Hernáez, 1994, 284). In France in 1780 there were 8 institutions providing 5,000 beds, and by 1882 there were 83 institutions and 100,000 beds (Demay, 1987, 70). In Ireland the first asylum for lunatics was built in Dublin in 1810. By 1900 0.5 per cent of the entire Irish population had been incarcerated in district lunatic asylums, and by 1958 this had risen to 0.7 per cent, a total of some 21,000 people and the highest to be found in Europe (Walsh, 1987, 108). By the end of the nineteenth century the almost inevitable consequence of being found insane was incarceration (Mangen, 1985, 7).

In the first half of the twentieth century there was some innovation taking place within the old mental hospitals. In the 1930s and 1940s many psychiatrists began to experiment with open-door policies, whereby patients gained some freedom of movement outside of the hospital ward. Efforts were made to increase the therapeutic value of the mental hospital, this including the development of industrial therapy as well as the introduction of a range of new physical treatments including electro-convulsive therapy, insulin coma therapy and psycho-surgery. Concurrent with these developments, admission rates tended to increase, while average lengths of stay tended to decrease. Overall, through the first half of the twentieth century asylums underwent a transition in function, from being primarily custodial institutions towards becoming treatment institutions.

Reflecting this shift towards a medicalized model of mental health care, terminology utilized in law began to alter. By the early 1950s around half the states in the United States had made statutory amendments changing the term 'insane' to 'mentally ill'. In England the Mental Treatment Act 1930 replaced the term 'lunatic' with 'person of unsound mind' and 'patient'. Similar changes occurred in Europe. In France the law of 1838 refers to *aliénés*, but was replaced by the term *malades mentaux* in a 1948 circular of the Ministry of Public Health. In Italy reference to *alienati di menti* (lunatics) was replaced by *infirmi di mente* (mentally sick persons), and in most other European countries the same trend is apparent (World Health Organization, 1955, 11). Equally, the terminology used to refer to institutional facilities has altered over time. The 'madhouse' was replaced by 'lunatic asylum' in the early nineteenth century, which itself was replaced by the 'mental hospital' a hundred years later. In France, for example, the term *hôpitaux psychiatriques* was first used in a Ministry of Health Circular in 1937, replacing the previously used *établissement d'aliénés* (World Health Organization, 1955, 13).

The origins of community care

During the latter part of the nineteenth century, as conditions within asylums deteriorated further, small-scale efforts to develop alternative systems of care and treatment emerged. Perhaps most famous of these schemes was that begun at Gheel in Belgium, where its shrines were reputed to offer a cure for lunacy. If no cure resulted within nine days, the lunatic would then be boarded out with a local family in order that they might continue to attend church. The practice of boarding-out lunatics with families subsequently developed in many European countries, including Germany, France, the Netherlands, Belgium and the Scandinavian countries (World Health Organization, 1955, 7).

In France public funds could be spent on extramural services as early as 1851, although very little expenditure was devoted to this (Bennett, 1991, 629). In Germany the concept of community-based care, with the aim of integrating people with mental health problems into society, was proposed by Griesinger (Rössler, 1992). A colony for people with epilepsy where they might live a near normal community life was established near Bielefeld in 1867, and this example was copied in some other European countries and the United States (World Health Organization, 1955, 6). There was also at this time the creation of a number of after-care associations which sought to help resettle ex-asylum patients (Scull, 1984; Mangen, 1985).

In the early twentieth century this new emphasis upon mental health care outside of the asylum continued to grow. Interest in the concept of prevention developed from the 1890s, this being most evident in the growing concern of eugenicists with mental hygiene. By the 1920s the mental hygiene movement had established associations in a number of European countries and in the United States. By the 1930s there were small-scale developments in a range of extramural services. This included domiciliary support, the development of child guidance, marital counselling services and out-patient services. While not common, these types of service began to emerge in various towns and cities across Europe and North America.

In many European countries World War II had a considerable effect upon mental health service provision. In France in-patient numbers fell dramatically, from 115,000 to 65,000, much of this reduction being a result of starvation due to the inability of mental hospital authorities to procure food. But there were also a number of initiatives to place people with mental health problems in the community as a means of ensuring their survival (Demay, 1987, 71). To some extent, however, this effect was temporary; after 1945 the size of mental hospital populations in many countries, at least in the short term, continued to rise.

Mental health service provision in the postwar period

In the 1950s the largest mental hospitals in Europe were to be found in France, the largest of these having some 4,000 beds. In the United States mental hospitals were larger still, with some containing as many as 10,000 beds (Mangen, 1985, 120). In Germany in the 1960s, there were 68 state mental hospitals with an average of 1,200 beds in each (Cooper & Bauer, 1987, 78). Since then, however, it has generally been recognized that these institutions are too large, too isolated, and in many cases too derelict to be of therapeutic use. Between 1972 and 1982 the number of mental hospitals with over a thousand beds fell considerably: from 4 to 2 in Denmark and in Ireland, from 10 to 4 in Sweden, from 14 to 0 in Spain, from 55 to 20 in Italy, and from 65 to 23 in England (Freeman et al., 1985, 34).

In the 1950s legislation governing the way in which people with mental health problems were provided for had for the most part been passed in the nineteenth century. Increasingly, however, it was coming to be seen as outmoded and in need of reform. The general trend since has been towards the introduction of new legislation allowing for early treatment and voluntary admission. Legislation safeguarding the rights of patients in hospitals, enabling them, for example, to appeal against detention, has also tended to follow. Many of the big old mental hospitals have been run down and in some cases closed. There has also been a general move towards the development of new community-based services, providing psychiatric treatment and support outside of the old mental hospitals. In the remainder of this chapter we will examine the particular outcomes of these general trends in a range of countries in Western Europe and North America.

England

In England mental health treatment services are the responsibility of the Department of Health. Local Health Authorities are responsible for the delivery of mental hospital services, and Family Health Service Authorities are responsible for the delivery of primary care services. These two bodies are, however, in the process of merging in the mid-1990s. There are also three special hospitals, administered separately, that are responsible for containment and treatment of the criminally insane. Social care, including services such as residential homes, day centres and social work support, is the responsibility of local government. Within each local authority area, social service departments are responsible for the delivery of social care services.

Following the enactment of the National Health Service and Community Care Act 1990, there have been substantial changes made to the administration of health and social services. An internal market has been created, whereby increasing emphasis is being placed upon involving the private and voluntary sector in the provision of services via a process of contracting with either the health authority or social service department of the local authority. Some state services, including most hospitals and many residential homes, have gained trust status and have become independent suppliers of services to state purchasing agencies.

While the organization and delivery of mental health services have been subject to considerable change, financial sources of treatment and care have remained relatively unchanged since 1948 when the National Health Service was created. For the most part mental health is funded by general taxation, and is distributed via the Department of Health to the health authorities. Local authorities also receive monies for social care services from central government, and gain some further resources through local taxation. The National Health Service provides services to all those in need of treatment. Local authorities, however, are increasingly using means tests for social care services in an attempt to control demand and raise resources.

The movement towards a more treatment-orientated service, together with the development of after-care services, was, as indicated above, apparent in many countries by the mid-twentieth century. But it was to be in England where these disparate trends were first to cohere within a clearly defined policy that advocated a shift towards community-based services. In 1954 the Ministry of Health instigated a Royal Commission to review existing mental health legislation and treatment. Its Report made clear the need for policy change:

> ... in relation to almost all forms of mental disorder, there is increasing medical emphasis on forms of treatment and training and social services which can be given without bringing patients into hospitals as in-patients, or which make it possible to discharge them from hospital sooner than in the past. (Percy Commission, 1957, 207)

Subsequently the Mental Health Act 1959 repealed all previous legislation concerning lunacy, mental treatment and mental deficiency. It placed considerable emphasis upon developing local authority community services, although it added few powers to aid such change, and stated that treatment should as far as possible be provided on an informal and voluntary basis. The passing of this legislation reflects the fact that a clear policy position had been established by this time in England, concerning the need to shift from an institutional to a community-based system of care and treatment (Goodwin, 1993).

In 1983 a further Mental Health Act was passed which introduced some safeguards to the process of compulsory admission, treatment and detention. But the basic policy of moving towards an increasingly community-based system of care and treatment established in 1959 remains firmly in place. Between 1954 and 1995 mental hospital bed space was reduced by two-thirds, and a range of new community-based facilities have been developed.

The United States

Historically, the individual states have been the main providers of mental health services. There is considerable variation between states as to the extent to which power over policy and service delivery is then delegated to counties or mental health agencies. The federal government has taken a relatively minor role, including the provision of hospitals for war veterans, limited funding of community mental health centres, and providing money through the Medicaid programme for in-patient care. Since the early 1980s there has been a growing trend towards the privatization of mental health services through the use of contracting out public services to private, mainly non-profit-making agencies. There has been a rapid expansion of private residential homes, as well as the development of private mental health clinics and sheltered workshops. Over half of the states now have well-developed programmes for contracting out services, and some states such as Massachusetts have shifted the bulk of their mental health services into the private sector by this means (Benson, 1994, 122).

Because of the highly privatized nature of health care in the United States, mental health services for which little financial demand exists have tended to be cut off from mainstream health care. A study in 1986 found that less than 2 per cent of those diagnosed with schizophrenia were served by private facilities (Hollingsworth, 1992, 902). Eighty per cent of the funding of mental health services for long-term care comes from the states, while only 15 per cent comes from federal government and 5 per cent from other sources (Hollingsworth, 1992, 904). Increasingly, however, the Medicaid programme has become a major source of finance for mental health services. Coverage of psychiatric services varies widely between states, but overall some 15 per cent of Medicaid funds are spent on mental health service provision (Benson, 1994). Many people with mental health problems, however, are ineligible for Medicaid benefits. State rules vary, but generally it is made available only to those in receipt of other cash assistance programmes. Until the early 1990s, most state Medicaid schemes were restricted to medical services only. In recent years, however, an increasing number are meeting some social care costs (Benson, 1994, 128).

Although not so early or so clearly developed and presented as a national policy as in England, the trend towards deinstitutionalization developed in the United States more rapidly than in any other country. The number of in-patients in public mental hospitals declined from 559,000 in 1955 to only 110,000 in 1990 (Mechanic & Rochefort, 1990, 301). Also unlike England, responsibility for the development of alternative services was not devolved to a local level, but was actively taken on by federal government.

In 1955 the Mental Health Study Act created the Joint Commission on Mental Illness and Health, and this body subsequently submitted to Congress a report entitled 'Action for Mental Health' in 1961. It recommended a reduction in the scale of mental hospital provision, and the development of community mental health Centres. These were to be 'a main line of defence in reducing the need of many persons with major mental illness for prolonged or repeated hospitalization'. It recommended one fully staffed, full-time clinic should be provided for every 50,000 people, implying the provision of 4,500 clinics across the country (Jones, 1988, 7).

This report was followed by the Community Mental Health Centers Act 1965, which was the first substantial attention given to mental health by the federal government. Federal funds were authorized for the construction of community mental health centres across the country; federal funds were to provide for the main construction costs, while the individual states would pay for the staffing of the new centres, and local organizations or groups of citizens would manage them. The rights to services were clearly defined and extensive. Everyone, irrespective of sex, race, age or ability to pay, was eligible for services, although those that could pay would be expected to do so. The responsibilities of the new community mental health centres were very wide, ranging from the provision of in-patient services through to emergency services, including 24-hour cover for anybody needing immediate care, as well as an emphasis upon prevention via public educational programmes.

By 1980 more than 700 community mental health centres had been funded under the programme. Under the Reagan Administration, however, their role was to decline following the dramatic reductions in their funding and authority brought about by the Omnibus Budget Reconciliation Act 1981. Community programmes funded by the Alcohol, Drug Abuse and Mental Health Administration, for example, were cut by 30 per cent between 1980 and 1982 (Marmor & Gill, 1989, 461). Since then the role of community mental health centres has been much less significant.

Conversely, since their inception in 1966 the role of the Medicare and Medicaid programmes in mental health service provision have grown rapidly. They have been largely responsible for the expansion of psychiatric services in general hospitals. Over 60 per cent of all psychiatric in-patient episodes in the United States now occur in short term non federal general hospitals (Kiesler, 1992, 1079). Medicaid has also been available to finance patients moving from state mental hospital to nursing home beds, and has been responsible for a rapid growth in private nursing homes, catering particularly for elderly people with mental health problems (Mechanic & Rochefort, 1990, 305). There has also been a rapid growth in other residential accommodation, including halfway houses, group homes and other facilities. Together, it is estimated that these provide accommodation for between 300,000 and 400,000 people with long-term mental health problems (Mechanic & Rochefort, 1990, 305).

Canada

In Canada the provincial and territorial governments are responsible for the delivery of health care services. The Canadian federal government provides funding via block grants, and imposes certain general conditions for their use concerning the provision of comprehensive and accessible services. The private health insurance schemes that emerged in the early part of the century rarely covered mental health problems, and have had a limited role in mental health service provision (Williams & Luterbach, 1976, 15; Bigelow & McFarland, 1994, 66).

The Ministry of Health in each province is responsible for the bulk of mental health costs, paying for hospitals and other services. To an increasing extent, provincial governments are contracting independent agencies to provide services (Bigelow & McFarland, 1994, 66). Admissions to mental health facilities, together with subsequent treatment and care, are governed by provincial mental health legislation. Residential care is subsidized, but service users meet some of the costs. The financial contribution of residents is set at 85 per cent of the old-age security pension and guaranteed income security (Bigelow & McFarland, 1994, 66). Canada has never had the federal programme of community mental health centres as developed in United States, and consequently there is more variation in service provision between the provinces than is to be found in the United States (Department of Health and Welfare, 1988).

In 1948 the federal government instituted a series of National Health grants designed to aid the provinces in a study of their mental health needs. Following this, in 1954, the Department of National Health and Welfare called for an improvement of existing mental hospital facilities via their integration with general hospital services, together with the development of community-based services (Williams & Luterbach, 1976, 15). It was only in the 1960s, however, that any real policy shift was to become evident when legislation was introduced to encourage voluntary admission in Saskatchewan. A policy of sectorization of services was introduced whereby catchment areas of around 200,000 people were created, the services of large mental hospitals were decentralized into small units, and out-patient and other new community-orientated services were developed (Williams & Luterbach, 1976, 17). This policy shift created a strong impetus towards community-based services in other provinces, with similar policy changes subsequently being introduced in many provinces such as British Columbia, Ontario, Quebec and New Brunswick. Other provinces such as Newfoundland and Manitoba have been far slower to implement change (Williams & Luterbach, 1976, 17).

Since the 1970s a policy of developing community-based mental health services has been clearly established in all Canadian provinces. Mental hospital bed space has declined rapidly, and a range of new services such as psychiatric units, day hospitals, residential units and community support services have been developed (Department of Health and Welfare, 1990). These developments have largely been stimulated by the federal government. The Canada Assistance Plan and the Vocational Rehabilitation of Disabled Persons Act provide for 50 per cent of programme costs for the provision of welfare and rehabilitative services to be met by the federal government.

France

Health policy in France is relatively centralized. The Ministry of Social Affairs and National Solidarity has overall national responsibility for mental health service provision. It determines the annual budget, organizes social insurance, sets fees and oversees the psychiatric hospitals. There is also a regional level of administration, but an increasing number of responsibilities for mental health service provision have since the 1980s been taken over at department level. The bulk of mental health services are provided by the state. The non-statutory sector role is very limited, with only some 10 per cent of beds being provided in private hospitals (Mangen, 1985, 125). The costs of hospital treatment are generally met by sickness insurance funds, which were expanded to provide cover for psychiatric cases in the 1920s (Mangen, 1985, 117). Extramural services receive central government subsidy, and long-term care and rehabilitation are provided by the *départements* (Mangen, 1985, 131).

In 1960 an exhortative circular was issued in which the principle of sectorization was presented as the basis for the future development of psychiatric services. This was to involve the country being divided into areas each with an average population of 70,000. It was intended that each sector would provide a comprehensive range of mental health services. This would provide whenever possible local in-patient facilities. Where this was not possible because of the existing geographical distribution of beds, mental hospitals in the region should themselves be divided into sectors, each serving a local community. In addition to in-patient facilities, mental health services should also provide locally based out-patient services, day hospital, night hospital and sheltered workshop facilities. Early treatment, counselling, domiciliary care, crisis intervention and follow-up treatment were regarded as essential parts of service development, in order to ensure that a full range of preventive, treatment and after-care services could be provided (Barres, 1987, 140–141).

This statement, however, had little effect on French services in the 1960s, with mental hospital in-patient numbers continuing to grow, albeit at a reduced rate. It was only in the 1970s, following a restatement of the French government's policy position in 1972, that a shift in policy commenced. By the late 1980s this had been largely implemented, with the full complement of sectors being realized. By 1979 approximately 800 multidisciplinary sector teams were in operation, each covering around 70,000 people (Freeman et al., 1985, 81). By 1991 there were 812 psychiatric sectors in operation, with each sector run by a multidisciplinary team, providing comprehensive care. Emphasis has increasingly been placed upon developing treatment facilities in the community such as day hospitals, out-patient services, day centres and crisis and emergency centres (Kovess et al., 1995, 132).

As well as developing sectorized treatment services, there has also been some development of community-based support services. In 1975 persons suffering from a severe mental illness became entitled to a pension plus a housing subsidy (Kovess et al., 1995, 134). In the 1980s and 1990s a more diverse range of services have been developed, including foster homes, sheltered apartments and drop-in centres (Kovess et al., 1995, 133).

Germany

The central principle in German welfare is that of subsidiarity. This concerns a basic predilection for organizing welfare provision at the lowest organizational level possible. Mental health services demonstrate this principle clearly. Considerable emphasis is placed upon the provision of family care of people with disabilities (Hollingsworth, 1992, 911). Local authorities (within each of the states) have some limited responsibility for social care services, although for the most part services are provided by voluntary groups. The federal states (the *Länder*) have overall responsibility for mental health services, and provide the administration of around a half of all mental hospitals. The remaining mental hospitals are run by voluntary and private groups, although they account for only one-fifth of psychiatric beds (Hollingsworth, 1992, 909). For the most part, community-based psychiatric care is provided by private office psychiatrists. They have been fiercely resistant to the development of hospital out-patient and day patient facilities, and to a large extent have been successful in hindering their development.

Mental health services in Germany are provided through an insurance-based system. The Ministry of Youth, Family and Health Affairs administers the social assistance programme which finances most social rehabilitation, and the Ministry of Labour and Social Affairs oversees the social insurance system, which includes the many health and disability insurance funds. There is a strong distinction between medical services for the cure or rehabilitation of patients, funded by insurance, and social care services for those with long-term needs, funded by social assistance. There is no comprehensive national or regional health planning system, although the federal government has some say over state policy (Mangen, 1985, 76).

In Germany there were some developments in community-based care in the nineteenth and early part of the twentieth century, but the Nazi regime swept this away, and in its place developed its own policies: compulsory sterilization and euthanasia. It is estimated that under the Nazis between 70,000 and 120,000 mental patients were killed, and between 200,000 and 350,000 were subject to compulsory sterilization (Bennett, 1991, 631). Many liberal psychiatrists fled Germany to take up posts elsewhere, and as a result more conservative forces came to dominate in the mental hospital. This tended to stymie innovation in mental health services: 'For many years a heavy silence hung over the mental hospitals and made any reform impossible, a situation exacerbated by the fact that many excellent psychiatrists had left the country before the war' (Haerlin, 1987, 105). After World War II people tended to want to ignore or forget what had been done to those with mental health problems. This tended to reduce public concern with mental health policy; indeed the most pressing priority was seen as the need to rebuild the old asylums (Cooper & Bauer, 1987, 78).

It was only in the 1960s that a new generation arose that felt less constrained by history, and sought to reopen the debate over how people with mental health problems should be provided for. This resulted in the establishment in 1970 of a major review of mental health services, the Psychiatrie Enquête, to inquire into the state of German mental health provision and to make recommendations. In 1975, it laid out a wide-ranging critique of existing services, and recommended the development of community-based mental health care. The Commission proposed a dramatic reduction of bed space in the old mental hospitals, and an increase in the number of beds in psychiatric units. It argued that care for people with mental health problems should be provided in or near their local community and that comprehensive care should be made available to all mentally ill persons. The various services should be coordinated so as to permit appropriate care at each stage of the illness, and care for the mentally ill should be of a standard comparable to that given to the physically ill (Cooper & Bauer, 1987, 80).

The federal government and the individual states tended to respond negatively to the report. They felt that it was overly critical of existing services, and made proposals that would prove expensive. A number of states did, however, subsequently agree to set up some model pro-grammes, and to improve conditions in the mental hospitals. In Solingen a range of new services were developed, including crisis and hostel beds, a day centre, social clubs and a cooperative workshop. An emergency team on permanent standby was established and the involvement of volunteers in service development and provision was encouraged. Over-all, however, these model programmes have left the bulk of German provision relatively unaffected (Bennett, 1991).

In 1988 the Experts Commission reported that service provision was similar to that found by the Psychiatrie Enquête in the early 1970s. Very few community services had been developed in the community, and conditions within mental hospitals and nursing homes were found to be poor. It was estimated that of the approximately 500,000 people with long-term mental health problems in Germany, between 150,000 and 200,000 were in psychiatric facilities. The remainder were to a large extent dependent upon family care, and had little contact with psychi-atric services (Mitzlaff, 1990; Hollingsworth, 1992, 911). Over the last few years, however, there has been some movement towards the develop-ment of community services, including the development of day centres and the provision of domiciliary support (Bock, 1994). In 1984 community-based support was given priority over institutional care within the social assistance law, and in the early 1990s compulsory care insurance was introduced (Tester, 1996).

Italy

Around half of Italian provinces are directly responsible for managing all of the psychiatric services in their area. The remainder rely to varying degrees upon contracting out of services, in particular to church-sponsored private psychiatric hospitals (Donnelly, 1992, 85). In 1978 Law 833 established a national health service, under which all those in need could gain treatment. Mental health service provision costs along with other health care costs are met by central government.

Seven months after the enactment of Law 833, Law 180 was passed by the Italian government. Under the influence of Psichiatria Democratica, a radical group led by Franco Basaglia, mental health policy took a highly distinctive and much publicized lurch towards a community-based system of care and treatment. Law 180 forbade the admission of new patients to state mental hospitals, limited voluntary readmission of new patients after 1 January 1981, and restricted the size of psychiatric units at the general hospitals to 15 beds. It was envisaged that within 10 years public mental hospitals would no longer be used for psychiatric treatment, except for the provision of services to a small number of long-stay patients. General hospital psychiatric units are the only setting in the public sector where psychiatric patients can be admitted (De Salvia & Barbato, 1993). New community-based mental health centres were to be established, and these would meet the bulk of psychiatric need within local communities, including all compulsory admissions. The new services had to be staffed from existing mental facilities, and were to be financed by centrally administered per capita funding.

Since 1978 the development of new district-based services has, at least in some areas, been quite slow. In 1984 there were only 298 district-based services, leaving 14.8 per cent of the population with no access to this type of service (Crepet, 1990, 28). Varying degrees of resistance to the proposals have occurred, with some regions in Italy still allowing readmissions to mental hospitals (Crepet, 1990, 28). Despite the clear emphasis upon deinstitutionalization, 40 mental hospitals remain partially open (Mangen, 1994, 239).

Overall, Donnelly (1992, 96–97) suggests three distinct patterns of implementation of Law 180 can be distinguished. The first pattern, to be found mainly in small to medium-sized towns in the north and centre of Italy, consists of a relatively full implementation of the reforms. This consists of a progressive shift of resources into the community, limited use of in-patient facilities, together with fairly good coordination between services. The second pattern is to be found most typically in large urban areas, and consists of the creation of new community-based services but not the running down of existing in-patient facilities. The result is a tendency towards diversification of services, rather than a sea-change in their orientation. There is little coordination between hospital and community-based services, and they tend to provide for different clienteles: in-patient facilities for the more disturbed, and community facilities for the less disturbed patient. The third pattern, typically found in the south of the country, consists largely of little change. Mental hospital-based services remain dominant, and the few community services that have developed tend to function as an adjunct to this, rather than provide an alternative type of service.

Spain

Historically, psychiatric services in Spain have been provided by a variety of agencies, and have been subject to little overall planning or coordination. Mental health service provision is mainly the responsibility of the provincial authorities, which supply approximately half of mental hospital beds, while the church and the private sector supply the other half (Comelles & Hernáez, 1994, 286). The social security system has expanded its role in mental health service provision over the past 30 years. It provides some in-patient and out-patient facilities, and operates independently of the provincial authorities. Mental health dispensaries provide some out-patient services, but are poorly funded and isolated from other parts of the mental health system.

While other European countries began to develop community-based policies in the 1960s and 1970s, Spain continued to rely upon a mainly institution-based psychiatric system. There was some small-scale development of day hospital and out-patient services, but these did little to alter the basically institutional nature of the system that had been in place since the 1860s. The reform of mental health services only became possible after the death of Franco and the transition to democratic government (Comelles & Hernáez, 1994, 283). This process first gained momentum in 1979 when left-wing candidates with the support of nationalist parties gained control of parliament. These parties were supportive of the shift from institutional to community-based systems of care, recognizing that this constituted part of the general modernization process that was required.

In 1985 a report of the Ministerial Committee for Psychiatric Reform laid out clear guidelines for the future development of mental health services. It argued for the integration of mental health services with general health services, and for a reduction in the number of in-patients. It also proposed the development of new community-based resources to enable discharged patients to find the support services they require within their local area.

As a result of this report, a new organizational structure for health care delivery was created, whereby primary health care teams were established, each with responsibility for their local health zone. These teams have specific responsibilities for encouraging more positive attitudes towards mental health problems, and for supporting people with mental health problems in the community. Their aim is to reduce the rate of hospitalization, and increase the level of support in the community (Poveda, 1987, 192).

In the 1980s and 1990s there has been some movement towards developing psychiatric services in general hospitals and in local clinics. There also have been some small-scale efforts made to develop support services with the community. Following the United States model, community mental health centres have been opened in many regions of Spain over the past 10 to 15 years. These now provide a substantial part of the mental health services available, and offer facilities for both the treatment and social support of service users (Poveda, 1987, 193). Overall, however, these developments have been slow, and considerable regional variations exist in the extent to which change has been implemented. In some regions mental health services have remained little changed, with an emphasis upon institutionalization remaining strong (Comelles & Hernáez, 1994, 290).

Denmark

In 1933 compulsory insurance for the funding of health care in Denmark was introduced, and between 1921 and 1976 a special national director-ate was responsible for the administration of state mental hospitals. But since 1976 the 14 counties and Copenhagen have taken over the pro-vision of health services and have been funded through general taxation. Hospital treatment and care in residential and nursing homes for long-term patients is free at the point of use.

In the 1950s a Commission was established by the government to review mental health policy. Its report in 1956 proposed wide-ranging change. It argued that mental hospitals should be scaled down in size, and should be made more accessible by locating them closer to existing general hospital facilities. Psychiatric units should be established in general hospitals and out-patient facilities should be developed. In 1960 the Glostrup hospital was opened in Copenhagen which provided a model for these proposals, but subsequent development was slow with only an additional four of the planned hospitals operating by the mid-1970s (Bennett, 1991, 637).

In 1970 the Danish Psychiatric Association published a set of proposals for the development of a sectorized psychiatric service. This was to involve the expansion of out-patient and day patient services and development of small and modern hospital psychiatric units, and in 1975 legislation was passed to implement these proposals. A Ministerial Report in 1977 stated that where mental hospital patients were more in need of nursing care than active treatment, they should be transferred to nursing and residential homes (Licht et al., 1991, 317). Since then there has been a substantial shift towards providing community-based psychi-atric services. Mental hospital bed space had steadily increased until 1976, but this has been followed by a period of rapid deinstitutionaliza-tion, with over half of mental hospital capacity being closed by the early 1990s. There has been some expansion of day hospital and out-patient services, and some development of support services in the community (Godt & Blinkenberg, 1992).

The Netherlands

In the Netherlands asylums were largely developed by charitable and voluntary groups, particularly religious organizations, and have continued to provide mental health services to a large extent (Grinten, 1985, 222). Mental health services are provided in three major settings: out-patient services, community-based facilities such as hostels and day centres, and hospitals (Dekker & Langenberg, 1994, 494). Services are paid for by insurance companies, and all citizens are required by law to make insurance contributions for mental health care. Systems of payment are made up of a combination of compulsory and voluntary insurance schemes. This provides for the costs of general practitioners, office psychiatrists, and so on, on a fee-for-service basis, and the daily fees of hospital care (Dekker & Langenberg, 1994). Government has had a relatively limited role, mainly involving the regulation of some aspects of service provision such as mental hospital conditions and admissions, and stipulating the size and budgets of the treatment programmes (Van Der Veen, 1988, 30).

The Netherlands was one of the first European countries to develop community-based treatment services. This started with the provision of clinics in the community in the 1920s, and led on to the development of a social psychiatric service, separate from asylum provision. This development was advanced by Arie Querido, who established a community-based system of psychiatric care in Amsterdam in 1934. He argued that approximately 10 per cent of the Amsterdam in-patient population at that time could live in the community if sufficient support facilities were available. He then engaged in the development of a number of after-care services, including an out-patient clinic, the placing of patients in the homes of former psychiatric nurses, and the development of a social psychiatric service that provided support to people in their own homes (Van Der Veen, 1988).

These early developments in community psychiatric care did not, however, herald a more general shift in mental health policy. Health insurance groups were unwilling to fund services that were not clearly concerned with the treatment and cure of patients, and the municipal and provincial authorities provided insufficient monies to adequately develop community services (Giel, 1987, 153).

The profusion of agencies involved in mental health service provision in the Netherlands has tended to hinder policy development. As a result, the trends towards deinstitutionalization and community support that were becoming evident in many countries by the late 1960s and early 1970s remained largely absent. Since then, however, there has been a slow shift towards community-based services. In 1971 the Hospital Act and several other government papers established a policy of stimulating the development of smaller, more locally based psychiatric services along with out-patient treatment and extramural care, and discouraging the use of in-patient facilities in the older and larger mental hospitals (Haveman, 1986).

In the early 1980s the government introduced a number of changes to mental health policy to encourage a shift from institutional to community care (Van Der Veen, 1988, 24). This included the delineation of catchment areas for emergency admissions to the mental hospitals and the creation of crisis intervention social psychiatric teams (Giel, 1987, 154). A policy of sectorization of psychiatric services was also established (Grinten, 1985, 218). Since 1982, community-based facilities, largely provided by non-statutory agencies, have been integrated into 59 'Regional Institutes for Out-patient Mental Health Care' (Van Der Veen, 1988, 28). These are available to everybody free of charge after referral by a general practitioner (Haveman, 1986, 456).

This policy shift has created a number of conflicts between different agencies providing services. Mental hospitals have clashed with each other over catchment areas, and they have clashed with agencies providing residential facilities in the community over who should provide for service users. Somewhat drily, Giel notes that 'continuity of care is not the most conspicuous achievement of Dutch mental health care' (1987, 152). Nevertheless, the shift towards deinstitutionalization together with the development of community services has now been clearly established.

Sweden

In Sweden, the 26 County Councils took over responsibility for the provision of mental hospitals from central government offices in 1967. The Health Act 1982 made the County Councils responsible for the finance of health services. Within the County Councils 286 local communities are, under the Social Welfare Act 1980, responsible for the provision of a range of welfare services, including financial support for people with mental health problems who have no insurance cover (Brink, 1994, 259). All health services are covered by the National Insurance System (Perris, 1987, 199).

Within each of the County Councils treatment services have for the most part been sectorized, with catchment areas averaging around 70,000 people. In each sector multidisciplinary local mental health teams, consisting of a psychiatrist, psychologist, social worker and a nurse, have been established. Each sector is responsible for in-patient and out-patient services. Most of the County Councils also have a specialist service for the whole county, providing for the more difficult-to-manage clients (Garpenby, 1993, 298).

The first indications of a policy shift occurred in 1963 when the National Board of Social Welfare stated that no further separate mental hospitals should be built, that the number of beds in the old asylums should be reduced, and that psychiatric units in general hospitals should be established (Perris, 1987, 199). In the early 1970s a policy aim of decentralizing services was established by the National Board of Social Welfare, and each county was required to draw up plans to achieve this (Perris, 1987, 202). The aim of closing down all the old mental hospitals

and replacing them with entirely community-based facilities was proposed in the mid-1970s, although it was only in the 1980s that a more
decisive shift towards deinstitutionalization took place in Sweden
(Garpenby, 1993, 298).

In 1982 the National Board of Health and Welfare laid out its views on
the future of mental health service provision: that large hospitals should
close, smaller psychiatric facilities be developed, and support services
be established in the community. In each county, Commissions were
established with the purpose of planning the shift towards a more
community-based system of care and treatment. County Councils have
considerable autonomy, and in consequence there is considerable variation in the extent to which policy change has been implemented (Brink,
1994, 258).

In the 1990s renewed efforts have been made to improve social
support services in the community. A Government Commission com-
pleted a study of Swedish psychiatric services in 1992, and presented
proposals for developing the shift of emphasis from the provision of
support in the community towards a more active programme of rehabilitation. Following this, in 1994 the Law on Support and Service to People
with Lowered Level of Functioning was introduced, in which the range
of responsibilities and activities of the local communities' social welfare
agencies was extended. Individuals gained the right to a needs assessment, and social welfare agencies gained responsibility for ensuring the
provision of outreach activities, and to ensure the provision of mean-
ingful daily activity for those unable to work. Monies for residential
facilities previously controlled by County Councils have been transferred
to them with the intention that they develop new and more local services
such as group homes and ordinary accommodation supported by staff.
Local communities have also been made responsible for the mental
hospital costs of all in-patients six months after the date of admission.
This has provided them with considerable incentive to develop alternatives to long-stay hospital accommodation (Brink, 1994, 265). There has
also been some reform of social insurance. Where previously many
people with mental health problems would gain a pension after a year of
disability, the insurance agencies can now use these monies in collaboration with the psychiatric services to develop and provide rehabilitation
programmes. Overall, there has been substantial progress made towards
establishing a new community-based model of care (Dencker & Långström, 1993, 110).

The global picture

Many other industrialized countries around the world are tending
towards developing community-based policies for people with mental
health problems. Malaysia, for example, has made substantial progress
in transferring mental health service users from institutional to com-

munity settings in recent years (Salleh, 1993). In Israel mental health legislation was implemented in 1991 which seeks to increase patient rights and to avoid unnecessary hospitalization (Levy, 1992). In 1992 the health ministers of all Australian states and territories, together with the federal government, endorsed a National Mental Health Policy. This laid out plans to promote the development of community-based services, together with their better integration with remaining institutional services (Whiteford, 1993).

Of the major industrial nations, Japan has proved to be the main exception to this general policy trend. Long-term institutionalization has provided the main method of treatment and care for people with mental health problems since the early 1920s. The average length of stay in a Japanese mental hospital in 1989 was 496 days, 41 times the average stay of patients in the United States. Nevertheless, the government has in recent years encouraged and supported the development of rehabilitation programmes. The Mental Health Law of 1988 provides support for a shift in policy towards supporting to some extent the reintegration of people with mental health problems into the community, although implementation of this has been slow (Koizumi & Harris, 1992).

Trends in policy and practice

Across Western Europe and North America a number of common patterns and trends in mental health services have emerged in the second half of the twentieth century. In many countries a variety of insurance schemes have developed which, over the twentieth century, have slowly expanded their sphere of activity to include first mental treatment, and subsequently mental health care. In fewer countries, including England, Denmark, Italy and Canada, services funded by general taxation have emerged.

There has been a general trend away from reliance upon long-term incarceration in the old asylums towards a more varied and more community-based pattern of care and treatment. Mental hospital bed space in each country has tended to reach a peak, and subsequently decline. Many of the older hospitals have been substantially run down or closed, while at the same time new psychiatric units in general hospitals have been established. There has also been the development of out-patient and day patient services. Outside of the hospital a range of new community-based treatment facilities have developed. These include community mental health centres, and the establishment of multi-disciplinary community-based psychiatric teams involving general practitioners, community psychiatric nurses, psychiatrists, psychologists and some other staff groups.

These developments in services have frequently taken place within a more general shift towards sectorized community psychiatric services. This involves a process whereby a country is divided into areas, which are then serviced by a specific set of mental hospital facilities. This may involve, for example, the division of existing mental hospital facilities between sectors. The resident population of each sector is often between 30,000 and 100,000, but sometimes rises to 300,000 in the cities (Katschnig et al., 1993, 33).

The consequences of these developments for service users have been substantial. The length of time for which patients are admitted has tended to fall, and the numbers admitted on a voluntary basis have increased. An increasing number of admissions are made to locally based and recently created psychiatric units in general hospitals, rather than the older mental hospitals. The number of admissions has demonstrated a tendency to increase sharply in many countries, although where deinstitutionalization proceeded earliest and most rapidly this trend has in recent years been reversed as increasing numbers of patients are treated in out-patient and community-based facilities.

These changes in the activities and functions of psychiatric services have resulted in a considerable reduction in the availability of care within the older, established services. The loss of beds and the reduction in the average length of stay means that many people with mental health problems find themselves living in community settings when previously they may have been institutionalized. To replace this shortfall, there has (to varying degrees) been an increase in the supply of residential homes, day care, social work support, domiciliary services and a variety of other facilities to help support service users in the community. In a number of countries there has been a large-scale transfer of patients to nursing and residential homes, many of these being in the private and voluntary sectors. Finally, the shift towards more community-orientated provision has resulted in greater emphasis being given to the role of lay help and support, particularly by the family members of service users but also by other members of the community such as friends and neighbours.

Overall, there has been a marked change in the way in which people with mental health problems are treated and cared for in the countries of Western Europe and North America in the postwar period. Attitudes towards what ideas and practices constitute good-quality services have, to a considerable degree, been turned on their head in a relatively short period of time. The question that arises, and provides us with the main focus of Part 2 of the book, is why has this occurred; what forces, in what combination, have resulted in such a rapid, widespread and dramatic policy shift?

PART 2: THE ANALYSIS OF MENTAL HEALTH SERVICES

Introduction

The early development of mental health services in Western Europe and North America is generally recognized to be a product of the emerging industrial societies. In the eighteenth and nineteenth centuries the shift of populations from rural to urban areas created a problem of maintaining social order, and of meeting the needs of a newly formed urban mass. Within the emerging market economies lunatics, more obviously than the physically sick, elderly and children, were less able to conform to labour market discipline and more able to create disturbance and disorder (Scull, 1979).

Not everybody could support themselves in the market, nor would they necessarily find support from church, charity or family. Or, where such support was made available by a family member, their own ability to participate in the labour market was constrained. The mentally ill, therefore, were one of the first potential welfare clients to be recognized by governments as a distinct group who had the right to social benefits without the need for labour market participation.

The creation of asylums in Europe and North America has been argued to represent one part of the response made to these issues: 'Throughout Europe, confinement constituted one of the answers the seventeenth century gave to an economic crisis that affected the entire Western world' (Foucault, 1973, 49). In his analysis of the origins and development of the asylums in the United States, Rothman develops a similar analysis:

> In this period, psychiatrists were more American than they were scientific, and the nature of their response to insanity cannot be comprehended unless one recognizes that they defined mental illness as a social problem, not just a medical one. . . . Prisons, poorhouses and orphan asylums grew up at the same time, and this coincidence suggest that the society was reacting to more than psychiatric doctrines. (1971, xv)

There is certainly some evidence for such theorization. As we saw in Chapter 1, the growth of institutional care, its peak, and its replacement by community care are themes that help organize an understanding of the development of mental health services in many countries over several centuries. These general trends should not, however, lead us too readily towards a view that mental health services are simply the product of more general forces, as some substantial variations in mental health service provision can be found. As was noted in Chapter 1, in the mid-twentieth century Ireland had the highest number of mental hospital beds per capita in Western Europe and this, it has been argued, resulted from the emigration of the younger and fitter population, thereby tending to leave behind a relatively impoverished population, more prone to mental health problems (Walsh, 1987, 114). In Sweden, which had the second highest number of beds per capita, the availability of institutional care was regarded as a measure of welfare provision (Perris, 1987, 222). Even between regions of countries considerable variations in policy can be found. In Italy, for example, the in-patient population of Lombardy declined by just 14.8 per cent between 1975 and 1986, compared to Veneto, where the decline was 70.4 per cent over the same period (Crepet, 1990, 28). Overall, the implementation of the postwar policy shift towards community-based services has been quite diverse. As Matthews notes:

> What is remarkable in the current period, and what should command our attention, is not the universality of decarceration, but rather its differentiation, even within neighbouring states. (1987, 343)

What this leaves us with is a conundrum of considerable complexity. The long-term trends that are clearly present imply that common economic, political and social forces have been, at least to some extent, responsible for the shaping of mental health service provision. The variety that is equally clearly present suggests that other factors, such as the different constitutional structures of countries, the different histories, cultures and national circumstances, the different means by which health and personal social services are financed and organized, are of importance in determining service development.

Most writers in the field of mental health would have little difficulty accepting this list of explanatory factors for why mental health services have developed in a certain way (and might add one or two more). But to develop an understanding of how and why mental health services have evolved in a certain way, identification of a list of explanatory factors in this way is of little use. What matters is their relative importance, and the nature of their interaction. On this point, we find far less agreement. As we shall see in subsequent chapters, there has been considerable argument over the nature of the process by which mental health service provision has tended to shift from an institutional to community focus.

Reflecting this situation, there exist today a range of propositions, some complementary and others not, for which their authors claim a place in the explanation of recent mental health policy development. In a discussion of postwar mental health services in North America, for example, Dear and Wolch argue that a combination of factors is responsible for the policy shift: 'The deinstitutionalization of hospital based populations was a response to new treatment philosophies, major advances in chemotherapy, a concern with patient's rights and fiscal pressures' (1987, 250). Hafner et al. (1989, 12) argue that there are three main reasons for the shift in policy in Europe: the neglect of mental hospitals and resulting criticism of their condition; the shift within psychiatry towards a more therapeutic orientation; and the increasing emphasis upon civil rights, liberty and quality of life for chronically sick and disabled people. The demand for deinstitutionalization was subsequently intensified by economic problems.

Within this range of factors concerning why community-based services have tended to replace institutional care, a pattern emerges in terms of the type of explanation developed in different accounts. Some tend to stress the importance of new drug treatments, and humanitarian concerns such as those contained in the anti-institutional critique. Others tend to stress the importance of structural factors, particularly those deriving from the nature of capitalist societies. This concerns factors such as the cost of service provision, and problems associated with the maintenance of social control. What we find, therefore, is a range of types of explanation, from the orthodox, which tend to stress the positive and beneficial aspects of the policy shift, to the radical, which tend to stress the negative and detrimental consequences of the shift to community-based systems of care and treatment. In Chapter 2 we review the first of these, and in Chapter 3 we examine the more radical explanations. In Chapters 4 and 5 we develop an analysis of service development that attempts to build upon the strengths, and avoid the weaknesses, of existing accounts.

2

Orthodox Accounts of the Policy Shift

By the term 'orthodox accounts', we are referring to those explanations and descriptions of policy development that offer a conventional understanding of policy change. Such accounts tend to be pluralistic, offering a range of factors to account for postwar change in mental health policy. Some of these, however, tend to be attributed greater significance than others, and in this review we draw out the most important of these and consider their explanatory worth.

The development of new treatments

The factor most often attributed greatest importance in propelling the shift from institutional to community-based services within orthodox accounts concerns the development and use of the major tranquillizers. These drugs, such as chlorpromazine and reserpine, were developed in the early 1950s and were in common use across much of Western Europe and North America by the mid- to late 1950s. Their use generated considerable optimism about the dramatic effect they would have upon the management of mental health problems. For the first time, the disturbed behaviour of more severely mentally disordered people could effectively and relatively easily be brought under control. As a result, it was argued that the public would be more tolerant of people with mental health problems being placed in the community, and that mental patients frequently no longer had need of long-term secure accommodation (Brill & Patton, 1959).

These views are reflected in an assessment made in the United States by the Joint Commission on Mental Illness and Health, which makes clear the optimism of the day about the scale of change then going on in the mental health services:

> Drugs have revolutionized the management of psychotic patients in American mental hospitals, and probably deserve primary credit for the reversal of the upward spiral in the state hospital in-patient load. (1961, 14)

Moreover, such views were to have considerable impact on the policy making process. President Kennedy, in an address to Congress in the early 1960s about the development of new community mental health centres, made this clear:

> This approach rests primarily on the new knowledge and the new drugs acquired and developed in recent years which make it possible for most of the

mentally ill to be successfully and quickly treated in their own communities and returned to a useful place in society. (cited in Gronfein, 1985, 450)

Such views as these continue to be presented. For example, a recent British policy document states:

> ... research and clinical experience showed that treatment was equally or more effective when less reliance was placed on long term inpatient care. .... Additionally, more effective drug treatments, such as the major tranquillizers which were introduced in the 1950s, transformed the prognosis of the most serious mental illnesses. (Department of Health, 1989, para. 7.4)

And a recent Canadian policy document makes similar claims:

> Pharmacological advances dramatically altered the course of some disabling mental conditions, allowing many patients to resume higher levels of functioning in the activities of everyday life, without constant supervision and care. (Department of Health and Welfare, 1990, 13)

As well as appearing in government policy statements, this position is also frequently to be found in the academic press. In Sweden, Windgassen argues that 'the transition from custodial to rehabilitative psychiatry would have been virtually inconceivable without neuroleptics' (1992, 405). In Ireland, Walsh maintains that 'The wide range of drugs becoming available for the treatment of mental illness was important in transforming a relatively sterile therapeutic situation into one with a reasonable degree of optimism' (1987, 110). In England, Jones maintains that 'Some patients were able to go home sooner; some did not need to enter hospital at all' (1993, 150). And in Italy, Donnelly contends that 'There can be no doubt about their dramatic effects on many chronic patients who rather suddenly seemed humanly reachable; or of the relief the drugs brought to those patients whose overpowering symptoms became less intrusive and compelling' (1992, 17).

Whether or not the introduction of the major tranquillizers significantly affected the numbers held in mental institutions constitutes perhaps the most important debate about mental health policy over the last 20 years. It contains two main strands. Firstly, are the drugs therapeutic; do they actually result in an improvement in the condition of a mentally disordered person such that early discharge might be made? Secondly, to what extent does the introduction of these drugs correspond with the reduction in mental hospital populations? The implication being that the more closely correlated these two variables are, the more likely a causal relationship exists between them.

An assumption of advocates of this position is that psychotropic drugs are effective; Jones, for example, maintains that their development 'has been one of the major success stories of modern pharmacology' (1988, 82). Whether this view reflects accurately the clinical trials of these drugs is, however, open to question. As early as the 1950s studies in the United States resulted in divided opinion over their therapeutic effectiveness (Gronfein, 1985, 445). Similarly in England many studies gave only guarded support for psychotropic drugs, often arguing that they provided no greater therapeutic effect than existing treatments (Charatan, 1954; Hordern & Hamilton, 1963). Scull, in particular, is highly critical of the studies that purported to demonstrate the therapeutic effectiveness of psychotropic drugs. He argues that many studies conducted in the 1950s lacked statistical rigour, and gave far more positive outcomes than those studies that were more rigorous: 'Remarkably few of the early studies of chlorpromazine's effects met even the minimal criteria of a scientifically acceptable research design' (Scull, 1984, 86).

Since the introduction of new drug treatments there have been very few studies that assess the cost–benefit ratio of psychoactive drugs compared with alternatives, including no treatment at all. Of the studies that do exist, there is some evidence to suggest that prognosis in schizophrenia is not necessarily any worse when drug treatments are not used (Fenton & McGlashan, 1987). Indeed it has been argued that the effects of drug treatments for people with schizophrenia still remain to be demonstrated (McGlashan, 1989). Pilgrim and Rogers (1993, 146) estimate that in 25 per cent of cases where major tranquillizers have been used they have had a therapeutic effect, in 50 per cent there has been little effect, and in 25 per cent of cases their impact has been damaging to the health of patients.

Similar views have been reached in relation to the use of minor tranquillizers. In the United States Caplan et al. (1985) undertook a series of interviews with 367 people who had taken diazepam (Valium) and 308 who had not during the period of the study. The overall effect of the drug was found to be minimal: 'numerous multivariate analyses controlling for levels of stress and health indicated no notable effects of Valium use on any of the social or psychological indicators, including anxiety' (1985, 887).

The relatively guarded assessments being reached of the new drug treatments in the 1950s were largely ignored by the policy-making community. In the United States the Joint Commission on Mental Illness and Health and the National Institute of Mental Health both placed more emphasis upon studies demonstrating the effectiveness of psychotropic drugs than upon those that did not (Gronfein, 1985, 450). In England also, policy makers presented a far more optimistic assessment of the new drugs than evaluative studies suggested should be the case: the view of government that 'It was only recently that powerful therapeutic weapons had been put into the hands of the medical staff, who for many years had had very limited prospects of curative work' (Ministry of Health, 1958, 22), was not at all well grounded within the available literature (Goodwin, 1989).

The second aspect of the claim that psychotropic drugs resulted in deinstitutionalization rests upon the apparent effect their introduction had upon mental hospital trends. The mental hospital in-patient population had grown since the early nineteenth century to stand at over 150,000 in 1954 in England and over 500,000 in 1955 in the United States.

Following the introduction of major tranquillizers in the mid-1950s the mental hospital in-patient population of each country began to decline. The apparent association between the two did not go unnoticed:

> Given the coincidence between the downturn in mental hospital populations and the introduction of the phenothiazines, one can readily understand why many simply assumed, and continue to assume, that deinstitutionalization was no more than a reflex response to another technological breakthrough of modern medicine. (Scull, 1987, 324)

Despite the emphasis that is frequently given to the coincidence of the introduction of psychotropic drugs and mental hospital populations reaching a peak, the correlation is in fact largely confined to just these two countries. The result of the introduction of major tranquillizers in France was to increase the medical dominance over mental health problems, not to reduce the mental hospital population (Demay, 1987, 71). Indeed in the 1960s, the Fourth and Fifth National Plans actually provided for an additional 20,000 psychiatric beds (Mangen, 1985, 124). In Spain between 1950 and 1981 the number of mental hospitals actually increased from 54 to 109, and the number of in-patients rose from 24,586 to 61,474 (Comelles & Hernáez, 1994, 284). And in most other European countries the link between the introduction of new treatments and policy change appears tenuous or non-existent. In Sweden and Denmark the mental hospital in-patient population demonstrated no sign of decrease until the late 1970s, while in Belgium it was not until the early 1980s that a trend towards deinstitutionalization became apparent (see Chapter 5 for fuller detail of these trends).

Given this variation in the pace and direction of mental hospital population trends, it is difficult to sustain the idea that psychotropic drugs and deinstitutionalization bear any particular relationship. Moreover, even when focusing just on England and the United States, the statistical basis of the argument proves to be tenuous. In an analysis of the trends in mental hospital discharge rates in the United States between 1946 and 1963, Gronfein found that the introduction of psychotropic drugs appeared to have had little effect on existing trends. The tendency towards an increased level of discharge was as apparent prior to 1954, when psychotropic drugs were first used, as it was after. Furthermore, considerable variations in mental hospital population trends existed between states, suggesting other factors were of greater importance in determining policy development. Gronfein concludes, therefore, that despite the mental hospital population reaching a peak in 1955, the impact of psychotropic drugs on this was minimal:

> While it is true that discharge rates were higher after the drugs were introduced than they were before, the mean percentage increase in discharge rates from 1946 to 1954 was greater than the mean percentage increase from 1955 to 1963. Also, while a majority of the states did experience a greater increase in discharge rates after drug introduction than before, fully 40 percent of the states showed the reverse trend. (Gronfein, 1985, 448)

In England, too, this apparent relationship between the use of psychotropic drugs and deinstitutionalization is ephemeral. As a percentage of the population, the mental hospital in-patient population peaked in the late 1920s (Chief Medical Officer, 1948), some 25 years prior to the introduction of the new drug treatments. Equally, trends in discharge rates in the period around the introduction of psychotropic drugs demonstrate similar patterns to those found by Gronfein in the United States. The mean percentage increase in discharge rate is no higher in the nine years after 1954 (when psychotropic drugs were introduced) than in the nine years prior (Ministry of Health, 1964).

These arguments are not intended to suggest that the impact of psychotropic drugs was anything other than profound. The effect on ward atmosphere was considerable, as was the effect upon the confidence of the psychiatric profession to be able to engage in what appeared to be a modern medical approach to mental illness. Indirectly, these effects contributed to the possibility of shifting from an institutional to a community care-based mental health policy. But what seems clear is that the claim that a direct and causal link exists between the introduction of the major tranquillizers and the onset of deinstitutionalization is, at best, unproven.

The basic problem with the argument is that it assumes something intrinsic to the effects of a chemical substance is directly responsible for the policy shift. But of course it is the way in which policy makers and mental health practitioners perceive the effects of the new drug treatments, within a context of what they consider to be their own and others' interests, that results in decisions about how they may be used. And it is this lack of a cultural context within which to locate an understanding of the impact on policy of the development of new drug treatments that vitiates the argument. As Sedgwick noted, to assume that the effects of a drug can be simply and directly related to a particular policy development amounts to a crude chemical reductionism:

> ... it is noticeable that the function of a particular medication, such as largactil or modecate, varies from that of an out-patient prescription with a specific anti-psychotic action to that of a general purpose bromide, doled out in massive frequency to long-term prison inmates or chronic mental patients as a convenient chemical straitjacket or liquid cosh. (1982, 200)

Social psychiatry and the interests and influence of the psychiatric profession

A further theme frequently appearing within orthodox accounts concerns the emergence of a new consensus of opinion about how people with mental health problems should be provided for. The claim often made is that in a variety of debates amongst various academic, professional and policy-making groups the move away from institutional and towards community-based care came to be readily associated with progressive and benevolent thinking. In 1953, for example, the World Health Organization's Expert Committee on Mental Health (World Health Organization, 1953) put forward a model of service provision proposing the development of a range of new psychiatric services within more locally based settings.

The most important source of this new and progressive thinking, it is often argued, was developments in psychiatric thinking (Jones, 1993). In France interest in social psychiatry grew strongly in the 1940s, and in 1952 a ministerial circular was issued supporting the use of trial leave and social therapies (Mangen, 1985, 119). In the 1960s a more liberal model of psychiatric practice emerged, associated with 'Évolution Psychiatrique' and led by people such as Henri Ey. It called for the modernization of hospitals, expansion of out-patient clinics, establishment of more day hospitals, and placed emphasis upon the importance of personal growth and the talking therapies (Demay, 1987, 72). In Amsterdam in the 1930s Querido (as we discussed in more detail in Chapter 1) developed a new model of mental health provision that placed emphasis upon the provision of social support. In Spain in the late 1960s younger psychiatrists began to demonstrate interest in the more radical and progressive ideas then coming into vogue.

By the 1970s a social model had to some extent replaced the previously dominant bio-medical model of mental health problems (Comelles & Hernáez, 1994, 288). Emphasis was also given in England in the 1940s and 1950s to the development of new models of care such as the unlocking of ward doors and the development of hostels and halfway homes. Perhaps most well known is the development of 'therapeutic communities' by Maxwell Jones. These European developments also had some impact in the United States, where similar patterns of experimentation with new models of service provision emerged in the mid-twentieth century (Kiesler, 1992, 1078).

This growing interest in and advocacy of a more socially orientated model within the psychiatric profession is often taken to represent an important shift in its position regarding how mental health services should be organized. Support for a more social rather than biologically orientated model of practice, however, does not amount to support for a shift from an institutional to community-based mental health system. The profession's origins and evolution lay largely within mental hospitals. A controlled environment dominated by medical rules and knowledge had constituted its working environment for over 100 years, and the shift towards community-based forms of treatment and care threatened this. It tended to take from it its power base and professional home, the mental hospital, and replace it with a more diverse working environment where team-work skills would be required.

Reflecting this history, the psychiatric profession has tended to demonstrate a reluctance to alter its working practices, and has generally opposed moves to erode the power and prestige of its hospital base

(Mangen, 1985, 132). In Italy, for example, where some of the more radical developments in thinking were taking place, a conference of psychiatrists held in 1965 clearly demonstrated their support of the institutional model. Emphasis was placed on the 'formative and educational function of the mental hospital', and concern was expressed about the 'antihierarchical notions equivalent to autodidacticism, contrary to the cultural and medical traditions to which we feel ourselves emotionally bound and rationally committed'. Overall it was argued that the mental hospital had made 'a significant contribution to the learning, research, and therapeutic achievements of science and society' (Pirella, 1987, 118).

The psychiatric profession has also tended to resist moves towards the development of new community-based services. In Canada, when proposals for developing new services were presented by the federal government in the 1960s, there was little response in the provinces. This was partly the result of a lack of money to make changes, but also a result of the role of existing interest groups, particularly the psychiatric profession, in maintaining the status quo: 'psychiatry in Canada had tended to be dominated by the British School, to maintain a physiological orientation, and to be hospital based' (Williams & Luterbach, 1976, 15). In France, while the asylum was dominant, the psychiatric profession had tended to emphasize chronicity of mental health problems together with the importance of maintaining patients for long periods of time in institutional care, and this attitude has tended to linger (Demay, 1987, 70).

In England the psychiatric profession has demonstrated a marked preference for maintaining its hospital-based role, rather than engage in the development of local community psychiatric services (Goldberg, 1986). In a 1984 study in Denmark, a total of 201 long-stay patients were examined to assess their need for continued hospitalization. The consultant psychiatrists found that 66 per cent of patients required continued hospitalization, whereas the investigators found only 20 per cent needed to be in hospital (Licht et al., 1991, 317). In Germany a similar attitude is taken: 'Community care is only one of the many objectives proposed and, in a country where psychiatrists have received a strong neuro-psychiatric training, it has often been viewed with suspicion as a means of undermining medical expertise' (Bennett, 1991, 633). In Ireland, too, community care has been hindered by medical interests. Following the publication of the Irish government's plans for the development of community-based services, laid out in 'Psychiatric Services – Planning for the Future' in 1984, considerable resistance from the psychiatric profession was encountered: 'A further but major constraint was the difficulty of the conversion to a community-orientated approach of doctors who relied heavily on their mental hospitals and whose professional identity was closely linked with the hospital' (Walsh, 1987, 114).

Alongside hospital psychiatry, there are also the interests and views of private psychiatry to consider. The development of new services, particularly out-patient provision at mental hospitals, directly threatens the business interests of private psychiatry. In Germany and the Netherlands, where 'office psychiatry' is widespread, this has resulted in considerable resistance to policy change. Equally, there are a number of other professional interests whose economic position is potentially threatened by policy change. The running down of a large mental hospital inevitably affects the job prospects of many workers, and hospital psychiatric nurses have displayed considerable wariness about supporting a policy that might lead to their own redundancy. This has proved a particularly pertinent issue in rural areas, where the local mental hospital has often been the main employer for many years (Kovess et al., 1995, 134).

Overall, the dominance of the psychiatric profession within mental health has had marked consequences for service development. The candid view of one psychiatrist in a review of European mental health services reveals its effect:

> Psychiatrists take a high proportion of the limited mental health budget, yet often pay little attention to chronically sick or disabled patients, long-stay institutional residents or the elderly mentally infirm who constitute the great bulk of psychiatric need. Neither do they necessarily involve themselves in service development work. Indeed, if trained in traditional patterns of work, they may represent a great force of inertia in traditional patterns of care, and therefore a constraint on the development of comprehensive, community-based services. (Freeman et al., 1985, 71)

Anti-psychiatry, anti-institutionalism and the civil rights movement

A further strand within this theme of the importance of new and progressive thinking is the development of radical analyses of mental health treatment and care. In the 1960s a number of critical accounts of psychiatric theory and practice were developed. Szasz (1961) argued that mental illness was a 'myth', concocted as a result of the interests of therapists in finding work and of the desires of people to absolve themselves of responsibility for their own 'problems in living'. Scheff (1966) developed the argument that mental illness was best understood as a form of residual deviance. By this idea Scheff means to refer to the actions of people who break rules, but not in ways that are immediately obvious and recognizable such as criminal activity. Those who are defined as displaying residual deviance are likely to be encouraged to perceive their own condition as one of mental illness.

A number of other writers, including Laing, Cooper and Esterson, also offered critiques of conventional, medically based psychiatry in the 1960s and 1970s. While they shared the umbrella term of anti-psychiatry, the analyses presented of the nature and causes of mental health problems varied widely. All, however, tended towards placing emphasis upon their social rather than medical origins, and upon understanding them as a product of unequal power relationships in society. Mental health problems were, for the most part, best understood as a form of deviance.

In addition to this critique of psychiatric theory and practice, a critique of institutions emerged. Barton (1959) developed the idea of 'institutional neurosis', to which, he claimed, people entering mental hospitals are prone. He defined this as being 'a disease in its own right characterised by apathy, lack of initiative, loss of interest' that came about because of the rigid and inhumane regimes within mental hospitals. Developing on this, Goffman (1961) formulated the concept of the 'total institution', central to which was 'the handling of many human needs by the bureaucratic organization of whole blocks of people', so that those admitted are 'shaped and coded' into the roles of psychiatric patients.

It is often argued that these critiques served to shift public and professional opinion against institutional and in favour of community mental health services:

> Both within and without the psychiatric profession a view criticising the ill-effects of prolonged stay within the large institutions emerged with increasing force. (Thornicroft & Bebbington, 1989, 740)

> The policy of deinstitutionalization in the 1960s received support because the public perception of the institutionalized mentally ill contradicted the social norms of what constituted humane care of the indigent. (Aviram, 1990, 83)

The views contained within anti-psychiatry and the anti-institutional critiques were often included in the civil rights movements of the 1960s, providing an impetus for their inclusion within demands for improved conditions and greater equality (Cooper & Bauer, 1987, 80; Aviram, 1990, 83).

> . . . 'anti-psychiatry' . . . harmonized with quite widely prevalent values and aspirations of the time. Models of mental illness which identified the patient (especially the sensitive young schizophrenic) with the radical critic of a dehumanizing society, his family with the oppressive forces of the established order, and defined the collusive psychiatrist as an agent of control and coercion, were dramatically congruent with the sharp questioning of established institutions and the quest for solutions. (Martin, 1984, 33)

There is certainly some evidence to support such views. In Italy, where the most radical policy initiatives took place, a marked shift occurred in the 1970s towards support for acknowledging the civil rights of marginalized groups. A number of social changes such as the decriminalization of the use of small amounts of some drugs, and the liberalization of the divorce and abortion laws were under way. The move against institutional care was very much part of this general change, and gained strength from it. In 1969, for example, a group of architecture students in Turin organized a conference with the billing 'It's a crime to build a mental hospital' (Pirella, 1987, 129). This social change resulted, in the local elections in 1975, in a shift towards more progressive provincial administrations. These were responsible for psychiatric services, and tended to shift mental health monies towards community-based projects and away from the mental hospital (Pirella, 1987, 129).

Within this context a radical democratic psychiatry movement was able to confront asylum-based psychiatric practice. It provided for a clear ideological position concerning the repressive nature of existing services, and the benefits of reintegration. These views were presented forcefully and effectively by the leaders of the movement:

> The external psychiatric services, in particular 'sectoral psychiatry,' are raising the first barricades capable of barring entrance into the asylum. But even if these structures should be able to reduce the influx of new patients, there remains the problem of the asylum as a forcibly imposed domicile, a place of perpetual institutionalization where the patient is constantly on trial and condemned, as Foucault says, under an indictment the text of which has never been displayed because it is sealed within the whole life of the asylum. (Basaglia, 1965, quoted in Pirella, 1987, 124)

The main areas of Italy where change in service provision has successfully been achieved are those where the Psichiatria Democratica movement was most active and influential, principally Trieste and Arezzo. This suggests that the influence of groups with strong and well-defined visions for change is an important factor in the policy shift. In other regions of Italy the influence of those supporting the status quo (in particular, those whose interests lie in maintaining existing mental hospital facilities) has been more influential.

While Italian mental health policy was clearly influenced by radical critiques, in most of Western Europe and North America their impact has been less distinct. While an element of psychiatric opinion was certainly affected by newly emerging critiques, for the most part the profession tended to either counter them or, perhaps more frequently, simply ignore them. A model of mental health problems as deviance never seriously threatened the long-standing and dominant bio-medical model. Moreover, the radical critique did not lead on to a more sustained critique of institutions in all countries. In the Netherlands Van Der Veen (1988, 29) suggests that the physical isolation of mental hospitals in the countryside resulted in their isolation from such outside influences. In Sweden, rather than focus upon the dismantling of the mental hospital, emphasis tended instead to be placed upon a critique of the biological orientation in psychiatry and advocacy of a more psychotherapeutic model of intervention. This generally had the effect of holding back the process of deinstitutionalization (Perris, 1987, 203).

A further problem with the assumed role of the anti-institutional critique concerns the timing of events. In the United States a comparable critique of the dangers of institutional care and the relative merits of community care had been developed in the 1870s, yet had had little effect (Scull, 1984). In England it is often argued that the critique of institutions that developed in the early 1960s provided a strong impetus towards reducing the number of psychiatric in-patients (Martin, 1984; Brown, 1985; Jones, 1993). Yet, by the late 1950s, a few years prior to the impact of the work of Goffman and others in England, the British government had already reached a clear view that care in the community was more therapeutic than institutional care:

> ... [there is] increasing acceptance by doctors of the view that for many patients treatment is likely to be more effective if the patient's links with his own home surroundings can be kept intact. Long term residence in a hospital – resulting in 'institutionalization' – may reduce the patient's prospect of eventual rehabilitation and discharge. (Ministry of Health, 1959, 7)

As with our discussion of the impact of new drug treatments on policy, the aim here is not to discount totally the importance of the anti-psychiatry movement and the critique of institutions. In the 1960s and 1970s their work was widely publicized and read, and undoubtedly contributed to the changing climate of opinion. This is not in question. But, as we have demonstrated above, to assume that such impact on public opinion is correspondingly important for the change of social policies is erroneous.

The poor conditions within the old mental hospitals

In addition to changing attitudes towards the therapeutic value of institutional care, increased attention began to be paid to the poor conditions often to be found in the old mental hospitals. In England in 1958 Aneurin Bevan, the Minister of Health, noted that 'some of our mental hospitals are in a disgraceful condition', and acknowledged that improvement was necessary (quoted in Klein, 1983, 31). In Germany in 1971, as was noted in Chapter 1, the federal government set up a commission, the Psychiatrie Enquête, to review mental health services. In an interim report in 1973 it found that conditions in the mental hospitals were very poor. Many patients were 'living in conditions which must be described as unsatisfactory and in part as unfit for human beings'. Two-thirds of patients were sleeping in dormitories with more than 20 beds. A whole range of items, including toilets, washing areas, lockers and other facilities, were found to be generally inadequate, and one building in eight was judged to require demolition (Cooper & Bauer, 1987, 78). Indeed, conditions in the mental hospitals of most other European and North American countries were generally recognized in the 1960s and 1970s to often be very poor (Mangen, 1985, 120; Walsh, 1987, 109; Rochefort, 1992, 1085).

Furthermore, overcrowding within mental hospitals was becoming increasingly common in the mid-twentieth century. Between 1945 and 1955 in the United States there was an average annual increase of around 13,000 patients, a rate of increase that if it had continued would have meant some 850,000 people being held in state mental hospitals by 1978 (Cockerham, 1992, 27). In France in the 1950s there was an estimated overcrowding rate of 40 per cent, resulting in considerable pressures upon the mental health system (Barres, 1987). Similar conditions pertained in English mental hospitals, with some reporting overcrowding levels of over 60 per cent in the early 1950s (Goodwin, 1993).

It is often argued that these circumstances provided an impetus towards developing new community-based services. In France, for example, Barres (1987, 142) argues that overcrowding and poor physical conditions of the old mental hospitals gave impetus to the development of new and more modern treatment facilities. This link, between poor conditions and a shift towards community-based provision was not made so clearly at the time, however. The initial response of the government in England was to make the expansion of institutional provision a priority policy: 'one of the biggest problems that faces the service in the future is the provision of more accommodation in mental hospitals' (Ministry of Health, 1952, iv). In the United States mental hospital superintendents were making stringent demands for more money and resources with which to expand and improve their services, such that 'Hospital growth seemed inevitable' (Gronfein, 1985, 449). In France, also, the main concern of hospital directors in the early 1950s was the development of more bed space, something that was to be achieved in subsequent years (Mangen, 1985, 120). In Spain, also, as admission rates and levels of overcrowding rose rapidly in the 1950s and 1960s, new mental hospitals were built and bed space was increased:

> The crisis of custodialism did not occur as a consequence of the unstoppable growth in the numbers of those admitted. In fact the state constructed mental hospitals in the period 1950–65 with the intention that they would act as psychiatric warehouses. (Comelles & Hernáez, 1994, 288)

Poor conditions combined with overcrowding certainly presented the mental hospital system with difficulties, but did not provide a direct impetus for deinstitutionalization. It was, instead, a combination of the growing criticism of the conditions in the old mental hospitals, combined with a lack of resources to overhaul them, which prompted policy change. It was increasingly widely recognized that the old asylums would required considerable refurbishment if public support for institutional care was to be sustained (Hafner et al., 1989, 12), and the potential costs of this provided a spur towards looking at alternatives to maintaining institutional care (Donnelly, 1992, 20). Policy makers within England were amongst the first to recognize this. We noted above that in 1952 the Ministry of Health advocated the development of more mental hospital bed space. Just four years later its position had already undergone considerable change:

> The extent of the problem of overcrowded mental hospitals could probably be reduced considerably by further development of all the resources of hospital

and community care in a comprehensive service. (Ministry of Health, 1956, 13)

Increased community tolerance

A further factor often presented to explain the policy shift is the idea that attitudes within the community are, or are becoming, sufficiently positive to ensure that people with mental health problems, once discharged, will experience a degree of tolerance sufficient to enable them to begin the process of reintegration. In England it was argued that there had been 'A substantial change in the general climate of public opinion' (Ministry of Health, 1958, 22), and that 'People are more ready to tolerate mental disorder' (Chief Medical Officer, 1958, 121). The impact of this, together with the recent development of new drug treatments, was held to be of considerable importance for the future development of mental health services:

> Because of the success of new methods of treatment combined with changed social attitudes, it may be expected that the recent decline in the number of hospital beds required for mental illness will continue. (Ministry of Health, 1962, 5)

Similarly in the United States, it was held that substantial changes in public attitudes towards people with mental health problems were occurring: 'It seems not too much to say that the community is at last developing an attitude of far greater tolerance toward the discharged mental patient, a greater readiness to accept him back into the community' (Overholser, 1958, 215). In Sweden, it was claimed that 'The attitude of the public as well as of officials outside psychiatry has been uninformed, vague, suspicious or frightened. This pattern is in a process of change' (National Board of Health and Welfare, 1993, 9). In France it has been argued that more positive attitudes towards the mentally ill have allowed for the discharge of people with mental health problems and for them to be supported in the community (George, 1992). And in Spain, too, similar views have been expressed: 'Today, mental patients are better understood than they were 25 years ago' (Poveda, 1987, 182).

However, while this view is often made explicit, far less clear is the basis upon which the claim is being made. Only in North America has the question of community tolerance been researched to any extent in the period over which deinstitutionalization has occurred. A number of studies were carried out in the 1950s that sought to establish how tolerant people were of discharged mental patients living in their local area. Generally, these studies made a negative assessment of community attitudes. Star (1955), in a large survey of United States public opinion, found considerable ignorance of the nature of mental illness, and little tolerance towards the condition. Cumming and Cumming (1957), in a study of a small, rural community in Canada, similarly found that attitudes towards people experiencing mental health problems were largely negative.

In the United States, surveys of public opinion continued to be made through the 1960s and 1970s. Researchers increasingly came to the view that the public was acquiring greater knowledge and understanding of mental illness, although attitudes to it remained largely negative (Cockerham, 1992). Moreover, research by Gove and Fain (1973) and Huffine and Clausen (1979) suggested that the negative attitudes held by the public are in fact rarely acted upon; that in practice the mentally ill are not actually subjected to the process of stigmatization and discrimination that might be expected given community attitudes. A recent national survey in the United States found that 84 per cent of respondents believed that most people with mental health problems are able to function normally in society when treated, and 71 per cent believed that mental illness could be cured (Thompson, 1994, 991). Overall, Cockerham suggests that 'although the stereotype of former mental patients is still negative, attitudes towards them have become somewhat more liberal in recent years ... however ... social rejection of such persons still persists' (1992, 281). Similarly, Taylor maintains that despite the fact that some opposition persists, 'findings on attitudes toward the mentally ill and community mental health facilities imply a relatively high level of public tolerance and support' (1988, 229).

The study of community attitudes towards discharged mental patients is far less well developed in Europe, although some evidence is now emerging. A study of community attitudes towards mental illness found that attitudes were generally more tolerant in Northern European countries (Neelman & van Os, 1994, 1220). In Italy, Graziani (1989) found that discharged mental patients were often perceived as being dangerous. This resulted in considerable difficulties being experienced by mental health service professionals when attempting to place mental patients in family and community settings. In England a number of studies have been conducted that indicate public support for community care. A survey by the National Schizophrenia Fellowship in 1990 found 69 per cent of the survey population agreed that quality of life for people with mental health problems would be 'a lot better in the community' (Sayce, 1994, 11). In 1994 the mental health charity MIND undertook a survey of public opinion, which again established that considerable support for community care policy exists. Seventy-two per cent of people were found to agree with the statement that 'as far as possible mental health services should be provided through community services'. There were also high levels of support for putting more money into community care services (67 per cent), and for improving the overall quality of service delivery and organization (69 per cent) (Sayce, 1994, 11).

While there is some evidence of a growing acceptance of people with mental health problems living within local communities, there is equally a growing body of evidence to suggest that the very notion of 'community tolerance' is overly simplistic. It has been found in some American studies that the responses of different groups to questions on mental health issues vary considerably. Older people, lower-class and less educated people all appeared to make a more negative assessment of mental health problems (Cockerham, 1992). A survey conducted in England in 1994 found that women demonstrated more commitment to the idea of community care than men, this being despite the fact that women experience the greater burden of care (Sayce, 1994, 12). There is a perception amongst older people in some countries, especially in Southern Europe, that young people are now less willing to care for elderly relatives than was the case previously (Means & Smith, 1994, 198).

Many studies have also found a hierarchy of levels of tolerance for certain groups of people with disabilities over others, and those with psychiatric disabilities consistently rank among the least favoured (Lyons & Hayes, 1993). For example, community-based facilities for mental health clients tend to be viewed far less favourably than those for people with learning disabilities or elderly people (Wilmoth & Burnett, 1987). It has also been found that the degree of acceptance of people with disabilities varies greatly between nationalities. Jaques & Davies (1970) found significant differences in attitude towards mental disability between American, Danish, Greek and Chinese samples. An Australian study of community attitudes towards disability found that the German community expressed greatest acceptance of people with disabilities, followed by the Anglo, Italian, Chinese, Greek and Arabic groups. However, the relative degree of stigma attached to the various disabilities by the communities was very similar. In all communities, people with mental health problems were amongst the least accepted of the disability groups (Westbrook et al., 1993).

Just what should be made of this evidence is, as yet, unclear. Certainly there is some reason for optimism. Taylor goes so far as to argue that 'The gradual shift in public opinion away from authoritarian and restrictive beliefs about the mentally ill toward a more benevolent and community-focused view of mental health care implies a growing tolerance, sensitivity to needs, and perhaps willingness to support facilities and services' (1988, 243). Supporting this view is the often-made proposition that over time increasing public acceptance of scientific medicine will result in a reduction in the level of stigma attached to disablement (Mechanic, 1968). Yet, as we have noted above, the level of knowledge about community attitudes towards the reintegration of people with mental health problems is low, and understanding of what processes contribute to the formation of attitudes is lower still.

While the available evidence is far from complete, what is becoming increasingly clear is that a gap exists between the assumptions made within policy statements and the reality of the situation concerning the extent of community tolerance. Policy statements have continued to demonstrate a simplistic and optimistic view of the reception discharged mental patients are likely to receive:

> Changes in the type of treatment available and in social attitudes to people suffering from mental illness, have continued to make the old pattern of health services based on long-term care in large isolated hospitals even more inappropriate. (Department of Health and Social Security, 1986, 23)

This is not to suggest, however, that discharged patients are all likely to receive a uniformly negative response. The research evidence suggests a far more complex reaction involving sympathy and fear, concern and indifference, that mix in different ways and amounts between different communities and between different social groups.

Increased understanding of the needs and desires of mental patients

The notion that people with mental health problems whenever possible prefer to live in the community and, when possible, in their own homes, has provided additional impetus to the policy shift. There is certainly some evidence to support this. In a survey of 48 long-stay patients discharged from a Scottish hospital, MacGilp (1991) found that every respondent preferred living in the community compared to being in a psychiatric hospital, and almost all respondents (46) were found to be satisfied with life in general. A Canadian study of 55 people discharged from in-patient psychiatric rehabilitation programmes came to similar conclusions. Following long periods of psychiatric hospitalization, these former patients had adapted to living in the larger community with considerable success. Ninety-six per cent felt that their quality of life had improved as a consequence of leaving hospital, and most were found to have the necessary basic domestic skills to live in community settings. They demonstrated appropriate behaviours and blended into the larger community without difficulty, and they used outreach support services provided by the hospital to help them in the transition to community living (Pinkney et al., 1991).

Less positive attitudes towards discharge into the community have, however, been found in other surveys. Abrahamson & Johnson, in a study of an English mental hospital, found that 'reluctance to leave hospital is in fact common amongst long-stay patients, and is one of the most frequent problems met by resettlement programmes' (1982, 95). In a study of 100 discharged psychiatric patients in London, it was found that although the majority preferred living outside hospital, 80 per cent were dissatisfied with their current housing (Kay & Legg, 1986). Ritchie & Jacobs, in a survey of the views of service users, found 'vociferous support for the continuation of psychiatric units which provide sanctuary of the kind hospitals now provide' (1989, 6).

In a review of the literature on patient satisfaction with service provision, Corrigan (1990) found that most patients were satisfied with the job performance of in-patient staff. A high staff–patient ratio was preferred, and patients were also pleased when doctors were readily available, and when they freely shared information regarding treatment (Corrigan, 1990, 157). A complaint often made about institutional care was the lack of privacy, and the lack of security for personal possessions it offered. The ready availability of food and provision of a warm and clean environment, however, tended to be regarded highly (Corrigan, 1990, 157). Somewhat equivocal views on the merits of discharge were expressed. Patients were often found to be concerned about the lack of preparation for discharge, and about whether community facilities would offer the same level of safety and cleanliness to be found in institutional settings (Corrigan, 1990, 159).

The level of satisfaction expressed by patients has been found to depend not just on the quality of services provided, but also on the patient's characteristics as well. In the United States older patients, better-educated and black people have been found to express greater satisfaction than other groups with out-patient services (Corrigan, 1990, 161). In a Danish study Kelstrup et al. (1993) found that patients who were diagnosed as suffering from affective disorders or from reactive psychoses were more satisfied than patients with schizophrenia or paranoia, and patients on anti-depressant medication were found to be much more satisfied than other patients with the services they received.

In a review of a number of studies of the preferences of service users, Weinstein (1979) undertook a comparison of professional opinions of consumer preferences for either institutional or community care derived from a review of 11 articles, and compared this to 38 studies that directly surveyed service user opinion. The survey of professional opinion was found to offer a far more pessimistic view of institutional care than those given by service users. Professional opinion tended to emphasize the lack of autonomy and bleak environment to which service users were often subjected. The service users themselves held a far more positive view of institutional care, and in particular stressed its value as a source of asylum.

The available research evidence tends to demonstrate what might be considered obvious: that, like any other group, people with mental health problems hold a diverse set of views about their own interests, needs and desires, and this is reflected in their varying views over the service provision that is available. While community care may be the preferred option of many, for some it may not. Overall, however, there is very little research undertaken to establish preferences for institutional or community care by people with mental health problems. The evidence that has been collected has tended to focus more upon the issue of how satisfactory service users have found services they are actually receiving, rather than upon inviting comparison between types of service

(Corrigan, 1990, 152). And perhaps what is most telling about this issue is that while governments have been active in stating what service users want, no effort was put into establishing their views prior to implementation of radical change in services.

The critique of institutions, together with the eulogization of community, has constituted the dominant discourse of academics, professionals and policy makers; but not that of service users. As Aviram notes, 'The widely shared belief that the preferred arrangement is for mentally ill persons to live with their families should be a subject for study rather than an accepted assumption' (1990, 81).

Constitutional structures

The federal constitutional structure of some countries is a further factor that it is argued can have substantial impact upon service development. In the United States the development of federally funded mental health programmes provided great incentives for the individual states to reduce rapidly their own programmes of mental hospital provision and develop new community care-based programmes utilizing federal funds (Scull, 1984). The introduction of Medicaid in the mid-1960s enabled both a transfer of obligation from state to federal budgets, and a more rapid transfer of patients to nursing homes (Mechanic, 1968). The introduction of the new Supplemental Security Income Programme in 1972 further enhanced the financial incentives of states to reduce mental hospital bed space (Scull, 1987, 322). The federal structure of Canada has also facilitated the creation of financial inducements for the provinces to respond to federal government policy-making. In 1957 the federal government introduced the Hospital Insurance and Diagnostic Services Act, which established a cost-sharing programme for hospital insurance between the provincial and federal governments. This provided financial support from federal government to cover hospital costs of mental patients in general hospital facilities, but not psychiatric hospitals. The provinces were therefore given a financial inducement to shift service provision towards the development of new services, resulting in a rapid shift towards running down provincial mental hospital facilities (Williams & Luterbach, 1976, 17).

These examples are, however, by no means typical of the effect on policy of a federal constitutional structure. In Canada the federal government and the Mental Health Association were both critical of the high levels of compulsory admission in the 1950s and 1960s in many of the provinces, but proved unable to do anything about it (Williams & Luterbach, 1976, 17). In European countries such as Germany, Belgium and the Netherlands, their federal or relatively decentralized constitutional structures have had the opposite effect, with the transition towards deinstitutionalization proceeding at a relatively slow pace. The division of responsibility and power between federal and state government, together with the involvement of voluntary groups, medical associations, hospitals and insurance funds who have their own interests, results in a situation where it is difficult to formulate and implement any national policies. The system tends towards inertia, and makes any attempts at planning or of coordination very difficult (Mangen, 1985, 82–83). Conversely, in England, where policy-making is more centralized, it has proved possible to implement reform in part because central government has relatively greater powers, thereby enabling it to overcome local resistance.

There is no clear relationship between constitutional structure and the speed with which community-based service provision has been developed. Federal governments are able to create inducements for their member states to follow, but are less able compared to more centralized governments to dictate change should resistance occur. Reflecting this, we noted in Chapter 1 that the United States and England were the first countries to proceed with deinstitutionalization and the development of community care. Yet the constitutional structures of these two countries are of course very different.

Funding systems

The organization of the finance of mental health services is often noted to have had considerable impact upon policy development. In countries such as Germany, France, Belgium, the Netherlands and the United States, the insurance system of payment upon which their mental health services are based has tended to create resistance to policy change (Verhaegey, 1987, 43). Mental hospitals have normally been paid on a daily fee basis for each patient provided for. As a result each mental hospital needs to maintain bed-occupancy rates in order to maintain its income. Consequently, this system of payment tends to discourage the development of day patient, out-patient and other community-based services, because they will tend to result in a reduction of in-patient admissions, and therefore a loss of income (Giel, 1987, 155).

This problem is compounded by the fact that the in-patients who could most readily be moved to residential or other community-based services will, in general, be the least dependent of the in-patient population and also therefore the cheapest to provide for. The daily fee system of payment tends not to distinguish between the most and least needy patients. As such the less needy patients provide a subsidy to the more needy. For the mental hospital this provides still greater incentive to avoid the loss of these patients to community facilities. The consequence of this in the Netherlands has been that patients moved from mental hospital to residential accommodation have tended to be old and highly dependent (Grinten, 1985, 221).

Compounding this problem, is the tendency of an insurance-based system to reinforce a medical rather than social model of service provision. This is because claims are made for identifiable mental health problems experienced by individuals. The emphasis in turn tends to be upon providing a specific treatment with the aim of curing the patient within a known period of time, and thereby ending the claim. This enables insurance funds to monitor and regulate claims made, and also control costs to a large degree. Mental health problems often do not fit this model. Compared to physical conditions they are relatively difficult to diagnose accurately, the treatments available are highly variable in their effect, and the problem often exists for a long period of time. As a result insurance schemes have proved slow to accept responsibility for mental health problems, particularly where the patient is primarily in need of long-term care or relatively non-specific treatment such as group counselling.

Reflecting these issues, in France 80 per cent of the costs of treatment by an office psychiatrist were reimbursed, while the dispensaries which offered a similar service but under the label of prevention received only a 30 per cent subsidy (Mangen, 1985, 131). In Germany it was only when the phenothiazines were introduced that statutory sickness funds were extended to provide for the treatment of psychosis. Mental hospital fees have tended to be only around half of those of general hospitals, and not all costs are adequately covered. Equally, the disability insurance funds accept liability only for providing rehabilitation that is likely to result in substantial improvement, and this has tended to exclude people with mental health problems (Mangen, 1985, 84). In a review of costs in one area in Germany in 1983 it was found that only some 20 per cent of the total mental health care costs were met by the insurance funds, and, of this amount, around 70 per cent went towards the costs of hospital in-patient care (Cooper & Bauer, 1987, 84).

In the United States insurance programmes have also tended to favour in-patient care. Most insurance schemes meet around 50 per cent of out-patient costs, but all of in-patient costs. The aim of insurance companies has been to meet the treatment costs of more serious psychiatric problems, but to inhibit the more general use of services by less seriously affected people (Kiesler & Sibulkin, 1987, 225). Mechanic (1980) notes, however, that this can result in a tendency for unnecessary hospitalization, in order that the patient may receive treatment. More generally, it tends to 'reinforce traditional, ineffective and inefficient patterns of mental health care, inhibit innovation and use of less expensive mental health personnel, and reinforce a medical as compared with a social or educational approach to patients' psychological problems' (Mechanic, 1980, 225).

This range of problems with insurance-based systems of allocating health care resources has resulted in some change. In France a unified mental health budget was introduced in 1984, which has helped remove some constraints. Mental hospitals are now guaranteed an annual budget, irrespective of bed-occupancy rates (Barres, 1987, 141–142). In the Netherlands in 1968 insurance cover was expanded to include long-term care needs, such as those of chronic mental patients. The social psychiatric services (voluntary community-based services) also gained access to funds through the insurance system (Grinten, 1985, 214). In 1982, sickness insurance liability was extended to clearly include preventive and counselling work, in addition to the more traditional notions of sickness, and in 1986 extramural services were incorporated into the social sickness fund insurance schemes (Haveman, 1986, 456). Fixed budgets for mental hospitals and for the combined out-patient and community-based services were introduced in 1982, the intention of this being to shift financial incentives for service providers away from hospital and towards community-based service developments (Giel, 1987, 154).

In Germany in 1969 the costs of rehabilitation of people with mental health problems became a statutory obligation of social insurance. More recently, the enactment of cost containment legislation in 1993 has resulted in considerable changes to the system of financing health care. The finances of mental hospitals are still determined to some extent by their activity rate, but other payments based on diagnostic-related groups and patient management categories have been introduced to help break the interest mental hospitals have had in admitting and retaining patients. These measures have helped remove some constraints upon the development of community-based services. Even so, some difficulties have tended to remain, particularly around the issue of categorizing the service of which a people with mental health problems is in need. The determination of which of these is required in turn determines which insurance fund is liable, and consequently provides ground for contesting of costs between insurance companies (Graf von der Schulenburg, 1994).

Summary

In Table 2.1 the main findings of the above discussion are summarized. It reveals a series of problems with many of the propositions that make up the orthodox analysis. Our argument is that the tendency of insurance-based funding systems to hinder policy change is the only proposition we have reviewed that can be accepted as being basically correct. This factor is, however, relatively marginal; its concern is only with the rate of policy change and not with its instigation. Other factors that are

Table 2.1   *A critique of the orthodox analysis*

Reasons for the policy shift	Evaluation
1. The development of new drug treatments.	There is little evidence to suggest a causal link between the use of drugs and the development of community care, although they certainly contributed to the possibility of policy change.
2. The development of social psychiatry.	While social psychiatry certainly contributed to innovative service developments, the influence of this upon policy development has been marginal in relation to other more conservative interests and concerns of the psychiatric profession.
3. The emergence of radical analyses, together with the civil rights movement.	The impact of these groups and movements upon public opinion was considerable. But their impact upon policy was less, and was not always in support of a move towards care in the community.
4. The poor conditions within the old mental hospitals.	The policy response in many countries to the overcrowding and poor conditions within the old mental hospitals was to plan for the building of new ones. In some countries this was subsequently undertaken, but not in others.
5. Increased community tolerance.	The assumption that increased tolerance in the community allowed for the discharge of mental patients lacks evidence in its support.
6. The wishes of people with mental health problems to live, whenever possible, within community settings.	As with community tolerance, the assumptions made about the wishes of service users have been without adequate foundation. What evidence does exist reveals a more complex set of views and desires than allowed for within policy development.
7. A federal constitutional structure has tended to facilitate a more rapid shift in policy.	A federal constitutional structure has proved both a help and a hindrance to governments seeking policy change. No clear relationship emerges between the two.
8. Insurance-based funding systems have tended to hinder the policy shift.	There is certainly some evidence to support this proposition, although developments towards overcoming these barriers have been made in many countries in recent years.

attributed greater importance within the orthodox analysis, such as introduction of new drugs, the role of social psychiatry and others, are all highly problematic. The available evidence is either insufficient to provide support for them, or indeed directly contradicts them.

3

Radical Accounts of the Policy Shift

Rather than focus upon particular ideological currents, administrative arrangements or other intricacies of public policy-making, Marxist and other radical writers tend to focus upon broad analytical themes associated with the more general nature of social and economic arrangements. A central contention is that the postwar mental health policies of Western European and North American countries have largely been shaped by financial pressures.

As a rough average, the countries of Western Europe and North America spend around 10 per cent of national income on health care, and around 10 per cent of the health care budget on mental health problems (McGuire, 1991, 375). In addition to these direct costs, the costs to families of caring and the economic costs of lost productivity add up to a total cost estimated to be as much as 4 per cent of gross domestic product in England (Mental Health Foundation, 1993, 1). In the United States it is estimated that total direct and indirect costs amounted to almost $2 billion in 1955, and by 1988 this had risen to $129 billion. In terms of national income, this represents a loss of 0.5 per cent in 1955 rising to 2.6 per cent in 1988. Fifty-five per cent of the costs of mental health problems in the United States are estimated to result from lost productivity (McGuire, 1991, 375).

Overall, therefore, the costs of mental health problems to a nation are substantial. This fact, together with the relatively difficult fiscal conditions faced by many governments over the last 20 years or so, leads most writers to accept the importance of economic factors in the determination of mental health policy. Jones, a leading advocate of the orthodox position, clearly acknowledges this:

> ... the discovery by governments that welfare policies had limits, and that citizens were liable to demand far more in the way of services than they were prepared to pay for through taxes; and a new economic situation after the crisis of 1973, in which monetarism was dominant, public sector expenditure was reduced, unemployment was widespread, and welfare services were cut to the bone. These factors, common to all countries in the Western world and involving some curious and contradictory reasoning, brought about similar results in quite different national contexts. (1988, 82)

The radical argument, however, is more specific than this. The argument presented is that the advanced capitalist societies are increasingly prone to ever more severe economic problems, and consequently ever higher levels of restraint within state welfare budgets are increasingly evident. It is not simply that the development of an adequate community care policy has suffered as a result of a lack of finance, but rather community care policy has arisen precisely because it allows for a cost-cutting process made necessary by the nature of the socio-economic system.

A leading advocate of this position is Andrew Scull. He maintains that over the postwar period governments in the advanced capitalist countries have become increasingly prone to 'fiscal crisis': a condition where tax revenues tend to decline while demands for social expenditure tend to increase, resulting in a growing fiscal deficit. The process of de-institutionalization has primarily been the result of a need to reduce costs, and the ideology of community care has provided the legitimating cover under which that programme has commenced:

> Once the drive for control of soaring costs is seen as the primary factor underlying the move towards decarceration . . . this change which formerly appeared either fortuitous or inexplicable becomes readily comprehensible. . . . In particular, it reflects the structural pressures to curtail sharply the costly system of segregative control . . . . (Scull, 1984, 140, 152)

This analysis has been very influential in discussions of mental health policy in recent years, with it often being argued that the transition from institutional to community care represents little more than a cost-cutting exercise. Less often evaluated, however, are the wide-ranging theoretical propositions assumed within such a contention. The theory underlying the idea of fiscal crisis suggests that countries with the largest public welfare expenditures might be expected to experience the greatest economic problems, the greatest pressure upon government finances, and would therefore be expected to demonstrate the greatest tendency towards deinstitutionalization. Contained within these propositions, however, are a range of assumptions about the nature of the policy-making process and the purposes and impact of welfare provision, many of which might be questioned.

High public welfare expenditure is a cause of economic problems

In a review of public welfare expenditure in a number of Western countries, Maddison (1984) argues that there is no convincing evidence to suggest that the welfare state inhibits economic growth. The OECD (1985) also came to a similar conclusion, finding no inverse relationship between the size of welfare states and economic growth rates, unemployment levels or inflation rates. Over the postwar period there has, Alber (1988) argues, been no statistical association between welfare state growth and fiscal problems. Since the mid-1970s, however, as economic problems have tended to increase, there is some evidence of such a linkage emerging:

... while there is little evidence showing that the growth of the welfare state is the root cause of budget imbalances, countries which failed to adapt their welfare state programmes to the recent changes in the economic environment were clearly most prone to run into mounting fiscal problems. (Alber, 1988, 198)

Western welfare states have in recent years found it increasingly difficult to harmonize their expenditure with their revenues, but just what the economic impact of this has been or will be is not clear (Alber, 1988, 193).

High public expenditure growth is associated with a tendency towards deinstitutionalization

A further assumption within the radical argument is that a tendency exists for countries with high rates of public expenditure growth to be more active in pursuing a policy of deinstitutionalization, as a means of reducing that expenditure burden. However, in the period 1965 to 1984, Alber (1988, 187) notes that of 16 Western welfare state countries (see Table 3.1), public spending generally grew at a faster rate than gross domestic product, and that this tendency was not stalled by the onset of greater economic problems after 1975. Within this general trend, three distinct rates of growth in public expenditure could be distinguished.

Table 3.1 offers little evidence of correlation between expenditure growth and deinstitutionalization. Germany has been relatively slow to deinstitutionalize its mental hospital population, yet is in the low expenditure category when the radical analysis would predict it should be in the high category. France has also been relatively slow to deinstitutionalize, but is in the fast category. England and the United States are the two countries where deinstitutionalization first started, and yet their rate of public expenditure growth has been slow when the theory of fiscal crisis would suggest that it should be fast. Overall, there appears to be no consistent relationship to be established between these two variables.

Table 3.1 *Rates of public expenditure growth (1965–1984)*

Fast	Medium	Slow
Denmark	Netherlands	US
Italy	Austria	Switzerland
France	Finland	Norway
Belgium	Canada	UK
Ireland	Japan	FR Germany
Sweden		

Note: Fast growth is defined by public expenditure ratio increases of between 9 per cent and 15 per cent, medium by increases of between 4 per cent and 7 per cent, and slow by increases of less than 3 per cent.
Source: Alber, 1988, 187

High fiscal deficits result in pressure for deinstitutionalization

Similar problems arise when considering the relationship between levels of government borrowing and deinstitutionalization. A high level of borrowing can be assumed to reflect greater fiscal problems. We should therefore expect to find the scale of government borrowing to be positively correlated with the rate of deinstitutionalization. For the period 1960–74, as Figure 3.1 demonstrates, there appears to be some degree of merit in this proposition. The three countries, Germany, France and Denmark, which had the largest increases in mental hospital bed space were also the three that hold a positive fiscal balance. Equally the three countries, Ireland, England and the United States, which had reduced their mental hospital populations all had a negative fiscal balance. However, the two remaining countries, Italy and the Netherlands, both had negative fiscal balances and yet increased their mental hospital populations in this period. Moreover, the scale of fiscal deficit or surplus appears unrelated to the scale of change in mental hospital bed space. It would, for example, be difficult to argue that bed space increased by a third in Germany because of an average 0.3 per cent surplus on government spending, and conversely that in the United States bed space decreased by a third because of an average 0.1 per cent deficit on government spending.

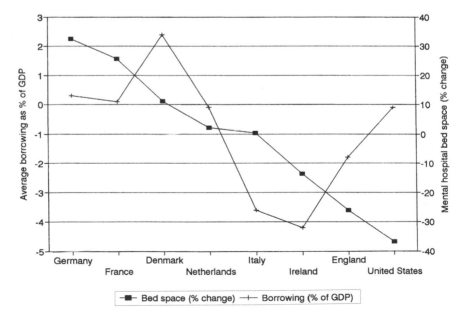

Figure 3.1 *The relationship between fiscal deficits and deinstitutionalization (1960–1974). Source: Average borrowing as a percentage of gross domestic product derived from OECD (1990). Percentage changes in mental hospital bed space derived from World Health Organization (1970) and Poullier & Sandier (1991).*

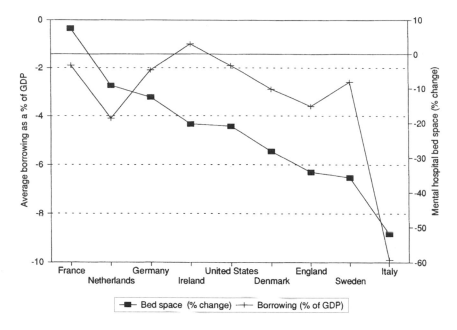

Figure 3.2 *The relationship between fiscal deficits and deinstitutionalization (1975–1985).* Source: *Average borrowing as a percentage of gross domestic product derived from OECD (1990). Percentage changes in mental hospital bed space derived from Poullier & Sandier (1991).*

In the subsequent period, between 1975 and 1985, a similar pattern emerges. As Figure 3.2 indicates, France has one of the lower borrowing requirements, and witnessed an increase in bed space. Conversely, Italy, with the highest borrowing requirement, had the greatest reduction in bed space. But there are also examples that clearly buck this trend. The Netherlands, for example, has one of the higher borrowing requirements and yet made little relatively little progress towards reducing its mental hospital bed space.

Overall, Alber concludes that general theoretical propositions concerning the supposed impact of welfare expenditure upon economic success (i.e. an economic burden), as well as assumptions about the likely reaction of governments to fiscal problems (i.e. welfare expenditure cuts generally, and deinstitutionalization in particular) lack general applicability. Rather, 'we find a growing heterogeneity in welfare state developments in recent years. The marked differences in national expenditure profiles illustrate that the analysis of welfare state developments requires much more specific hypotheses than the dominant "grand theories" suggest' (Alber, 1988, 189). Certainly, the evidence available does not support the proposition that fiscal problems are likely to result in a general tendency towards deinstitutionalization. There is little evidence of correlation between the two, and there are a number of examples where the opposite of what the radical arguments predict has actually occurred.

The retention of institutional care results in increasingly large opportunity costs

As a result of the growth of welfare states over the twentieth century it has become possible for groups such as the elderly and people experiencing mental health problems to survive within the community. As a means of supporting people this should prove far more cost-efficient:

> ... with the advent of a wide range of welfare programs providing support, the opportunity cost of neglecting community care in favor of asylum treatment – inevitably far more costly than the most generous scheme of welfare payments – rose sharply. (Scull, 1984, 135)

The development of pensions, social assistance and other benefits enables dependent people to survive in the community, with the consequence that the mental hospital becomes an unnecessary expense.

To consider this proposition, we will use social security expenditures as a percentage of gross domestic product as a measure of the extent to which community-based welfare provision has been developed. The radical position holds that we should expect to see an inverse correlation between trends in the level of social security transfers, and trends in the extent of deinstitutionalization. Yet, as Figure 3.3 demonstrates, this is not readily apparent. All the countries included experienced some increase in the level of social security transfers as a percentage of gross

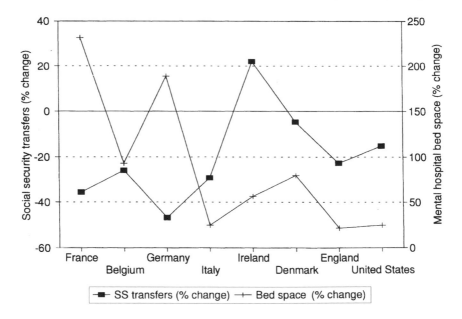

Figure 3.3 *The relationship between opportunity costs and deinstitutionalization (1962–1985). Source: Data on social security transfers, OECD (1990). Percentage changes in mental hospital bed space derived from World Health Organization (1970) and Poullier & Sandier (1991).*

domestic product, yet in two (Germany and France) there was actually an increase in mental hospital bed space between 1962 and 1985. Ireland experienced the greatest increase in social security transfer growth, and yet was only in the mid-range of countries that experienced reductions in mental hospital bed space.

In total, it would appear from this sample of countries that the opportunity costs of institutional care, which Scull maintains should rise with increased social security spending, are either not apparent or are not having the assumed effect.

An inverse relationship can be found between levels of unemployment and mental hospital bed space

Brenner (1973) develops a variation on this economic argument, concerning the importance of levels of unemployment. It is based on a study of New York State from 1841, and of all American states from 1922 through to 1968. From this, he concludes that there is a clear and consistent inverse relationship between rates of unemployment and levels of mental hospital admission. It is, he claims, 'clear that instabilities in the national economy have been the single most important source of fluctuation in mental-hospital admissions or admission rates' (Brenner, 1973, p. viii). This basic fact holds even when allowing for differences in admission rates based on gender, ethnic origin and a number of other variables.

In a study of the Hamilton Psychiatric Hospital in Hamilton, Ontario, between 1960 and 1977, Dear et al. also found evidence of a link between economic activity and rates of mental hospital admission. Variations in the level of unemployment were not found to be significantly correlated with the provision of bed space, but did seem to be of some importance in determining the level of mental hospital bed vacancies. It was found that for a 10 per cent increase in unemployment the vacancy rate would decline by 4.8 per cent. Inflation also appeared to be an important factor, whereby a 10 per cent increase in price inflation would induce an increase of 17.4 per cent in the vacancy rate. Overall, these conclusions differ somewhat from those of Brenner concerning the importance of unemployment in determining mental hospital use. Nevertheless the basic contention, that changes in mental health policy are largely economically driven, is very similar: 'trends in mental health policy are strongly related with indicators of economic activity' (Dear et al., 1979, 53).

The position adopted by Warner (1989) provides further variation on this theme. He maintains that two key economic forces have been at work in determining the mental health policies of Western European and North American countries in the postwar period. Firstly, following Scull, Warner argues that the opportunity for cost savings has given governments great economic incentives to reduce the level of mental hospital bed space. However, because of the considerable international variations in the onset and pace of this shift in policy and also in the quality of alternative service provision that has been developed, he maintains that this factor alone is insufficient to fully explain what has occurred.

Warner maintains that the missing variable in this analysis is that of the demand for labour. In countries where the demand for labour has been greatest, such as England, the Netherlands, Norway and Switzerland, Warner argues that deinstitutionalization was introduced relatively early, and that the quality of rehabilitative services developed has been higher. The result, Warner argues, is that 'It seems reasonable to conclude that such a heavy demand for labour can be a stimulus to the rehabilitation of the marginally functional mentally ill' (1989, 24). Then, in the 1960s as the demand for labour declined, the quality of these programmes deteriorated sharply. In the United States, where the demand for labour never reached particularly high levels, the early onset of deinstitutionalization can be mainly attributed to the desire for cost saving, and the poor quality of rehabilitative services reflects the lack of demand for the labour of people experiencing mental health problems.

Warner's argument is that trends in the rate of unemployment and trends in deinstitutionalization should, in general, be inversely correlated. If we take the level of unemployment as an indicator of the demand for labour, then we should expect to find an inverse relationship between higher levels of mental hospital bed space and lower levels of unemployment. Between 1960 and 1974, as Figure 3.4 demonstrates,

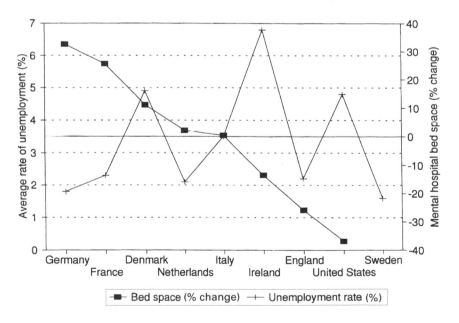

Figure 3.4 *The relationship between unemployment and deinstitutionalization (1960–1974). Source: Average rate of unemployment derived from OECD (1990). Percentage changes in mental hospital bed space derived from World Health Organization (1970) and Poullier & Sandier (1991).*

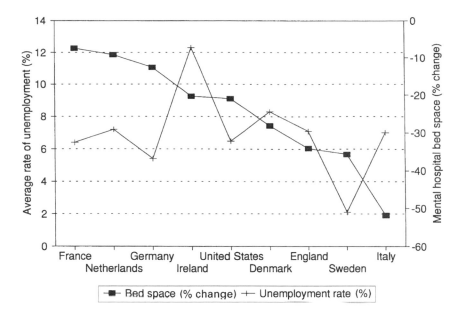

Figure 3.5 *The relationship between unemployment and deinstitutionalization*
(1975–1985). Source: *Average rate of unemployment derived from OECD (1990).*
Percentage changes in mental hospital bed space derived from World Health
Organization (1970) and Poullier & Sandier (1991).

there is no clear relationship between these two variables. The highest
rate of decline in bed space was in England and the United States, yet the
level of unemployment in these countries is in the middle range.
Conversely, Denmark and Ireland have the highest rate of unemployment yet the former actually shows an increase in bed space, while the
latter shows a relatively small decrease.

In the subsequent period, between 1975 and 1985, as shown in Figure
3.5 this pattern is repeated. Denmark and Ireland again have the highest
rates of unemployment, while their rates of deinstitutionalization are in
the middle range. Sweden and Italy have the greatest reductions in bed
space, and yet their rates of unemployment are in the low to middle
range.

Community care is cheaper than institutional care

A key assumption of the radical analysts is that community care represents a cheaper option than institutional care, this providing the under-
pinning of their analysis of the economic reasons for the policy shift. This
assumption has been the subject of much study in a number of countries
over recent years. In a study of the Californian state mental health
services, Leavin (1984) estimated that deinstitutionalization had produced a net annual saving of $1.3 billion. A study of a comprehensive
urban psychiatric service for 172 patients in London found that in-

patient stays, and hence overall costs, were significantly reduced by the provision of an active community care programme. Mental hospital care was found to cost nearly twice as much as care provided in the community, although considerable variations in the costs of caring for different patient groups in the community were also found. Care for patients with schizophrenia was, on average, twice as expensive as care for patients with other mental health problems. This was mainly the result of increased in-patient care, which averaged 33 days for the patients with schizophrenia and only 7.6 days for non-schizophrenic patients (Burns & Raftery, 1991).

In a study of 148 patients with schizophrenia discharged from mental hospital in Germany, Hafner et al. (1989) found that when comparing the mean costs of comprehensive community care per case with those of hospital care, community care was less than half as expensive as traditional hospital care. There was, however, considerable variation around this mean, with many people with mental health problems living in the community requiring levels of support that approached the cost of institutional care and, in 6 per cent of the cohort studied, actually resulted in higher costs. Moreover, this latter group, who generally were more disturbed, were likely to place a far greater burden upon their families. As such, the support offered for community care is strongly qualified:

> ... there is not only a monetary, but also a non-monetary threshold value, above which community care seems to be no long appropriate. Beyond this threshold it is not only cheaper, but probably also more humane to place chronically ill patients requiring long-term inpatient care in mental hospitals providing 24-hour medical and nursing care, good accommodation, occupation, and leisure-time activities, as well as rehabilitation units. (Hafner et al., 1989, 16)

Overall, studies of service costs have tended to reveal that care in the community is generally cheaper than care provided in hospital, although there are always some patients in the community whose care costs are more than that of the average hospital patient (Goldberg, 1991, 454). Also, for some patients, such as those with organic brain disease or people who are severely disabled, community care will always be inappropriate. Studies have often excluded such individuals for the purpose of their study (Goldberg, 1991, 454). They have also tended to follow up selected groups of patients over inadequate periods of time, and vary considerably in the completeness of estimating community care costs. The more comprehensive community programmes tend to show less short-term cost saving and to require forms of bridging finance. Conversely, the least expensive successor services have been shown to offer an equivalent or worse standard of care than the mental hospital. The balance of current evidence is that adequate community care is no cheaper than inadequate hospital care (Thornicroft & Bebbington, 1989).

Analysis of the relative costs and effectiveness of institutional care and community care is beset by a number of methodological problems. One such problem with assessing the costs of mental health service provision is that the very policy of deinstitutionalization itself tends to impact upon the costs of both community care and institutional care. As mental hospital bed space is reduced, the unit costs of institutionalized mental patients have tended to rise. This has partly been because of the loss of economies of scale, and also because the least severely disabled and therefore least costly patients have tended to be discharged first. Hoult (1986) takes this analysis a stage further, arguing that a consequence of community care is that when patients are admitted to mental hospital their condition is often worse than might have been the case if they had be institutionalized earlier, which in turn raises the costs of institutional care still further. As a result the appearance of cost efficiency in the development of community-based provision tends to be enhanced by the very changes in policy that are being evaluated.

Assessment of the relative effectiveness of institutional and community-based care requires an agreed set of criteria by which this can be measured. This might include hospital statistical information such as average length of stay, number of admissions and readmissions, but would also require other measures such as the degree of social competence and independence achieved, and the lost opportunities and additional burdens experienced by informal carers. Equally, there are certain potential benefits of discharge, such as gaining employment, which could be included in the overall equation. In general, it has been found that the more sophisticated the evaluation in terms of the range and number of costs considered, the less apparent is the cost advantage of home-based care (Thornicroft & Bebbington, 1989). Furthermore, attempts at measurement of the effectiveness of different treatment regimes are subject to difficulties. Ideally, such measurement should involve the random placement of patients in each setting, but this of course raises considerable ethical problems (Hafner et al., 1989).

Because of these issues the available evidence on the relative cost-effectiveness of institutional care and community care remains ambiguous. Reflecting this, in a review of some 18 studies Braun et al. (1981) found that problems with the design and implementation of the research programmes meant that none were able to prove any greater level of effectiveness in community-based rather than institution-based systems of care and treatment for people with mental health problems. These problems are highlighted by the view of two professors of psychiatry working in California, where deinstitutionalization has been vigorously pursued:

> ... the elimination of state hospital beds and other highly structured 24-hour care over and above the clinically demonstrated need for it does not save money. This point is illustrated by the situation in California, where a shortage of long-stay psychiatric beds has resulted in chaos not only for chronically and

severely mentally ill persons but for the mental health system itself. The resulting pressure for more acute in-patient care, the most expensive mental health care of all, will in the end drain more scarce funding from urgently needed expansion and up-grading of community care. (Lamb & Shaner, 1993, 976)

The problems involved in deciding what to measure, and how to measure the costs of mental health services, have resulted in the debate over the relative costs of institutional care and community care becoming increasingly sterile. Intuitively, we might argue that good-quality care is expensive, and poor-quality care is not. Whether this is provided in institutional or community settings may well prove to be marginal to this perhaps more fundamental point. What the shift towards community care does allow for, however, is increased scope for the shifting of the costs of care from the state on to informal carers. It also allows for the neglect of at least some patients, who, following discharge, may not receive any community support services whatsoever. Community care policy creates the possibility of cutting costs in a way that institutional care does not allow and, as we review in more detail in Chapter 5, there is some evidence of governments having chosen this route.

Government policy is determined by economic issues

A further assumption underlying the radical analysis is that governments are largely driven by economic imperatives. It is argued that the tendency to shift from institutional to community care since the 1970s has been driven largely by cost considerations: 'As the crisis of the welfare state has deepened, official preoccupations with community care have progressively narrowed down to the paramount question of cost' (Mangen, 1987, 77). Indeed Ungerson claims that the desire to save money has been key to the process of deinstitutionalization. In many European countries 'these policies are driven largely by ideas of reducing expenditure – namely that it is cheaper and more cost-effective to care for people in the "community"' (1995, 39).

There is certainly some evidence to support this contention. In England, government concerns with the costs of service provision and the possibilities community care presented for reducing costs were evident at its inception.

> The advantages to, for example, the housewife or the salary earner of being able to secure the needed treatment, while continuing to live an ordinary life, are obvious, and one should not overlook the economic advantages which accrue to the community at large. (Ministry of Health, 1958, 24)

In the Canadian federal government in the 1960s there was considerable concern with the cost of institution-based mental health service provision. Around 60 per cent of costs were hospital-based, and the development of community care was intended to provide a means of reducing these costs (Williams & Luterbach, 1976, 18). This concern has continued to influence policy development:

> An over-arching objective is the development of a continuum of care and support capable of responding sensitively and effectively to the needs of individual, families and communities. At the same time, all governments are working to control the growth of public-sector expenditure and to make the best use of limited fiscal and human resources. (Department of Health and Welfare, 1990, 169)

In the Netherlands it is argued that the development of community-based services in Amsterdam in the 1930s by Querido was primarily a product not of humanitarian, but of economic concern. The city was facing financial problems, and the development of alternatives to mental hospital was seen as potentially cheaper (Grinten, 1985, 211). More recently, it was only with the onset of economic problems in the 1980s that the government demonstrated substantial support for deinstitutionalization (Van Der Veen, 1988, 30). This was reflected in the creation of the 'Commission on Choices in Care', whose remit was to review ways in which health care monies could be spent more effectively (Spanjer, 1992, 7). Even in Sweden, with its strong tradition of state welfare, it is argued that economic problems have resulted in a reduction in the commitment to welfare provision, and a shift towards community-based care because of its assumed relative cheapness (Carrol, 1993).

While a concern with welfare costs within governments is relatively easy to demonstrate, the assumption that this tends to promote a shift towards cheaper community-based care is not so clear. Rather, cost constraints may actually stultify new policy development. In the 1980s the French government reduced its commitment to the development of community-based services because of the cost of developing new facilities (Demay, 1987, 75). Indeed, a concern with cost containment has hindered the shift from institutional to community care in a number of European countries because of the costs of developing new programmes (Breemer ter Stege & Gittelman, 1987, 7). This constraint upon policy development has been of particular importance in countries where power is relatively decentralized, such as Germany, Belgium and the Netherlands.

Even in more centralized countries, such as England, the development of community care has been hindered by the lack of 'bridging finance' to fund new services whilst older services are maintained (Goodwin, 1993). The Department of Health has made repeated claims that community care can only be adequately developed as and when mental hospitals are closed, thereby releasing money for the development of new services. In fact, the Department has not kept any central record of land sales or change of use that would allow for quantification of this issue (Sayce, 1994, 11).

Summary

The radical analysis of the development of mental health policy rests upon a number of propositions about the nature of the relationship between capitalist economies and welfare provision. They are considered to exist within an antagonistic relationship; successful development of one is considered to have adverse consequences for the other. The role of the state is to manage this conflict, the postwar manifestation of this process being the shift from institutional to community care. As with the orthodox analysis, however, our review of the evidence available to support this position has found that many of the propositions are poorly supported.

As Table 3.2 demonstrates, the concerns of governments with the economic cost of welfare provision and the possibility of achieving cost

Table 3.2 *A critique of the radical analysis*

Reasons for the policy shift	Evaluation
High public welfare expenditure is a cause of economic problems	Since the mid-1970s there has been a tendency for countries to experience greater difficulties in meeting welfare expenditure commitments, but there is not sufficient evidence to support fully a burden model of state welfare provision.
High public expenditure growth is associated with a tendency towards deinstitutionalization	This proposition appears to have little foundation. High public expenditure growth is not an accurate predictor of a tendency towards deinstitutionalization.
High fiscal deficits result in pressure for deinstitutionalization	There is little evidence of a correlation between these two variables.
The retention of institutional care results in increasingly large opportunity costs	There is no apparent relationship between the development of community support, the apparent creation of opportunity costs, and deinstitutionalization.
An inverse relationship can be found between levels of unemployment and mental hospital bed space	While some evidence of a correlation between these two variables has been established in the United States for a certain time period, trends in the level of unemployment and mental hospital bed space in many other countries demonstrate no clear relationship.
Community care is cheaper than institutional care	Community care is not necessarily a cheaper method of service delivery. It does, however, allow for the possibility of greater neglect of service users, and, therefore, greater cost savings.
Government policy is determined by economic issues	Governments are certainly strongly influenced by economic concerns, but the relationship between service costs and service development is variable and complex.

savings through the shift towards community care are evident. But there is a lack of evidence to support propositions within the radical analysis about the dramatic impact these factors are likely to have upon policy development. Moreover, there are a number of variables argued to exist in a certain relationship to each other, but which largely fail to demonstrate the expected patterns.

4

Problems and Issues Within Existing Accounts

Orthodox analyses of postwar changes in mental health policy tend to emphasize its progressive nature. Attempts to increase the independence and dignity of the individual are considered to be the prime force underlying why a shift from institutional to community-based systems of care and treatment has occurred. Radical accounts tend to emphasize its regressive nature. It is not the interests of people with mental health problems, but the economic requirements of the capitalist system that have provided the main impetus towards policy change. Both these accounts, as we have argued, are problematic. Many of the propositions and assumptions made are simply not supported by the evidence available.

The contention of this chapter is that existing accounts fail to provide an adequate account of the policy, in part at least, as a result of their lack of an adequately developed conceptual and analytical base. Two issues are of central importance. Firstly, what are mental health problems; what exactly is it that requires intervention and management? Secondly, what is the role and status of governments in relation to the provision of mental health services?

Now the orthodox and radical analyses do of course contain assumptions about these issues. The orthodox analysis views mental health problems largely within the dominant medical model subscribed to by the psychiatric profession, that the problem is one of illness requiring treatment. The role of government is, at least in part, to address the welfare needs of its population, and the development of mental health policy represents the efforts it has made to do just this. The radical analysis holds largely to a sociological model of mental health problems, as behaviour patterns that break certain rules. Rather then being concerned with an illness, the problem is one of deviance. The role of government is one of social control; to ensure that threats to system functioning are contained and minimized. The main purpose of mental health service provision is to achieve this goal.

Just what constitutes mental health problems, what exactly it is that requires treatment or control, and what the position of government is in relation to these issues, are central themes to the development of an adequate account of mental health policy. There are, as we discuss below, a number of weaknesses with both the orthodox and radical analyses in relation to these issues. The aim of this chapter is to review these in more detail, and to attempt to create a more coherent and adequate platform from which an analysis of postwar mental health policy might be attempted.

Why provide mental health services at all?

As we reviewed in Chapter 2, writers within the orthodox camp tend to utilize dominant conceptions of mental health problems, largely as offered by the psychiatric profession. The problem tends to be defined as illness, or as the behaviour patterns of individuals that result. Jones, for example, maintains that mental illness is

> ... the condition of people who are suffering from lasting and disabling stress for no ascertainable or sufficient cause, or whose behaviour is so bizarre or so unacceptable that it is causing considerable stress to those around them. (1983, 218–219)

This position is taken to be relatively unproblematic within the orthodox model. It reflects conventional thinking within the psychiatric profession, and to a large extent is taken to be self-evident. The central claim within this, however, that the problem is one of illness or the behaviour resulting from illness, is problematic.

In Jones' definition the two reasons given for designating somebody mentally ill – lasting and disabling stress without ascertainable or reasonable cause, and bizarre or otherwise unacceptable behaviour – are both dependent for their meaning upon a social and value-based context. Taking the first of these, it must be asked, how is it possible to assess what constitutes ascertainable or sufficient cause without making reference to an ideological stance of some sort? For the notion being tested here is capacity for rational action, and the base-line for such a test would seem to be the dominant conception of rationality within a society. While such an approach may not subscribe to any particular model of mental distress, its overall ideological stance is clearly one in support of the status quo.

Equally, the criterion of bizarre or unacceptable behaviour is open to similar criticism, where the values used to judge such behaviour are likely to be based on dominant conceptions of normal or acceptable conduct. The orthodox model tends to make the assumption that a consensus exists that can be appealed to in order to justify the designation of people as mentally ill. Any apparent absence of ideology within the diagnostic procedure, rather than being taken to imply that a value-free judgement is being made, could instead be taken to imply the presence of a hegemonic value system.

This point is substantially developed by those more supportive of the radical position. In the early 1970s it increasingly came to be argued that mental illness is a socially constructed category, increasingly utilized by capitalist states in the twentieth century as a means of enforcing conformity to certain norms. The American sociologist Irving Zola was amongst the first to argue along these lines:

> ... medicine is becoming a major institution of social control, nudging aside, if not incorporating, the more traditional institutions of religion and law ... this is not occurring through the political power physicians hold or can influence, but is largely an insidious and often undramatic phenomenon accomplished by 'medicalizing' much of daily living, by making medicine and the labels 'healthy' and 'ill' relevant to an ever increasing part of human existence. (1975, 170)

More specifically in relation to mental health, Friedson argued that there was an increasing tendency for a growing number of 'deviant' behaviour patterns such as heavy gambling, high levels of alcohol consumption and shoplifting to be redefined as mental illnesses, awaiting treatment:

> The medical mode of response to deviance is thus being applied to more and more behaviour in our society, much of which has been responded to in quite different ways in the past. In our day, what has been called crime, lunacy, degeneracy, sin and even poverty in the past is now being called illness, and social policy has been moving toward adopting a perspective appropriate to the imputation of illness. (1975, 249)

A concern with the expanding orbit of psychiatric practice, and the consequent tendency for a 'therapeutic state' to emerge, is shared by many other writers (e.g. Lasch, 1977; Castel et al., 1979; Conrad & Schneider, 1980). The central point of all these analyses is that the primary function of mental health policy is the regulation of behaviour:

> The major social forces that drive public policies about the mentally ill ... rest largely on social control considerations. A concern with the maintenance of order and the need for consensus lead to the adoption of policies that constitute a social response to deviancy. (Aviram, 1990, 82)

This conception of mental health problems as the pathologizing of rule-breaking behaviour has proved to be a popular model of explanation, but just exactly what constitutes this deviance, and exactly what specific threat it poses to the existing organization of societies, is rarely considered. As Ingleby (1983, 180) notes, it is relatively easy to demonstrate that the boundaries of mental illness categories are culturally determined, but it is far more difficult to relate those boundaries to perceived threats to a social system, hence provoking a social control response.

From a Marxist perspective, Scull (1984, 26–30) claims people with mental health problems are incapable of supporting themselves and are therefore a living threat to bourgeois rationality, including the sanctity of the market, and the wage–labour relationship. Consequently, these people are subject to a process of social control; a process analysed as part of the overall project of class domination, where the state's labelling of certain deviants as mentally ill constitutes the mystification of an essentially oppressive relationship by transmuting antagonistic class relationships into the individual psychiatric problems of the proletariat (Scull, 1984, 29).

This analysis does leave open a number of questions, however. Just why the fact that people with mental health problems tend not to work should pose a threat is never made clear, for continued capital accumulation does not depend upon every able-bodied proletarian being involved in wage labour. Moreover, continued capital accumulation is not simply dependent upon this one dimension of the economic productiveness of the proletariat, but also involves cultural reproduction. Yet how the definition and application of the category of mental distress is affected by this is not considered. As Cockburn notes:

> If capitalism is to survive, each succeeding generation of workers must stay in an appropriate relationship to capital: the relationships of production must be reproduced. Workers must not step outside the relation of the wage, the relation of property, the relation of authority. So reproducing capitalist relations means reproducing the class, ownership, above all reproducing a frame of mind. (1977, 56)

The perceived nature of the threat

To develop an understanding of what it is about mental health problems that provokes a policy response, we need to consider the way in which the condition has been understood. Central to this is psychiatric theorization about the nature and causes of mental health problems, and central to this, in turn, is the medical model. The origins of this model can be traced back as far as the sixteenth century, but it was in the nineteenth century that it came to achieve dominance in relation to mental health problems. Its core claim is that bizarre or disturbed behaviour is the result of a disease process; mental problems are illnesses in exactly the same way that physical problems can be.

In Europe psychiatrists such as Wilhelm Griesinger, a German practitioner, popularized this view of mental health problems, and in the early twentieth century its position was reinforced by the discovery of a cure for syphilitic insanity by malarial therapy. As this treatment began to be used, the death rate from general paralysis (as the condition was known) fell rapidly, in England, for example, from 1,353 in 1923 to 164 in 1948 (Chief Medical Officer, 1948, 128). Through the twentieth century the medical model has retained its dominant position. Driven on by the development of new physical treatments such as electro-convulsive therapy and psychosurgery in the 1930s, the major tranquillizers in the 1950s and a number of other drugs in subsequent decades, it has continued to provide the organizing framework within which the large bulk of psychiatry is practised. In Sweden, for example, Gustafsson notes that 'The medical hierarchy is imbued with a professional science-based ideology' (1989, 122).

Through the twentieth century there have, however, been a number of additional themes added to the basic medical model. Of importance in this regard was the development of Freudian theory, which presented mental illness as something comprehensible. The concept of mental illness, particularly of neuroses, came to be applied to an increasingly large range of behaviour patterns, and the impact of the social environment on these conditions was increasingly recognized (Rose, 1986, 49). In England, for example, it was noted that:

> The concept of the unconscious and recognition of the importance of past experience and of instinctual drives have led the way to a vastly increased interest in and understanding of psychopathology and the role of psychotherapy. (Chief Medical Officer, 1948, 128)

The two world wars further contributed to the development of a psychosocial, behavioural perspective. The graphic evidence of 'shell shock' presented by soldiers gave increasing weight to the view that social conditions were of importance in determining mental health. During World War II many soldiers in the United States army who were ineffective in their duties were discharged through medical channels, often with a diagnosis of psychoneurosis. Previously, they might well have been shot for cowardice (Ginzberg, 1987).

These developments contributed to a substantial shift of orientation within the psychiatric profession. Whereas, in the early part of the twentieth century, 'faith in the construction of a neurologically based psychiatry was evident throughout most of Western Europe and North America' (Prior, 1993, 59), by mid-century the possibility of a model of psychiatry existing outside the orbit of neurology was increasingly being recognized.

A second tendency within psychiatric theory in the first half of the twentieth century was to integrate the concept of mental illness with that of physical illness. This is not simply a case of understanding both by the same conceptual model – the medical model – but also involves the claim that the two are more closely related entities than was once thought; where mental illnesses may have physical effects and vice versa. The development of this trend in psychiatric theory was noted in England by the Royal Commission on Lunacy and Mental Disorder in its report in 1926:

> It has become increasingly evident that there is no clear line of demarcation between mental and physical illness. The distinction as commonly drawn is based on a difference of symptoms. In ordinary parlance, a disease is described as mental if its symptoms manifest themselves predominantly in derangement of conduct, and as physical if its symptoms manifest themselves predominantly in derangement of bodily function. (cited in Jones, 1972, 240)

While psychiatrists share a common background in the medical model, there are some variations of emphasis to be found. Some diagnostic categories are used only locally, such as that of 'reactive psychosis' in Scandinavian countries. Some treatments, such as electro-convulsive therapy, have fallen out of favour in some countries, such as Germany and the Netherlands, but remain in frequent use in Spain, Denmark and France. There are also national variations in the perceived therapeutic value of many drugs, as well as variations in the frequency and quantity of their prescription (Neelman & van Os, 1994, 1218). Overall, however, these differences amount to little more than minor variations within a basic consensus around the idea that mental problems are illnesses requiring treatment.

These developments in psychiatric theory, towards a more eclectic but still fundamentally medical view of the nature of bizarre behaviour, have had a profound effect upon the nature of mental health service provision. Through the early and middle part of the twentieth century there was a general shift away from a custodial towards a more medically orientated service. Reflecting this, in Spain a decree in 1931 introduced to the asylums the Kraepelin system of classification of mental disorders, and encouraged a reduction in the numbers of long-term in-patients (Comelles & Hernáez, 1994, 285). In Denmark a report in 1956 recommended the integration of psychiatric with general medicine (Bennett, 1991, 637). In France statutes determining the legal status of psychiatric hospitals were amended in 1968 so that their position was similar to that of general hospitals (Kovess et al., 1995, 132). In Belgium the new policy for mental health care laid out by the Minister for Social Affairs in 1975 placed emphasis upon developing a more medical and curative approach (Verhaegey, 1987, 43). Across the whole of Western Europe and North America through the middle part of the twentieth century the medical model of mental health problems was thoroughly absorbed and institutionalized within the practice of psychiatric treatment.

The apparent scale of mental health problems

Concurrent with this process of the medicalization of mental health problems went a rise in the confidence of the medical profession to treat a growing range of mental disorders. Rather than just reserve the mental illness label for the seriously disturbed, an increased range of behaviour patterns came to be seen as products of mental illness. In particular, the concept of neuroses was used more frequently and applied to larger areas of social life in the twentieth century (Rose, 1986, 49). Increasingly, mental illness has been seen not just as a severe affliction confined to relatively few, but as a condition of varying levels of severity that affects many. No longer are the sane and the insane to be regarded as opposite types sharing little if any common ground. While still representing opposite ends of an axis, that axis has totally changed in nature. It has become graduated, and it can be more easily traversed. The apparent range of psychiatric competence, and the confidence of the psychiatric profession itself, increased dramatically as a result of these developments in theory and practice.

> Psychiatry can be proud that at long last it has woken up and that it now produces therapeutic results which are at least as good as those attained by most other branches of medicine. (Rees, 1966, 14)

Whereas the recovery rate from psychosis had not varied by more than a few decimal points for more than eighty years up to World War II, we now have a situation in which roughly 70 per cent of those who need inpatient care in mental hospitals are within three to four months fit to be back at work and with their families. (Rees, 1966, 14)

At the beginning of the twentieth century the primary concern of the psychiatric profession was with the custody of relatively few, and relatively disturbed, people with mental health problems. By the middle of the twentieth century its primary concern was with the provision of treatment for a far larger percentage of the population, most of whom experienced relatively minor and temporary mental health problems.

It is in this context that we have witnessed in the second half of the twentieth century a massive expansion in the apparent scale of the problem of mental illness. In the United States, the National Institute of Mental Health estimates that 20 per cent of the adult population suffer from a mental disorder in any six-month period, and that 33 per cent suffer a disorder in their lifetimes. A recent survey in the United States conducted by Ronald Kessler of the University of Michigan found that 48 per cent of the population had suffered a mental disorder at some point in their lives, and that 30 per cent had suffered a mental disorder within the previous year (cited in Goleman, 1994). In England, in the 1950s, it was claimed that some two million people a year receive treatment from general practitioners for psycho-neurotic disorders (Chief Medical Officer, 1958, 126). More recently the Mental Health Foundation (1993, 1) has estimated that 25 per cent of the population have a mental disorder, and that over three million people suffer from severe mental illness. At any one time, around 20 per cent of women and 10 per cent of men in England are taking some form of behaviour-altering drug. In Canada it is estimated that one in eight of the adult population will be hospitalized for mental illness at least once in their lifetime (Department of Health and Welfare, 1990, 5). In the Netherlands it is estimated that 24 per cent of the adult population have a mental health problem (Giel, 1987, 156).

Overall, the apparent increase in levels of mental health problems in the twentieth century is quite dramatic. Studies from both Western Europe and North America have found approximately 18 per cent to 23 per cent of all adult females and 8 per cent to 11 per cent of adult males have experienced a serious depression at some point in their life (Cockerham, 1992, 142). Moreover, many of these receive little if any treatment. In the United States it is estimated that fewer than 20 per cent of those with a recent mental disorder seek help for their problem (Bourdon et al., 1992), and of those experiencing depression 92 per cent do not seek professional help (Cockerham, 1992, 142).

For the future, the psychiatric profession generally predicts that these trends will continue. The ageing of populations that is occurring in most advanced industrial nations is likely to increase the numbers of those with Alzheimer's disease, while more generally it is argued that the increased pace of life within modern industrial societies tends to generate ever larger numbers of psychiatric problems:

> Rampant urbanization, fragmentation of life, uprooting of populations, increasing fluidity of social networks in the future, and the almost osmotic intermingling of cultures of the world are among the trends we can distinguish already. (Sartorius, 1987, 151)

The distribution of mental health problems

This apparent expansion in the perceived scale of mental health problems has not, however, been evenly distributed across populations. Rather, in the diagnosis and treatment of mental health problems distinct patterns have emerged.

Social class A relationship between social class and the incidence of mental health problems is long established. In the 1930s in Chicago Faris and Dunham (1939) found that the highest rates of schizophrenia were to be found in the poorest residential districts. In New Haven in the 1950s, Hollingshead and Redlich (1958) found that the lower social classes tended to experience higher rates of schizophrenia, while higher social classes tended to experience higher rates of anxiety. More recently, a study in Germany found a clear inverse relationship between levels of psychological distress and social class (Cockerham et al., 1988). Overall, many studies have been undertaken that confirm this relationship between the incidence of mental health problems and social class.

While this evidence is fairly clear, the reasons why this relationship exists are argued over. Genetic factors could account for the concentration of mental illness amongst certain groups. It is also argued that those who suffer from mental health problems may in consequence tend to experience 'downward drift' into a lower social class. Neither of these explanations, however, is able to fully account for the scale of inequality in the distribution of mental health problems (Weiner, 1985). A third model is that of social causation. Poverty and generally poor social conditions are argued to result in increased levels of mental health problems, and to exacerbate existing mental health problems (Bruce, 1991; Borga et al., 1992). In reality, it is perhaps likely that all three factors may be of some importance, but the exact balance of their relative importance is difficult to determine (Cockerham, 1992).

Race A further dimension of inequalities in the apparent scale of mental health problems is race. In the United States black patients are over-represented in mental institutions, and have become increasingly so over the postwar period. This has particularly been the case within state mental hospitals, where minority groups constitute 35 per cent of the hospital population, and are subject to higher rates of admission and readmission (Wade, 1993, 538). In a review of eight epidemiological studies conducted in the United States between the late 1950s and mid-1970s, Kessler and Neighbors (1986) found that among persons with low incomes black people exhibited significantly more distress than white people. They claimed, therefore, that race is an important independent variable in determining the likelihood of an individual becoming mentally ill.

There is some dispute over what to make of this evidence. Cockerham maintains that the majority of studies on the incidence and distribution of mental health problems suggest that race is not an independent variable: ... 'race alone does not appear to produce higher rates of mental disorder for particular groups' (1990, 217). Rather, it is because more black people are in the lower social classes that they tend to demonstrate more signs of mental distress. Others, however, disagree. Halpern (1993) argues that minority status can be demonstrated to result in a tendency towards psychiatric problems.

As with gender, a number of studies have been conducted indicating that racial bias exists in the assessment, diagnosis and treatment of mental health problems. It has been found, for example, that white therapists generally rated their black clients as being more psychologically impaired than did black therapists. Patients who are uncooperative, threatening or abusive are more likely to be diagnosed as being mentally ill if they have minority status. In particular, it has been found that being black tends to increase the chances of a person being diagnosed as being schizophrenic (Wade, 1993, 541). Certain groups such as people of Afro-Caribbean origin tend to be more likely than whites to receive electro-convulsive therapy and higher doses of medication, and are less likely to receive psychotherapy (Littlewood, 1980). Minority groups have proved less able to make use of community-based services. This is partly because they have lacked the resources to participate in the development of community care, and partly because of the lack of interest in or understanding of the specific cultural needs of minority groups when establishing services (Wade, 1993, 539).

Gender   Women experience more mental health problems than do men. Community-based surveys of psychoactive drug treatment in a number of countries in North America and Western Europe have found that generally twice as many women as men are likely to be treated (Allgulander et al., 1990, 420). This is particularly the case with certain conditions. Studies have tended to find that women experience higher rates of anxiety and affective disorders, while men tend to experience more personality disorders. This applies as much to reported mental illness as it does to community surveys of unreported mental illness. Women tend to experience depression more often, particularly where they are married and even more so when they have children (Dennerstein & Astbury, 1995). Ninety per cent of people with eating disorders are women.

There are some biological aspects of women's lives that account for increased levels of mental health problems. Pregnancy and childbirth have been found to be related to mental health problems. It is estimated that 10 per cent of women suffer post-natal depression, and in one study it was found that women are 22 times more likely to be admitted to a psychiatric hospital with a psychotic illness in the first month after childbirth than during the two years beforehand (Dennerstein & Astbury, 1995). Women, on average, live four to five years longer than men, and this, too, tends to result in higher levels of mental health problems. The majority of people aged over 85 are women, and some 25 per cent of this group have Alzheimer's disease (Dennerstein & Astbury, 1995).

Overall, however, there is little evidence to suggest that women's higher rates of mental health problems are the result of hormonal or genetic factors (Cockerham, 1992, 171). Rather, the available evidence suggests that the underlying cause of these differences in the mental health profile of men and women is the sexual division of labour. The roles that women occupy as wives and mothers, daughters and carers of others, tend to result in high levels of stress that in turn precipitate mental health problems. The resulting lack of outside contact and alternative sources of status and income have been found to be negatively correlated with mental health. Other factors such as discrimination at the workplace have also been found to have a negative impact on women's mental health (Cockerham, 1992, 171). Domestic violence is a further cause of women's relatively poor mental health status. In the United States it has been found that 90 per cent of physical and sexual assaults reported by psychiatric patients were committed by family members, with as many as two million American wives being battered each year (Dennerstein & Astbury, 1995).

In addition to sexual inequality, it has also been argued that mental health professionals hold certain sexist assumptions that in turn influence their practice. One reason suggested for why women consume more psychoactive drugs is that general practitioners are more likely to give them to women with social problems in addition to health problems (Allgulander et al., 1990, 424). In a survey of psychologists in the United States, Broverman & Kline (1970) found that men were generally seen as being more emotionally stable, more objective, less conceited and more independent. This assessment of men and women was matched against the psychologists' own assessment of what human characteristics constituted adult status, and the assumptions made about women were found to seriously undermine their status as adults. A number of other surveys of mental health professionals have also been conducted that reveal a similar tendency to devalue women.

These sexist assumptions have been found in the United States to result in women being less readily perceived as experiencing mental health problems, because the symptoms of mental health problems overlap to some extent with presumptions about normal female behaviour patterns. This, it is argued, helps account for the substantially higher rates of male admission to state and county mental hospitals (Cockerham, 1992, 182). This pattern of admission, however, is not common to all countries. In England women have traditionally been subject to higher levels of mental hospital admission, and this is particularly so for certain types of mental illness. In 1986 in England, for example, 16,526 women and 8,107 men were admitted to a mental hospital with a diagnosis of affective psychosis, and 10,291 women and 4,978 men were admitted with neurotic disorders (Department of Health, 1989).

Conclusion   The relationship between minority status and mental health is an area in which a considerable amount of research has been undertaken, and considerable dispute exists over the reasons for the prevailing distribution of mental health problems. Overall, however, there is evidence to indicate that in terms of the three main dimensions of power in the Western capitalist nations – class, race and gender – there is considerable evidence to indicate that those at the powerless ends – the working class, black people and women – tend to be more prone to psychological problems. The precise extent to which this distribution is a product of those power relationships is difficult to determine. That the relationship exists, however, seems clear.

The relationship of capitalist societies and mental health

Mental health and social control

Through the twentieth century there have been enormous changes in perception of the nature, scale and distribution of mental health problems. As the century progressed it has increasingly been recognized that it is a condition that affects a relatively large proportion of society, in ways that require managing with somewhat more sophistication than incarceration: 'Today there appears to be a growing consensus that mental illness is not the private misery of single individuals but a social problem for which the whole community shares responsibility' (David, 1966, 4).

The apparent explosion in the range and frequency of mental health problems has widely been perceived as a matter of considerable concern, and also a matter requiring the development of new methods of regulating human behaviour. Amongst health professionals a growing realization of this is readily apparent in the mid-twentieth century. In England, for example, the Chief Medical Officer noted that, 'The practice of medicine is not wholly a matter of the diagnosis and treatment of diseases as they occur in individual patients; its field extends into the world of everyday life' (1959, 143). Amongst the psychiatric profession it would seem that at times its ambition to colonize responsibility for new areas of human behaviour could hardly be contained:

What are the major medical problems which have not been effectively dealt with? The first and most important is of course insanity and feeble-mindedness; probably the next is functional disease of the nervous system, with its manifestations in the psychoneuroses and psychosomatic disorders. It would be in line with modern thought to add that crime, delinquency, and general bad manners are hardly distinguishable from the medical manifestations. (Burnett, 1953, 104)

In Britain, if you take any of the less distinguished Sunday papers, you will find on the front page stories of loss of memory, drunkenness, child neglect, industrial unrest, delinquency, sexual offences, and many more things. These of course are social problems. Sometimes their causes may be economic. But every one of these problems has considerable psychological factors, and we need to understand these factors if we are to attempt to treat the causes and not just the symptom. (Rees, 1966, 19)

Reflecting these trends in thought and resulting concerns, the World Health Organization Expert Committee on Mental Health in its Second Report argued that:

Mental health, as the committee understands it, is influenced by both biological and social factors. It is not a static condition but subject to variations and fluctuations of degree; the committee's conception implies the capacity in an individual to form harmonious relations with others, and to participate in, or contribute constructively to, changes in his social or physical environment. It implies also his ability to achieve a harmonious and balanced satisfaction of his own potentially conflicting instinctive drives – harmonious in that it reaches an integrated synthesis, rather than the denial of satisfaction to certain instinctive tendencies, as a means of avoiding the thwarting of others. (World Health Organization, 1951, 4)

As well as being of concern to the psychiatric profession, the apparent changes in the nature and frequency of mental health problems and their implications for the maintenance of social order are evident in the government policy statements of many countries through the second half of the twentieth century. In England the definition of the problem of mental illness was widened to include a range of behaviours, newly defined as 'socio-psychological' problems, that, it is argued, mental health services should increasingly be seeking to address:

For good mental health one would postulate good physical health, a modicum of intelligence, lively instincts with a sufficiency of reasonable control, full participation in family and social life, giving and receiving in a warm-hearted way; an eye to the welfare of the self, the family, the community and the nation. (Chief Medical Officer, 1954, 104)

It is new advances in scientific knowledge and understanding that have enabled recognition for example of the suffering of the housebound phobic or the young girl starving herself through anorexia nervosa for what they are – namely the manifestation of mental illness for which it is both humane and realistic to offer professional help. (Department of Health and Social Security, 1975, para 1.2)

Not all those who need help are in fact getting it: some are unwilling to receive it; others have fallen out of the system. It is the behaviour of those people that often worries the community. (Department of Health and Social Security, 1986, 3)

The definition of mental health below is that given by the Department of Health and Welfare in Canada:

> Mental health is the capacity of the individual, the group and the environment to interact with one another in ways that promote subjective well-being, the optimal development and use of mental abilities (cognitive, affective and relational), the achievement of individual and collective goals consistent with justice and the attainment and preservation of conditions of fundamental equality. (1988, 2)

This definition clearly demonstrates the importance of the economic, political and social context within which behaviour is understood. As the report goes on to make clear:

> Our interactions with others take place within a framework of societal values; therefore, any definition of mental health must necessarily reflect the kind of people we think we should be, the goals we consider desirable, and the type of society we aspire to live in. We cannot isolate our ideas about mental health from such wider social values as the desire for equality among people, the free pursuit of legitimate individual and collective goals, and the equitable distribution and exercise of power. (1988, 3)

Perhaps the most clearly articulated statement on the relationship of mental health problems to social order is provided by Article 196 of a Health Code introduced in Argentina in the 1950s:

> Mental illness is any deviation, defect, deficiency, deterioration, perturbation, disintegration, disjunction, extirpation or affection of any kind, whether temporary or permanent, of the mental functions, manifesting itself as an incapacity for community life and for active, logical, and ethical adaptation to the environment. (quoted in World Health Organization, 1955, 12)

Overall, the perception of an increase in the range and frequency of mental health problems has become widespread. Governments have demonstrated a tendency to fully recognize and support developments in psychiatric theory concerning the nature of the problem to be dealt with, as well as the threat to social disorder this creates and hence the need for the development of services to manage the problem. These changes in the field of mental health are generally recognized to represent a necessary reaction to the increased understanding of the way in which mental illness can manifest itself. And for the future, it is often argued that modern-day societal trends are liable to maintain this trend:

> The standard of living has increased markedly since 1945, but unrestrained urbanization, fragmentation of life and uprooting have been detrimental to the mental health of many people . . . in many big cities, one has the impression that depression and suicide are connected with loosening family ties, increasing divorce rates and a weaker social network. (Kringlen, 1993, 298)

Capitalism, government and mental health

Through the twentieth century, governments have readily accepted a medically based interpretation of the behaviour patterns of millions of people offered by the psychiatric profession, and lent it considerable support in the development of new services to provide the treatment assumed to be required. But why should governments do this? Why take on such a project when previous responses were so much more straightforward; for the most part simply not acknowledging the existence of people with less severe mental problems and occasionally, should they prove particularly problematic, shooting them (as we noted above in relation to wartime cowardice).

To address this question we need to consider the role of government. Offe (1984) provides an analysis of this which has had considerable impact on debates over the nature of government activity in capitalist societies. He argues that within capitalist countries governments are dependent upon the flow of revenue through taxation on private capital. Governments lack the power to take control of the organization of the production process, and so have little option but to attempt to maintain the conditions for private capital accumulation in order to safeguard their own revenues. Thus the argument presented is that there are structural pressures on government personnel to sustain to the best of their ability the capitalist economic system:

> Since state power depends on a process of accumulation which is beyond its power to organize, every occupant of state power is basically interested in promoting those political conditions most conducive to private accumulation. This interest does not result from an alliance of a particular government with particular classes or social strata also interested in accumulation; nor does it necessarily result from the privileged access of the members of the capitalist class to centres of state decision-making, a privilege which in turn makes it possible for that class to 'put pressure' on the incumbents of state power to pursue their class interest. Rather the institutional self-interest of the state in accumulation is conditioned by the fact that the state is denied the power to control the flow of those resources which are nevertheless indispensable for the exercise of state power. (Offe, 1984, 120)

The conception of government being presented here is of an institution with its own interests and concerns, whose problem is how to survive within the increasingly hostile environment of the capitalist social formation. The implication of this is that governments will tend to show an interest in economic, political and social issues which affect their own revenue base, and in turn their own ability to function. Moreover, governments must devise policies that muster sufficient support for them to be effectively implemented. In relation to mental health problems, the institutionalization of the medical model has proved particularly successful. The presentation of certain kinds of behaviour as an illness has proved broadly acceptable, and providers of treatment services gain a source of business which in turn tends to ensure their support of the policy. This is particularly so with the psychiatric profession and with drug companies.

It is often noted that conceptions of mental illness vary considerably over time and between places. However, one common characteristic that has united the vast majority of people with mental health problems is poverty. As a potential client group, relatively few are able to purchase private services, and most tend to rely upon what is made available by the state, and by charitable organizations. In consequence, the income and status of the psychiatric profession are dependent upon addressing the concerns of service providers, rather than upon meeting the stated or perceived needs of people with mental health problems. In the same way as the state is dependent upon and therefore actively involved in maintaining the continuation of successful capital accumulation, so, too, is the psychiatric profession largely dependent upon the state.

This is not to imply that the psychiatric profession does not have its own concerns, interests or volition, or that individual psychiatrists will always act in accordance with the more general interest of the profession in maintaining its economic and social position. But it does imply that over time the psychiatric profession is faced with a choice. It either develops theories and practices that are concordant with the position of the state, or it does not. The former option will of course tend to reinforce its dominant role in the management of mental health problems, and conversely the latter option will tend to erode that status.

The economic interests of drug manufacturers are a further factor helping to reinforce the pre-eminent position of the medical model of mental health problems. In the United States the pharmaceutical company Smith, Kline and French held the marketing rights over chlorpromazine, the first of the new major tranquillizers to be developed in the 1950s. This company was to make massive profits from this drug, and devoted a considerable part of its efforts to its early marketing:

> Over a seven year period, both state legislatures and state hospital staffs were bombarded with a hail of sophisticated propaganda designed to convince them of the virtues and advantages of the drug as a cheap, effective form of treatment suitable for administration on a mass basis to mental hospital patients. (Scull, 1984, 81)

This economic interest has escalated since, as new drugs have been developed and marketed. In the United States in the late 1980s drug companies were spending some $2 million just on advertising to doctors working with elderly patients (Phillipson, 1989). Perhaps the best known in the 1990s is 'Prozac', the worldwide sales of which in the first six months of 1995 totalled $970 million, a 30 per cent increase on the same period in 1994.

The shifting boundaries of social control

Explanations for the apparent incidence of mental health problems tend to focus on two main factors. Firstly, inequalities of power and of access to resources and opportunities are often argued to precipitate mental health problems. Secondly, discrimination and prejudice tend to result in a focus of psychiatric attention upon certain groups (Pilgrim & Rogers,

1993). The results are as outlined earlier: poor people, black people and women tend to suffer from, and to be more often defined as suffering from, mental health problems.

Such arguments as these are of course important. But still left unanswered in all of this, is why should mental health problems be so readily identified and responded to by governments? What is it that has led to such a huge expansion in the scale and type of mental problems that governments across the whole of Western Europe and North America have in the twentieth century actively sought to acknowledge and respond to?

Answers to such questions are difficult to assemble. Necessarily, they involve making broad generalizations for which little if any specific evidence can be accumulated to offer either support or opposition. But the need for answers is made necessary by the graphic evidence we reviewed earlier of the massive expansion in the use made of the concept of mental illness as a means of categorizing some people in terms of their failure to conform to certain social conventions.

In general terms, we might argue that the development of industrial capitalism over the last two hundred years has made necessary an increasingly regulated population. This starts with economic regulation, concerning the need for and acceptance of a concept of time and punctuality around which to organize factory production. It requires an acceptance of authority, and a willingness to provide labour power in return for a wage. Over time the trend has been towards ever more regulation. With the movement towards mass production in the twentieth century the regulation of consumption became important, this concerning the construction of a consumerist culture and the defining of lifestyle.

These themes are of course familiar ones of the nineteenth and twentieth century. The Marxist theme of alienation and the Weberian theme of rationalization constitute much of the theoretical framework of such views. Writing in the mid-twentieth century, Mills argues that the growing tendency towards regulation of everyday life was leading towards a loss of individuality and personal autonomy: 'among contemporary men will there come to prevail, or even to flourish, what may be called The Cheerful Robot?' (1959, 189). Earlier in the twentieth century, in his *Brave New World*, Huxley clearly anticipates such dangers should the power of mass production grow.

Given the increased regulation of greater areas of social life, it follows that an acceptance of roles, in terms of our class, gender and ethnic position, has become of greater importance in relation to the continued success of the socio-economic system. In turn, it might be anticipated that governments become progressively more concerned with regulating the borders of acceptable behaviour, and that increasing numbers of people may tend to transgress these limits.

These arguments are not intended to imply that all mental health problems are a form of deviance. Conditions such as Alzheimer's disease and perhaps some other more serious mental health problems such as schizophrenia have been found to have, or may well prove to have, an organic basis. Others may experience mental health problems because of the prejudice, discrimination and oppressive conditions they experience, and some may simply be the victims of experimentation. Equally, not all new forms of service development constitute an expansion of social control. As Matthews notes, a problem with much of the social control literature is that it fails to differentiate between types of intervention:

> Much of what parades under the heading of 'net-widening' may be constructive and progressive. Social workers, community workers, youth workers and the like are not simply 'agents of social control', nor are they just 'clearing up after capitalism' or 'papering over the cracks', for if nothing else these agents have undoubtedly brought much needed resources into deprived areas. (Matthews, 1987, 344)

But these points only constitute qualifications, albeit perhaps important ones, to the basic theme we have identified: it is the increasing sensitivity of governments to mental health problems, and their inclination to support a medicalized response, that largely accounts for what is often perceived as a dramatic increase in mental health problems in the twentieth century. The reasons for this derive from the need for regulation of an increasingly broad range of behaviour patterns.

Whether this analysis will hold for the twenty-first century is perhaps as yet unclear. The era of mass production is being replaced, to some extent, by post-fordist production processes and economic relationships that are more small-scale, fragmented and less uniform in nature (Jessop, 1994, 19–21). The implications of this for mental health policy can only be speculated upon, but it may be that the mass regulation of behaviour patterns that has developed in the twentieth century will give way to a more differentiated and fragmented social world in which common norms and values are of declining relevance. In turn this might presage a reversal of governments' interest in the psychological condition of their populations. This may be evidenced by predictions for the future that the less serious mental health conditions will in future be returned to the ownership of individuals, as personal problems (Sartorius, 1987). For the moment, however, within the countries of Western Europe and North America, government interest in the regulation of mental health appears to be strong and rising.

Summary

Through the twentieth century the relationship between governments and the mental health of their populations has altered dramatically. Ever larger areas of behaviour have come under medical scrutiny and control, resulting in a massive expansion in the number of people diagnosed as being mentally ill. Our argument has been that these developments have been very much led by the psychiatric profession, under the patronage of governments and supported by other vested interest groups such as drug companies. We have argued that the underlying reasons for these developments lie within economic and social changes that have occurred in capitalist societies. This changing model of psychiatric practice has had considerable implications for mental health policy. The old asylum-based model may have been an effective response to the problem of lunacy in the eighteenth and nineteenth centuries, but social and economic changes in the twentieth century made it increasingly out-dated. And it is to an examination of this change in policy that we turn in Chapter 5.

5

Specialization, Accessibility and Variation: Themes in the Analysis of Postwar Mental Health Policy

Within the old institution-based mental health system it would have been impossible for any government in the twentieth century to have developed sufficient bed space to meet all recognized mental health care needs. Moreover, many of the newly recognized cases of mental health problems have not necessarily required in-patient care. While institutional care may have served a function in the containment and control of lunatics in the nineteenth and early twentieth century, it was of rapidly declining relevance to the needs of people experiencing anxiety states, depression and other conditions that have become far more widely recognized. In short, the mental hospital has over the twentieth century to a large extent become outdated. Its lack of capacity, and the increasingly superfluous hotel costs associated with in-patient treatment, have both proved to be major impediments to its ability to address changes in the scale and type of mental health problems.

The shift towards community care represents the policy response to these changes in the nature and treatment of mental health problems. Firstly, treatment has become more accessible. The provision of treatment in general hospitals, community mental health centres, health centres and other readily accessible locations allows for increasing numbers of people to be treated. In the United States, for example, a primary goal of the community mental health centres programme was to increase access to treatment to people who previously were unable to obtain services (Kiesler, 1992, 1078). In the new sectorized organizational structure of many mental health services, there has been a tendency for a higher proportion of the population to enter the psychiatric care system (Hansson & Sandlund, 1992, 255). Overall, 'developments in the name of community care have reorganised and, indeed, extended the psychiatric field' (Mangen, 1985, 18).

Secondly, mental health services have become increasingly specialized. The old mental hospitals can be characterized by the fact that they met the entire range of needs a patient might have: for custody, treatment and care. These functions have gradually been separated. Custody still remains the province of mental hospitals, but (as we review below) the numbers subject to compulsory detention have been greatly reduced.

Treatment services have been developed in a range of new locations, including psychiatric units in general hospitals and community mental health centres. Finally, care services in the community such as residential homes and day centres, as well as the informal support of family, friends and neighbours, have become of increasing importance in the support of people with mental health problems.

These trends, towards increased accessibility and greater specialization, have enabled psychiatric services to address more adequately the changing nature and scale of mental health problems. Greater accessibility enables services to be provided to more people. The costs of this are contained to some extent by a process of specialization, whereby the specific costs associated with treatment are borne by the state, but increasingly the costs of providing care are off-loaded by placing people with mental health problems in cheaper residential accommodation, or, cheaper still, discharging them into the local community. The result of this development is an increasingly stark divide in the pattern of expenditure on mental health services. Statutory financing of services has tended to be concentrated upon the provision of treatment services, while financial responsibility for the care of people with mental health problems concerning their need for accommodation, employment, transport, and so on, has tended to be delegated to non-statutory and informal sources of care. In Belgium, for example, until 1974 there was a fixed daily fee rate for all mental hospitals, but since then the level of reimbursement for new facilities that specialize in the treatment of patients with more acute problems has been greater than that for the older mental hospitals; overall 'there is increasing differentiation in the types of institutions, professionals, and technical facilities and resulting increase in the utilization of services' (Verhaegey, 1987, 50). In Germany long-term patients are less eligible for insurance-based benefits than those receiving active treatment, and are more reliant upon state-funded social assistance. This division in funding tends to result in poorer standards of hospital care for this group (Bock, 1994, 277).

This increasing focus of statutory mental health services upon the provision of treatment rather than care is reflected in the criteria commonly used to measure success in the new community-based model of service provision. These include measures such as the hospital re-admission rate, the interval before readmission, social role performance, social adjustment and symptom levels (Thornicroft & Bebbington, 1989). The central concerns here are with achieving a level of functioning sufficient to maintain independence, and conformity to norms of behaviour associated with an absence of mental illness. The concerns of mental health services are mainly negative ones: that once discharged, patients do not return to mental hospital; that once treated, they do not display symptoms of mental illness. More positive concerns with the quality of life experienced by people with mental health problems, while often acknowledged, constitute a relatively marginal concern.

This is not to suggest that in all cases, at all times, the themes of specialization and accessibility will constitute the sole explanatory variables in the development of mental health service provision. Specific factors such as the nature of funding and constitutional structures (as we reviewed in Chapter 2) can have a particular, if not always predictable, impact on policy development. Moreover, as we shall see there are a number of variations on these themes to consider. But the argument of this chapter is that while a range of influences may be observed on how postwar mental health policy has evolved, the tendency towards increased accessibility of and specialization within mental health service provision, and the resulting bifurcation of treatment and care, are central to an understanding of that policy. We can demonstrate the centrality of these themes by reviewing various aspects of the development of postwar mental health services.

The decline of the mental hospital

In the 1950s the largest mental hospitals in Western Europe were to be found in France, where 44 per cent had over 1,000 beds and the largest had 4,000 beds (Bennett, 1991, 630). In Germany in the 1960s, there were 68 state mental hospitals with an average of 1,200 beds in each (Cooper & Bauer, 1987, 78). In the United States in the 1950s, mental hospitals of up to 10,000 beds could be found (Mangen, 1985, 120). Since then, however, it has been generally recognized that these institutions are too large, too isolated, and in many cases too derelict to be of therapeutic use. Between 1972 and 1982 the number of mental hospitals with over a thousand beds fell considerably; from 4 to 2 in Denmark and in Ireland, from 10 to 4 in Sweden, from 55 to 20 in Italy, and from 65 to 23 in England (Freeman et al., 1985, 34).

In the United States the number of in-patient beds has been reduced from a peak of over half a million beds in 1955, to a little under 300,000 in 1988 (Manderscheid & Sonnenschein, 1993). In 1955 there were 339 beds per 100,000 population in state and county hospitals. By 1992 this had been reduced to 40 beds per 100,000 and, in California, just 14 beds per 100,000 population (Lamb & Shaner, 1993, 973). In England the number of in-patient beds peaked in 1954 at around 152,000. By 1993 89 mental hospitals were closed and 100,000 mental hospital beds were lost, leaving just 41 hospitals and some 50,000 beds (Department of Health, 1995). In Canada between 1948 and 1959 an additional 20,000 mental hospital beds were created (Williams & Luterbach, 1976, 16). However, bed space peaked in 1962 at some 55,000 and then dropped rapidly to only 12,000 in 1977 (Rochefort, 1992, 1085). By 1990 there were just 42 psychiatric hospitals, with 15,792 beds (Department of Health and Welfare, 1990, 17).

In many other countries the mental hospital population peaked later, and the subsequent decline in bed space has been slower. In Germany and France there was a perceived deficit in in-patient capacity in the 1960s, and consequently a rise in mental hospital bed space (Mangen, 1987, 79). In France, between 1960 and 1972, 33,000 beds were added to psychiatric hospitals' in-patient capacity (Mangen, 1985, 141). The in-patient populations of both countries then peaked at around 120,000 in the early 1970s before slowly subsiding to a little over 100,000 in the early 1990s. In the Netherlands the in-patient population remained stable at around 25,000 through the postwar period, before beginning to decline in the mid-1980s. In Belgium, meanwhile, the in-patient population remained at around 27,000 until the early 1980s (Verhaegey, 1987, 44, 54), before falling back to around 20,000 by the early 1990s.

The bed stock of a number of other Western European countries also peaked in the 1960s and 1970s, but has since experienced a more substantial fall. In Italy the number of beds increased from 78,964 in 1954 to 98,544 in 1963. The number of beds slowly subsided to 85,000 in 1972, before falling more dramatically to 47,481 beds in 1981, although the decline in the in-patient population has been more pronounced in the north of the country than in other areas (Pirella, 1987, 119). Between 1975 and 1987 the in-patient population declined by 57 per cent in the Emilia Romagna region, while in Sicily the decline was only 26.4 per cent (Crepet, 1990, 28). In Denmark the in-patient population remained stable until the mid-1970s, but then declined by 48.6 per cent between 1976 and 1989, falling from 8,889 to 4,816 (Godt & Blinkenberg, 1992, 263). A similar pattern is to be found in Sweden, where the in-patient population peaked in 1977 at 28,787 beds (Perris, 1987, 200), before declining to around 14,000 by 1992 (Garpenby, 1993, 298).

Amongst Southern European countries, there has been (other than in Italy) little evidence of a decline in bed stocks at all. In Greece, Spain and Portugal it has only been since the mid-1980s that attention has been focused upon replacing institutional facilities with community-based services (Madianos, 1994).

Within the English language-based literature the United States, England and Italy are the most frequently discussed examples of de-institutionalization, and provide evidence of a substantial policy shift. Rafferty, for example, claims that 'Along with many other countries, both the United States and the UK have been running down psychiatric in-patient facilities since the mid-1950s' (1992, 589). This position, as the above evidence indicates, offers too simplistic a summary of policy development. While a shift from institutional to community care is generally taking place, the timing of its inception and its pace of development vary greatly between countries.

The development of new treatment services

As mental hospital bed space has declined, a range of new, treatment-orientated services have emerged. Together, they allow patients easier access to a service that places greater focus upon treating the specific mental health problem they are experiencing.

Psychiatric units in general hospitals

Concomitant with the decline of the old mental hospitals has been an increase in the number of beds available in psychiatric units in general hospitals. The new facilities are intended to provide a more local, more accessible, modern, treatment-orientated service where patients are generally expected to remain for at most only a few months. In France there were only around 1,500 beds in psychiatric units in general hospitals in the immediate postwar period, almost all in the university sector, where admission policies were highly selective (Mangen, 1985, 120). By the mid-1980s, however, there were 112 psychiatric units (Barres, 1987, 140) and 15 per cent of all psychiatric beds were in psychiatric units in general hospitals (Kovess et al., 1995, 133). In England 82 psychiatric units had been established by 1960, providing approximately 5,000 beds (Rehin & Martin, 1968, 10). By 1987 over half of all admissions were made to psychiatric units in general hospitals (Department of Health and Social Security, 1987). In Italy the number increased from 35 in 1972 to 236 in 1984, providing 3,113 beds (Freeman et al., 1985, 38; Donnelly, 1992, 91).

Many other European countries demonstrate similar trends. In Belgium the number of psychiatric units in general hospitals rose from 8 to 26 between 1972 and 1982 (Freeman et al., 1985, 38). In Germany the number of units increased from 21 in 1975 to 76 in 1987 (Grinten, 1985, 221). In the Netherlands a number of new psychiatric units in district general hospitals have been built since the 1970s, with the result that over 10 per cent of all psychiatric beds are in psychiatric units (Grinten, 1985, 221). In Sweden there has been a rapid increase in psychiatric unit beds since the mid-1970s, rising from around 4,500 to over 9,000 beds in the late 1980s (Perris, 1987, 202). A psychiatric unit in a general hospital now exists in each county (National Board of Health and Welfare, 1993). In Denmark it became a legal requirement in 1980 that every general hospital provide a psychiatric unit.

Similar trends are evident in North America. In the United States the number of in-patient psychiatric units increased from 664 in 1970 to 1,425 in 1988. The number of beds within these units increased from 22,394 to 48,421 over the same period. In 1988, beds in separate psychiatric in-patient services of non-federal general hospitals comprised 18 per cent of all psychiatric beds, compared to 4 per cent in 1970 (Manderscheid & Sonnenschein, 1993). In Canada the first psychiatric ward in a general hospital was opened in 1930, but it was not until the 1960s that a more substantial shift in mental hospital services occurred (Department of Health and Welfare, 1990, 15). In 1960 there were just 26 psychiatric units in general hospitals, and 151 mental health clinics, many of which were open only on a part-time basis and often operated out of existing out-patient departments (Williams & Luterbach, 1976, 17). Their develop-ment since then, however, has been rapid, with psychiatric units in general hospitals now making more than five times as many psychiatric admissions as mental hospitals (Rochefort, 1992, 1085).

Day and out-patient treatment

In Europe, as with the development of psychiatric units, it is in France and England where the earliest developments were made in the pro-vision of out-patient and day hospital treatment services (Freeman et al., 1985, 85). Out-patient counselling facilities were first developed in France in the 1930s (Demay, 1987, 71). In England 45 psychiatric day hospitals had been established by 1959 (Rehin & Martin, 1968, 11), and the number of new out-patients being seen was rising rapidly in the 1950s (Goodwin, 1993). Since then there has been a substantial expansion of out-patient and day patient facilities. Between 1979 and 1987 the number of day hospital units for mental patients increased from 315 to 500 (Department of Health and Social Security, 1987). In Canada day treatment services were first introduced in 1946 in Montreal, and by the mid-1950s had become widespread (Thompson, 1994).

Most other countries have been slower to develop day patient and out-patient facilities, but nevertheless are now clearly in the process of doing so. In the Netherlands a policy of expanding out-patient services was introduced in the 1970s (ten Horn et al., 1988, 271). There has been some expansion of day hospital places, with 513 places for this form of treatment being created in the general psychiatric hospitals between 1986 and 1991 (Spanjer, 1992, 20). The Netherlands government has attempted to prompt the development of out-patient facilities by making available funds to local bodies for this purpose; since 1982 a network of regional non-residential centres open 24 hours a day, seven days a week, has been established (Freeman et al., 1985, 85).

In Sweden there are now around 400 out-patient departments, and some day treatment facilities have been developed (National Board of Health and Welfare, 1993). In Germany the bulk of mental health treatment outside of the mental hospitals has been provided by general practitioners and office psychiatrists. As a result of their concerns about protecting this business there was no development of out-patient ser-vices until 1977, except in the university clinics. After 1977, following an amendment to the Reich Insurance Order, psychiatric hospitals were able to open out-patient services (Mangen, 1985, 98). Health clinics also exist which provide some psychiatric care.

In the United States the state mental hospitals have to a large extent shed their out-patient and day care patient responsibilities, as other community-based organizations have increasingly taken on this role. By 1988, only around one-quarter of state mental hospitals provided out-patient and day patient services. Reflecting this, the number of out-patient attendances at state mental hospitals fell from 164,232 in 1969 to 94,067 in 1988 (Manderscheid & Sonnenschein, 1993). In the non-federal general hospital psychiatric services, however, the number with out-patient units and/or day care patient facilities has increased rapidly (Manderscheid & Sonnenschein, 1993, 13). Between 1955 and 1975 there was a ten-fold increase in episodes of out-patient care (Hafner et al., 1989, 12).

Community mental health centres

In many countries, including the United States, Canada, Italy, Belgium and England, there have been some developments in the creation of community mental health centres. As we noted in Chapter 1, it is in the United States that this model has been most fully developed. In England community mental health centres first appeared in the 1970s, and by the early 1990s over 100 had been established. This has involved the development of a range of services, including the provision of some in-patient care, out-patient clinics, counselling facilities, emergency facilities and educational services. Access to these services is often gained by self-referral. The main aim of the movement towards the creation of com-munity mental health centres has been to provide a more accessible psychiatric service to a greater range of people: 'a commitment by the federal government to help support easily accessibly and locally con-trolled mental health centers, reflected the objective of modern treat-ment' (Cockerham, 1992, 294). Reflecting this extension of services to new client groups, in the United States in 1977 the median family income of patients treated in community mental health centres was only approx-imately $100 (Kiesler, 1992, 1078). In England it has been noted that these services have tended to focus upon the worried well, who previously may well have received no services at all (Pilgrim & Rogers, 1993, 133). Commenting on United States services Jones maintains that 'The scope of the new services was so wide and so undefined that there seemed to be almost no areas of social concern which could not be subsumed under its interests' (1988, 11).

Primary care

In many European countries the role of general practitioners in the identification and treatment of mental health problems has been encour-aged. In England it has been estimated that somewhere between 9 per cent and 35 per cent of their time is taken up with dealing with mental illness (Royal College of General Practitioners, 1985). There has also been some small increase in the number of psychiatrists providing clinics in primary care settings. It is estimated that some 20 per cent of psychi-atrists spend some time working in general practitioner clinics (Uffing et al., 1992, 268). In many other countries an increased role for general practitioners has been encouraged. In the Netherlands, for example, since the 1970s there has been some development of facilities such as clinics offering psychosocial guidance and psycho-therapeutically orientated treatment. There were also a whole range of child guidance clinics, and marital and family guidance centres (Van Der Veen, 1988, 28). Overall, however, the role of general practitioners remains quite limited in the provision of mental health care (Freeman et al., 1985, 86).

The impact of policy developments on the treatment received by people with mental health problems

A result of these developments in service provision has been to greatly increase the range of services available, and the number of people treated for mental health problems. In the United States there were approximately 7.5 million patient care episodes in 1986 (exclusive of the veterans' programmes), a more than four-fold increase over the 1.7 million patient care episodes in mental health organizations observed 31 years earlier in 1955 (Redick, 1990). The number of mental health organizations providing ambulatory services increased from 1,372 in 1970 to 2,139 in 1988 (Manderscheid & Sonnenschein, 1993). Within this general trend, there have been a number of changes in the way in which people with mental health problems have been provided with services

Trends in mental hospital admission rates

In many countries the admission rates to mental hospitals rose rapidly in the immediate postwar period, before falling back as bed space was reduced. In Sweden the mental hospital admission rate rose from 96,739 in 1970 to 127,992 in 1977, but subsequently fell to 109,502 in 1984 (Perris, 1987, 200). In Italy the number of admissions rose from 46,532 in 1954 to 102,617 in 1972, but then rapidly dropped to 27,322 in 1981 (Pirella, 1987, 119).

In other countries, the tendency for mental hospitals to admit increasing numbers of patients has continued longer. In England in 1950 there was a total of 60,266 mental hospital admissions and in 1989 there were 194,000 admissions; more than a three-fold increase in the admission rate despite a two-thirds reduction in bed space (Ministry of Health, 1951; Department of Health, 1991). In the Netherlands between 1970 and 1982 mental hospital admissions rose by 79 per cent (Haveman, 1986, 462). In Denmark the number of patients admitted to mental hospital increased from 37,591 in 1970 to 41,683 in 1987 (Kastrup, 1987). In the United States the number of in-patient admissions to mental health organizations increased from 1,282,698 in 1969 to 1,996,522 in 1988 (Manderscheid & Sonnenschein, 1993). Overall, however, as the tendency towards a contraction of mental hospital bed space continues, the rising number of admissions that tended to characterize service provision in the mid-part of the twentieth century has been or is being reversed.

The declining use of compulsory mental hospital admission

The admission of most mental patients was, until the mid-twentieth century, the result of a formal legalistic process. However, most countries have since introduced legislative change allowing for voluntary admission. In Ireland the Mental Treatment Act 1945 and in England the Mental Health Act 1959 both allowed for voluntary admission, and many other countries have since followed suit.

The impact of this shift in admissions procedure has, however, been quite slow-moving in many countries. In the early 1970s some 25 per cent of patients in Europe were detained compulsorily. In Germany in the 1960s 70 per cent of admissions were compulsory, and 80 per cent of patients were contained in locked wards (Cooper & Bauer, 1987, 78). In Belgium until 1974 two-thirds of patients were held under compulsory detention (Bennett, 1991, 634). By the early 1980s, in a review of 18 European countries Freeman et al. (1985, 52–53) still found an average of 16 per cent of admissions were involuntary. Within this average a wide range existed, with Sweden making 30 per cent of admissions on an involuntary basis, England 12 per cent, and Spain only 1 per cent. In the United States 26 per cent of admissions were involuntary (Riecher-Rössler & Rössler, 1993, 233). In the Netherlands involuntary detention declined rapidly in the 1970s, and by 1982 only 12 per cent of patients were compulsorily detained (Giel, 1987, 154). In Canada the mental hospital retained its custodial orientation until the late 1960s, and it was only in the 1970s that the majority of patients were admitted on a voluntary basis (Williams & Luterbach, 1976, 17).

In Italy, with the passing of Law 180, the number of involuntary admissions dropped rapidly. In 1977 there were 32,551 compulsory admissions, and in the year from June 1978 to May 1979 there were just 13,375. In the same period voluntary admissions rose from 51,137 to 67,498 (Donnelly, 1992, 83). In many other countries the number of compulsory admissions has dropped significantly in recent years. In France less than 10 per cent of admissions have been compulsory since the early 1980s (Barres, 1987). In Denmark in 1990 there were 40,000 voluntary admissions, compared to 1,348 involuntary admissions (Vestergaard, 1994, 192). In Sweden compulsory admission declined from around 10,000 a year in 1979 to 3,000 in 1991 (Brink, 1994, 262). In Ireland by the early 1980s compulsory admissions comprised just 10 per cent of the total (Walsh, 1987).

Within some countries there are widely varying rates of use of compulsion. In Italy in the 1970s the number of mental patients who were involuntarily committed varied enormously, between an average of around 80 per cent in mental hospitals in the south of the country, and 45 per cent in the north (Donnelly, 1992, 87). In the German states rates of involuntary admission vary between 3.9 per cent and 44.8 per cent, the higher rates tending to be found where less emphasis has been given to the development of social psychiatric services. In Switzerland also there is considerable variation between the cantons, with between 50 per cent and 93 per cent of admissions still being made on a compulsory basis (Riecher-Rössler & Rössler, 1993, 233). In the United States around 75 per cent of admissions are on a voluntary basis, but in a few states, such as Connecticut and Alaska, voluntary admissions make up only 25 per cent of admissions (Pilgrim & Rogers, 1993, 148).

Overall, there has clearly been a trend towards a declining use of compulsory admission procedures. It has been argued, however, that while the possibility of compulsory detention exists, there can be no such thing as a genuine voluntary decision (Szasz, 1961). There is certainly evidence to suggest that people facing admission are informed that unless they enter voluntarily then compulsion will be used, and also that voluntary patients frequently regard themselves as being under coercion. In England, it is estimated that over 8,000 detentions each year are made after a patient has been admitted to a mental hospital on a voluntary basis (Pilgrim & Rogers, 1993, 145). Compulsory admission to in-patient treatment occurs almost always during emergency interventions. Reflecting this, in England 90 per cent of compulsory admissions are carried out under Section 4 of the 1983 Mental Health Act (Katschnig et al., 1993).

Average length of stay

A substantial fall in the average length of stay in mental hospitals has been common to all countries. In the United States the average length of stay in 1970 was 41 days, and by 1986 this had fallen to 15 days (Cockerham, 1992, 294). In Italy the average hospital stay had declined to just 12.5 days by the early 1990s (Donnelly, 1992, 91). In the Netherlands between 1974 and 1982 the number of in-patients discharged within three months rose from 53 per cent to 77 per cent (Haveman, 1986, 462). In France the average length of stay dropped from 247 days in 1971 to 131 days in 1980 (Barres, 1987), and in Denmark between 1972 and 1987 the number of patients occupying a mental hospital bed declined by 75 per cent (Licht et al., 1991). In 1975 the average length of stay in one mental hospital in Barcelona was 21 years, although the national average was 413 days and this has since declined substantially (Comelles & Hernáez, 1994, 293).

These reductions in the average length of stay are due, in part, to the emphasis given in the psychiatric units in general hospitals to patient throughput. In these units the average length of stay is generally lower than those in the older mental hospitals. In the psychiatric units of general hospitals in France the average length of stay in 1980 was only 51 days (Demay, 1987, 71). In most psychiatric units in England patients generally stay for a maximum of three weeks (Freeman et al., 1985, 49). In Canada the throughput of psychiatric units is twice that of the older mental hospitals (Rochefort, 1992, 1086). In 1984 the average length of stay in a state mental hospital in Baden-Württemberg (one of the German states) was 59 days, and in the psychiatric units it was 33 days (Rössler et al., 1992, 448).

While the trend is towards a reduction in the length of stay, there is considerable variation around the average, with it still being the case that a large number of patients experience protracted hospital stays (Lelliott & Wing, 1994). A comparative study of psychiatric services, for example, found 'remarkable differences in the pathway in care of patients from Mannheim and Groningen' (ten Horn et al., 1988, 278) concerning such variables as the numbers admitted to mental hospital and the length of in-patient stay. In the Netherlands in 1970, 71 per cent of mental hospital patients had been resident for two or more years, and 47 per cent had been resident for ten or more years (Haveman, 1986, 463). By the mid-1980s, two-thirds of beds were still occupied by a patient who had been resident a year or more. There is some movement of older patients to residential homes, but their place in the old mental hospital is in part being taken by the 'new long-stay' (Grinten, 1985, 221). In Germany there are still 60,000 long-term in-patients in mental hospitals (Bock, 1994, 277).

Out-patient and day patient services

An increasing number of psychiatric patients receive treatment services without undergoing hospital admission. In the United States in 1955, 77 per cent of people provided a psychiatric service were admitted to a mental hospital, and the remaining 23 per cent were seen as out-patients. By 1986 in-patient care episodes constituted only 27 per cent of the total, while 68 per cent were out-patient episodes, and 5 per cent were partial care episodes (Redick, 1990). Between 1969 and 1988 the number of out-patient attendances increased from 1,146,612 to 2,289,779, and the number of day care patients increased from 55,486 to 276,185 (Manderscheid & Sonnenschein, 1993). In-patient admissions to the community mental health centres increased rapidly in the 1970s from 83,168 in 1969 to 270,446 in 1979, but, as a result of their subsequent loss of funding in the 1980s (see Chapter 1), decreased substantially to 167,715 in 1988 (Manderscheid & Sonnenschein, 1993).

A similar pattern of service use is to be found in other countries. In France the dispensaries, which provide locally based psychiatric services, saw their number of new patients increase by 350 per cent between 1960 and 1980 (Mangen, 1985, 136). Over 50 per cent of the country's psychiatric patients are now treated in facilities outside of the mental hospital (Barres, 1987). In Denmark between 1972 and 1987 the number of day patients increased by 500 per cent (Licht et al., 1991). In England between

1975 and 1985 the number of new out-patients rose from 187,000 to 201,000, while the total attendances of out-patients rose from 1.55 million to 1.8 million. The number of regular day patients has also risen, with 36,000 new patients in 1975 and 58,000 in 1985 (Goodwin, 1993).

Within this general trend there is some variation between countries in the experience of treatment services by service users. In a comparative study of services in towns in Italy, Germany and the Netherlands it was found that out-patient care was the most commonly received service, but considerable variation of factors such as the number of consultations and the time span of treatments existed. Single consultations, for example, were found to be three times more common in Verona than Groningen. In Mannheim it was found that 76 per cent of patients have finished their treatment after six months, whereas in Groningen the figure was only 43 per cent (Hansson & Sandlund, 1992, 259). Overall, however, out-patient treatment has expanded rapidly over the last 30 years, and constitutes the most common form of treatment in many countries (ten Horn et al., 1988, 275).

Variations in the type of treatment offered

A number of studies of psychiatric care service utilization have examined patient background characteristics and have generally found distinct differences in the admission characteristics of different groups in society. Men generally make heavier use of services than women, although more women are admitted to mental hospital than men (Hansson & Sandlund, 1992, 259). In a survey of mental health service use by people with long-term functional psychoses in Sweden, Borga et al. (1991) found that the frequency of admission amongst men and women was similar, but men were on average admitted for twice as long as women. Because women spent less time as in-patients, they tended to make greater use of out-patient facilities, but there was no gender difference in the use of social welfare and primary health care. Patients with long-term functional psychoses were found, on average, to spend on average two months of the year in a psychiatric institution. Overall, men were found to spend around twice as long as women as in-patients, and this gender difference has been found in a number of other studies (Lassenius et al., 1973; Shepherd & Tester, 1989).

There are also considerable class differences in service utilization. In England in areas defined by the government as socially deprived, admission to psychiatric hospital is three times higher than the national average. Unemployed people are 11 times more likely to attempt suicide than are those in employment (Mental Health Foundation, 1995).

Amongst ethnic minorities there is some evidence in the United States of under-use of available services. One possible explanation for this, Neighbors et al. (1992, 59) suggest, is that ethnic minorities are more likely to use alternative informal support systems or indigenous practitioners. Also, because of the overrepresentation of ethnic minorities amongst low-income groups, they are more likely to obtain mental health help from the public mental health care sector. This means than in comparison to those receiving private mental health care, minorities are seen less often, over a shorter period of time, and are more likely to get drug therapy (Neighbors et al., 1992, 59). Overall, however, there is insufficient evidence to fully determine the extent to which black people are underrepresented in comparison to whites (Neighbors et al., 1992, 61). For some black people, however, there is clear evidence of over-use of services. A study in England found that amongst the younger Afro-Caribbean population incident rates were 12 to 13 times higher than those of the general population (Harrison, 1988). Littlewood and Lip-sedge (1988) found that first-admission figures for British-born Afro-Caribbean men were 7 times the white rate, and for Afro-Caribbean women they were 13 times higher.

While in recent years admission rates have tended to drop (as discussed above), this reduction is unevenly spread amongst different patient groups. In Denmark, admission rates have tended to decrease for all diagnostic groups except schizophrenia, which has increased. The number of in-patients diagnosed with neurotic conditions has decreased most rapidly (Munk-Jorgensen & Jensen, 1992). Similarly in England, in the first report of a national audit of new long-stay psychiatric patients conducted in 1992, it was found that younger patients (aged 18–34) were mostly single men with schizophrenia. Forty-three per cent of these had a history of serious violence, dangerous behaviour or admission to a secure hospital, and over one-third were formally detained (Lelliott & Wing, 1994).

The elderly tend to be overrepresented in in-patient population statistics (ten Horn et al., 1988), but there is some evidence that the overall age profile of in-patients is lowering (Haveman, 1986, 461). In Denmark, between 1972 and 1987, the proportion of patients aged 15–44 increased from 11.7 per cent to 23.6 per cent, while the proportion of patients aged 65 or over decreased from 58.4 per cent to 49.1 per cent. Overall, the mean age of the mental hospital population declined from 65.8 to 61 (Licht et al., 1991). Amongst older patients (aged 55–67) in England, most have been found to be married or previously married women, most often with a diagnosis of affective disorder or dementia and with poor personal and social functioning; over half were at moderate or severe risk of non-deliberate self-harm (Lelliott & Wing, 1994).

There is also considerable variation in the use of compulsory admission amongst different groups. People diagnosed as being schizophrenic have been found to be far more likely to be subject to compulsory admission. People with personality disorders, Alzheimer's disease and mania have also been found to be more likely to experience compulsory admission. Committed patients are also more likely to be lower class, and unemployed. They are mostly male, single and live alone (Riecher-

Rössler & Rössler, 1993, 233). But perhaps most clear is the fact that black people are overrepresented in compulsory admission figures, and in secure mental health facilities (Knowles, 1991, 176; Pipe et al., 1991). In England, amongst male offenders in the 16–29 age group, Afro-Caribbeans are 17 times more likely to be admitted to a mental institution (McGovern & Cope, 1987). It is argued that psychiatrists perceive a greater likelihood of violence from a black than from a white patient, and are more likely to suggest that the police should be involved when dealing with the former. Overall, black patients are more likely to receive enforced treatment, more likely to be prescribed psychotropic medication, more likely to be kept in hospital longer, and more likely to be compulsorily detained (Lewis et al., 1990).

The care of mental patients

The changing pattern of postwar mental health services has had substantial consequences for the availability of care services. As in-patients, service users receive treatment within a context of being provided board and lodging. The decline in the number of in-patients, the decline in average length of stay and the decline in the number of people admitted to mental hospital have all tended to reduce the availability of this aspect of psychiatric services. The increased role of out-patient, day patient and other services has maintained the availability of specific treatment services but provides little care in terms of the provision of a safe and secure environment where a bed, meals and some activity are provided. To a large extent, greater specialization and increased accessibility of mental health services have resulted in the separation of treatment and care. More people now receive a greater range of treatments for mental illness than ever before. But this has been achieved, in part, as a result of unit cost savings gained from a reduction in the number of hospital beds and increasing throughput in those that remain.

As this process began in the middle of the twentieth century, little thought was given to the problems that people with mental health problems might face upon discharge, and little attention was paid to the range of services they might require. As Bennett and Morris note:

> The community care facilities that were established were frequently viewed as transitional, a step between acute hospitalization and full reintegration into the community. The notion that some patients might require no less than life-long support in some sort of sheltered, protected setting was either ignored or denied in the hopeful therapeutic climate that prevailed. (1983, 9–10)

But as treatment services have become more specialized and more accessible, the separation of care and treatment services has appeared increasingly stark. By the 1970s it came to be recognized that the problem of mental illness cannot be so radically and simply separated from the wider range of problems experienced by people with mental health problems:

... there is always an interaction between clinical and social problems. It is rarely possible to separate the two in a way that would be convenient for the development of independent medical and social services. (Wing & Olsen, 1979, 172)

Thus a radical separation of treatment and care services has come to be seen as overly simplistic: 'the assumption that medical and social needs can be dealt with separately, which is built into the present administrative structure, will have to be modified' (Wing & Olsen, 1979, 185). In the old mental hospitals, it has come to be recognized that for many patients it will remain their home for long periods, and that for those being admitted their treatment is likely to be more effective if the quality of their surroundings is improved. Similarly, in the community it has come to be recognized that the effectiveness of treatments depends in part upon the patient receiving social support.

Refurbishment of the old mental hospitals

A policy of improving the quality and numbers of staff and the quality of furnishings in the remaining mental hospitals has been introduced in many countries. In the Netherlands considerable efforts have been made since the late 1970s to reduce the size of wards, and improve the general standards of accommodation. Seventy-six per cent of general psychiatric hospital buildings were deemed to be in good or reasonable condition in 1991, as opposed to 33 per cent in 1978. In 1978 37 per cent of the buildings were of poor quality, but this had dropped to 7 per cent in 1991 (Spanjer, 1992, 20–21). It has even been suggested that the extent of improvement has been too great:

Large amounts of money are spent making housing conditions more adequate as regards modern treatment and way of life. However in times of frozen budgets these costly investments put serious limits to the growth of non-residential mental health facilities. (Haveman, 1986, 458)

In England this process of refurbishment started in the immediate postwar period. By the late 1950s, these efforts allowed the Ministry of Health to claim that 'great improvements have been made by upgrading, reconstruction and new building. The effect has been to make the hospitals both pleasanter places for patients and staff, and better suited for their therapeutic purpose' (1958, 26). Nevertheless, in the mid-1970s there were still 79 mental hospitals where some patients did not have a full range of personal clothing, and many patients did not have their own personal cupboard space (Department of Health and Social Security, 1976, 59), although since then these issues have been largely addressed. In Germany the number of people sleeping in large dormitories has been greatly reduced, and conditions are generally much improved in the remaining mental hospitals (Cooper & Bauer, 1987, 87).

While there is a general tendency of governments to refurbish the remaining mental hospitals, this trend is not apparent in all countries. In

Southern European countries conditions in many of the old mental hospitals remain poor (Madianos, 1994). In Italy, for example, 'it is the opinion of many practitioners that the "quality" of the care provided by the psychiatric hospitals today is, except in a few praiseworthy exceptional cases, even worse than that which existed before the reform' (Crepet, 1990, 29).

Residential homes

A result of the decline in mental hospital bed space has been that many patients have been discharged into cheaper residential homes, many of these being within the private sector (Mangen, 1988, 28). In the United States private nursing homes have expanded rapidly since the 1960s to cater for those patients discharged from the mental hospital but unable to cope in the community. Of around 1.5 million people in nursing homes, it is estimated that as many as 75 per cent may have a mental disorder. Additionally, there has been the growth of a range of new private residential services such as group homes and halfway houses which cater for between 300,000 and 400,000 people (Mechanic & Rochefort, 1990).

In England in 1962 only 967 residential places in local authority and voluntary hostels existed (Ministry of Health, 1962, 70). By 1975 this had increased to 1,366, and by 1989 reached a total of 6,237 (Department of Health and Social Security, 1981; Department of Health, 1991). Following a change in social security regulations in 1980 there has also been a rapid expansion in the provision of privately run accommodation. In France, the 1975 Handicapped Persons Act encouraged the transfer of long-stay mental hospital patients into residential homes. The Ninth National Plan (1984–9) laid out plans to reduce the number of unoccupied beds by 12,000, and to replace 28,000 beds occupied by chronic patients with new residential accommodation in the community (Barres, 1987, 142). In Germany in the 1980s, many discharged patients were transferred into residential homes, many of them in the private sector. In the mid-1980s, there were around 50,000–60,000 in such homes (Mangen, 1985, 103; Cooper & Bauer, 1987, 81).

Other European countries are also moving in this direction, but at a slower pace. In the Netherlands in 1980 there were only 4,200 places in day care and residential accommodation for people with mental health problems, although numbers have begun to increase (Grinten, 1985, 212). Similarly in Denmark, since 1980 there has been some increase in the number of residential homes in the community for people with mental health problems, although numbers remain relatively small (Licht et al., 1991, 317). In Italy, despite the dramatic reductions in mental hospital bed space, there has also been relatively little development of residential facilities for people with mental health problems.

Increased emphasis on the role of informal carers

As community care policies emerged in the 1950s and 1960s informal carers constituted a relatively hidden part of service provision, with little thought being given to their role (Benson, 1994, 119). More recently, however, and particularly since the economic downturn of the 1970s, the importance of informal carers has been increasingly recognized. In the United States, Rice & Jones (1990) estimated that the value of time contributed by family members for the care of people with mental health problems was $2.5 billion in 1985. In a survey of the experience of care by families, mostly by parents caring for adult offspring diagnosed as having schizophrenia, Franks (1987) found that on average these families spent $3,539 per year on their ill members, and gave 798 hours each year to their care.

This economic situation, together with increasingly evident assumptions about the duties and obligations between family members, has brought informal carers closer to the centre of the policy-making process. In France and Italy there has been a considerable increase of responsibility upon families to provide care and support of their members who have mental health problems (Donnelly, 1992, 93; Kovess et al., 1995, 134). In the United States, a similar position is evident, where 'current policies seem to based on the often unstated belief that the preferred place for the serious mentally ill is with their families' (Aviram, 1990, 81). In England this increased emphasis upon the role of informal support reflects in the fact that the term 'carer' entered the political vocabulary only in the early 1980s. By the late 1980s it had gained a central position within the policy-making process:

> The great bulk of community care will continue to be provided by family, friends and neighbours. The majority of these carers take on these responsibilities willingly and I admire the dedicated and self-sacrificing way in which so many members of the public take on serious obligations to help care for elderly or disabled relatives and friends. Our proposals are aimed at strengthening support for those many unselfish people who care for people in need. (Department of Health, 1989)

In addition to this increased emphasis upon the role of informal carers, some new resources have been made available. In Germany a new statutory long-term care insurance scheme has recently been introduced. It provides benefits on a scale according to the person's level of dependency to pay for home and institutional care. This system is intended not to replace family care, but to support and bolster it where needed (Rickford, 1995). In England, since 1991, emphasis within community care policy has been placed upon providing support to carers. This has involved the development of services such as respite care, where people with mental health problems might receive residential care for a short period of time with the specific intention of providing the carer with a break from their role. In 1995 carers gained a legal right to have their own needs assessed, in addition to those of the people they cared for.

Overall, however, as is often noted within discussions of community care policy, the increased emphasis upon the role of informal carers has not been matched by a proportionate increase in resources to support them. A result of community care policies, therefore, has been that the burden of care has increasingly been shifted from governments to informal carers:

> ... despite the well documented needs of these families, efforts by policy-makers and mental health professionals to provide supportive services to family care givers have, until recently, been rare. As a result, many families with mentally ill members have felt virtually abandoned by treatment pro-viders. (Benson, 1994, 119)

The skewing of state mental health expenditures

We have argued in this chapter that the shift from institutional to community care has involved a process of increased specialization in service provision, allowing for ever-growing numbers of people to receive access to psychiatric treatment. A consequence of this policy development has been that statutory provision has increasingly been concentrated upon the treatment of mental patients, while responsibility for the more general support of people with mental health problems has to a large extent been devolved to private, voluntary and informal sources of care. Yet, the process of deinstitutionalization, together with the increasing emphasis upon care in the community, means that the problems faced by mentally ill people in gaining adequate accommoda-tion and social support are of growing importance. The result has been a tendency for patterns of expenditure to be increasingly skewed, where treatment services to address the problem of mental illness have tended to be prioritized, while the importance attached to addressing the problems of mentally ill people is reduced.

This tendency towards the skewing of mental health expenditures is apparent in a number of countries. In the United States, despite the fact that deinstitutionalization has progressed more rapidly than in any other country, psychiatric in-patient facilities absorb over 70 per cent of money spent on mental health (Hollingsworth, 1992, 904; Kiesler, 1992, 1079). In some states, such as New York, the hospital tranche is as high as 85 per cent (Aviram, 1990, 80). In recent years the general emphasis in the United States has been upon developing short-term acute services where the federal government, through the Medicaid and Medicare pro-grammes, has funded an expansion in the numbers of in-patient admis-sions to general hospitals, but provided little money for the development of other community-based services (Kiesler, 1992, 1081).

In Canada, between 1970 and 1980, spending on community mental health programmes amounted to just 0.71 per cent of Ministry of Health spending, and by 1988/9 it had dropped to 0.66 per cent. In the late 1980s the majority of provinces were found to spend between 10 per cent and 30 per cent, and only one province (Saskatchewan) spent more than 50 per cent of mental health resources on community-based services (Rochefort, 1992, 1087). In Ontario, despite the emphasis given in policy statements to the development of community-based services, only 16.5 per cent of provincially controlled mental health expenditure was allocated to community mental health programmes in 1989/90 (Lurie, 1992, 13).

A similar picture emerges in Western Europe, where on average over 80 per cent of the mental health budget continues to be spent upon in-patient services (Mangen, 1987, 76). In France hospitals consumed 80 per cent of resources in 1960s and 1970s (Demay, 1987, 75). In 1980 just 4.5 per cent of the costs of psychiatric personnel were spent outside of the mental hospital. Of overall expenditure, the mental hospital received 80 per cent (Mangen, 1985, 130). In the Netherlands in 1980 the mental hospital still employed 90 per cent of all psychiatric staff and spent 83 per cent of the budget (Grinten, 1985, 221). In 1983 91 per cent of total expenditure and 94 per cent of staff were allocated to hospital facilities (Haveman, 1986, 457), and this was cut back to around 70 per cent only in the early 1990s (Dekker & Langenberg, 1994). In 1991 in England, 77 per cent of the NHS mental health budget was still being spent on hospital and prescription costs, and only 23 per cent on out-patient, day patient, community health and primary care services combined.

While the role of informal carers is being increasingly stressed, little money has been diverted into supporting them. In Ontario, expenditure in support of families and other carers amounted to $3.2 million in 1991/2. This represents just 20 cents of every 100 dollars spent on mental health (Lurie, 1992, 13). In England local authority social service departments, which are responsible for meeting the social care needs of people with mental health problems in the community, spend just 3 per cent of their budgets on mental health (Sayce, 1994, 12). In the early 1990s, it is estimated that on average £80 per person per day was spent on those in English mental hospitals and just £1 per person per day was spent on those in the community (Mental Health Foundation, 1993, 48).

Responsibility for the costs of providing care can also be passed over to families. In a review of costs in one area in Germany in 1983 it was found that 60 per cent of total mental health costs were met by social security funds, of which over a quarter was subsequently recovered from the patient or their family (Cooper & Bauer, 1987, 84). In England since the early 1980s local authorities have increasingly sought to obtain some part of the costs of service provision from service users.

The three different relationships of capitalist societies and mental health service provision

These general trends, of increased specialization, accessibility and the resulting skewing of expenditure patterns in the postwar development of mental health services, reflect the common concerns, interests and pressures that countries in Western Europe and North America have tended to experience. At the same time, however, the development of services in different countries has, as we examined in Chapter 1, been diverse. The onset and the pace of deinstitutionalization have varied considerably, as have the style of new services that have replaced the older mental hospitals. Thus, while certain common patterns can be established, we need also to be able to account for variations within these.

In his recent work, Esping-Anderson maintains that within advanced capitalist countries there are 'three highly diverse regime-types, each organized around its own logic of organization, stratification, and social integration. They owe their origins to different historical forces, and they follow qualitatively different development trajectories' (1990, 3). While a common analytical base concerning the history of political class coalitions is utilized, he nevertheless concludes that liberal, conservative and social democratic regime-types can be clearly identified (Esping-Anderson, 1990, 26–28).

Liberal regimes are characterized by the importance that is attached to the maintenance of market relationships in economic and social affairs. The role of the state is minimal, intervening only when and where the market has failed, and even then doing only sufficient to ensure basic needs are met. Consequently, state welfare benefits tend to be means-tested, flat rate and of limited value, and are often stigmatized.

Conservative regimes are characterized by a tendency towards economic and social status maintenance. Welfare services have often developed within pre-democratic regimes with the purpose of impeding the development of working-class political parties. Consequently the role of social policy tends to be one of reinforcing the existing order of society. Welfare services will tend to reflect this where, for example, the value of social security benefit payments tends to correspond to the previous wage of each claimant, and where pre-existing welfare arrangements such as those provided by the church and the family are not replaced by the state.

Social democratic regimes are characterized by the importance attached to the social and economic rights of citizens. The state tends to be far more proactive than in either conservative or liberal regimes. Social and economic relationships are based upon a social contract, often involving objectives such as equality and a commitment to addressing a wide range of social needs. Consequently, state welfare services tend to be universal, relatively generous, broad in scope, and have the role of reducing inequalities. To the extent that welfare benefits are graduated, this is intended to encourage allegiance to the insurance-based benefit system rather than to maintain differentials amongst recipients.

Esping-Anderson's model provides a means of characterizing variations in the basic social and economic arrangements of what are all basically capitalist countries. This is not to imply that any one country provides a discrete example of any one regime type. Liberal regimes may well demonstrate aspects of social democratic regimes, conservative regimes aspects of the other two, and so on. Equally, over time the social and economic arrangements of a country may alter such that the balance of regime characteristics is substantially altered. But, overall, Esping-Anderson contends in a wide-ranging analysis that industrialized capitalist countries tend to exhibit more features of one model than the other two. As such, we can identify a tendency towards a clustering of certain countries around each regime-type. The United States, Canada and England exhibit predominantly liberal regime characteristics; France, Germany, Italy, Belgium and Spain are examples of conservative regimes; and Denmark, Sweden and the Netherlands are examples of social democratic regimes.

Attempts such as this to categorize the welfare arrangements of different countries have been the subject of a variety of criticisms concerning the extent to which such typologies can be determined. (Deacon, 1992). Issues of race and gender have tended to be ignored or downgraded in importance. Esping-Anderson in particular has been singled out for criticism as a result of his focus upon paid work only (Tester, 1996). Nevertheless, the argument developed in the remainder of this chapter is that while the mental health policies of all countries considered in this study demonstrate the more general trend from institutional to community care, the clustering of regime-types identified by Esping-Anderson can also be detected within the varying trends apparent in the development of postwar mental health services and policy.

The decline of the mental hospital

In all the countries we have examined, the mental hospital population has risen, peaked and subsequently fallen. The timing of the peak and the speed of the subsequent fall has, however, varied considerably. As Table 5.1 demonstrates, the mental hospital population of countries with liberal regimes peaked earliest, while the peak in countries with conservative and social democratic regimes tended to follow some 10 or 20 years later.

Further differences between regime-types are also revealed when we consider the rate of change in the mental hospital in-patient population of various countries. As Table 5.2 demonstrates, between 1950 and 1985 conservative countries have been the slowest to deinstitutionalize, social democratic countries have been in the mid-range and liberal countries have proved to be the fastest to deinstitutionalize people with mental health problems. There are some countries that clearly do not fit this pattern. Italy, for example, is untypical of conservative countries, perhaps because of the distinctive and specific contribution of the Psichiatria Democratica movement. The Netherlands is untypical of the social

Table 5.1   *Mental hospital populations: peak years*

Liberal:	
England	1954
United States	1955
Canada	1962
Conservative:	
France	1972
Germany	1973
Italy	1963
Belgium	1981
Spain	1981
Social democratic:	
Denmark	1976
Sweden	1977
The Netherlands	1979

Sources: Scull, 1984; Mangen, 1985; Perris, 1987; Pirella, 1987; Verhaegey, 1987; Godt & Blinkenberg, 1992; Novack, 1992; Rochefort, 1992; Goodwin, 1993; Comelles & Hernáez, 1994

Table 5.2   *Changes in mental hospital population totals (per cent)*

	1950–85	1970–85
Liberal:		
England	−51.2	−44.8
United States	−47.7	−18.9
Total of above countries	−49.8	−25.5
Conservative:		
France	22.5	−6.0
Germany	27.1	−11.0
Italy	−36.1	−50.2
Belgium	7.2	−20.2
Spain	46.7	−26.3
Total of above countries	−4.8	−21.7
Social democratic:		
Denmark	−29.9	−28.6
Sweden	n/a	−40.0
Netherlands	−3.0	−9.4
Total of above countries	−11.2	−27.0

Source: Figures derived from Poullier & Sandier, 1991

democratic countries, perhaps because of the particularly devolved and complex nature of its social welfare arrangements, and also because of the influence of the principle of subsidiarity which is unusually high for a regime which is primarily social democratic in character. Moreover, to the extent that overall trends are apparent, they were very much established in the 1950s and 1960s. For the more recent period, between 1970 and 1985, the pace of deinstitutionalization varies widely and demonstrates no consistent pattern between regime-types.

Community-based treatment and support

Comparable statistical material on the emergence and speed of development of community-based services is more difficult to find than that on mental hospital use. However, there are some general trends to be identified that suggest different styles of development between regime-types.

Within liberal regimes the shift towards developing new services tended to be made relatively early, and more quickly than in either conservative or social democratic countries. We noted earlier in this chapter how the development of residential accommodation for chronic patients came to be seen as a means of enhancing the treatment function of the remaining mental hospital bed space. In England this shift towards the specialization of functions in service provision can be detected as early as the late 1940s. The National Assistance Act 1948, Section 21, stated that 'it should be the duty of every local authority to provide residential accommodation for persons who are by reasons of age, infirmity or any other circumstances in need of care and attention which is not otherwise available to them'.

In the United States, too, there was an early shift towards a diversification of services, together with a clear emphasis upon the focusing of services on treating increasing numbers of people. As we noted above, the number of residential homes, mainly in the private sector, has expanded rapidly and massively since the 1960s. The development of community mental health centres also arose in the 1960s and, at least until the 1980s, when they fell out of favour, provided a substantial new resource for the treatment of people with mental health problems.

Conservative regimes have tended to be slower, and relatively late, to place emphasis upon developing community-based services. In France, as we discussed in more detail in Chapter 1, it was only in the mid-1970s with the enactment of the Handicapped Persons Act 1975 that emphasis was given to moving long-term patients out of the mental hospital, and it was only in the 1980s that substantial movement in this direction was achieved (Barres, 1987, 142). Similarly in Germany it was only in the late 1970s that the large-scale movement of long-term patients into residential homes began (Cooper & Bauer, 1987, 81). In Spain this process of specialization has only really begun in the 1990s, and has still to take effect in all parts of the country (Comelles & Hernáez, 1994, 290).

The pace of development of other community-based support services has also proved to be relatively slow. In Germany, as we noted in our review of mental health services in Chapter 1, the Report of the Experts Commission in 1988 found very little development of community-based services. Similarly in Italy, Spain and Belgium we noted there has been relatively little development of services such as day centres and domiciliary support. Moreover, there is also a strong tendency within conservative regimes to place greater emphasis upon family care. In France, Italy and Germany there has been a considerable increase of responsibility upon families to provide care and support of their members who have mental health problems (Kovess et al., 1995, 134; Donnelly, 1992, 93; Rickford, 1995).

Social democratic countries were also relatively late to develop the new style of service provision. In Sweden, as we discussed in Chapter 1, the development of residential homes in the community first received emphasis in the late 1970s, while in Denmark and the Netherlands it has been only in the 1980s that residential accommodation has been developed to any extent (Grinten, 1985, 212; Licht et al., 1991, 317). However, as the shift towards community care has become more established, emphasis upon addressing the social rights of service users has resulted in a more rapid development of new services. As deinstitutionalization has proceeded, the state has largely taken on responsibility for meeting the welfare needs of discharged patients, while the role of the family in providing care has been relatively limited (Tester, 1996, 82).

The 'three worlds' of mental health policy

Liberal regimes

In the nineteenth century it came to be accepted that lunatics were unable to provide for themselves within the market and, more than most, required the assistance of the state in order to survive. In this context, the development of institutional care might be characterized as a process of administrative decommodification (Offe, 1984), whereby it came to be generally recognized and accepted that lunatics should be segregated from the wider processes of a market economy.

In the twentieth century, with the expansion in the numbers of mentally ill people together with the identification of a whole new range of mental problems requiring treatment, it made less sense to incarcerate all those deemed in need of treatment. The status of madness as a source of rights to benefits outside of market relationships, which appeared so clear-cut in the nineteenth century, was making far less sense by the twentieth century as those deemed to be mentally ill generally appeared to be less disabled. By the 1950s, as the demand for labour rose and a range of new drug treatments became available that appeared to allow for the suppression of symptoms, the administrative separation of people with mental health problems and the market economy began to collapse.

Since the 1950s the policies of deinstitutionalization and the development of community-based services can be understood to have constituted a process of administrative recommodification; a reversal of nineteenth-century policy, with the aim being to restore people with mental health problems to the status of (wholly or at least partially) functioning members of a market economy. This framework for the development of postwar mental health policy has had a marked impact on service development within the countries representing this regime-type. Deinstitutionalization, as noted above, started early and has proceeded rapidly. Specialization of service functions, and increased accessibility of treatment facilities, have equally been vigorously developed.

The primary aim of these developments in service provision has been upon rehabilitation; the underlying theme of this being that people should be helped to regain their independence within a market economy. In England, for example, concern over the effects of mental health problems upon industrial efficiency rapidly became apparent in the immediate postwar period. In 1938, with unemployment still at high levels, 47 per cent of all mental patients had been regarded as unemployable, yet by 1953/4, with full employment, some 75 per cent were employed (Fox, 1954, 1087). It was often suggested that approximately one-third of absence due to illness was due to neurosis (Falop, 1955, 858), which amounted to 20 times more days work lost than through strikes (Strauss, 1957, 930). As the Chair of the Board of Control noted at the time, 'This is a very serious economic problem' (Armer, 1957, 1031). Moreover, these concerns rapidly had impact upon policy-making. In 1957 just 1 per cent of mental hospitals containing over 300 beds had occupational units. By 1961 some 64 per cent had such units, which it was hoped would provide patients with 'training not only in work skill but also in earning money with a view to resettlement in open employment and independent living' (Chief Medical Officer, 1961, 101).

This focus of service development upon the restoration of mental patients to labour market activity also characterizes other liberal regimes. In the United States, as deinstitutionalization got under way and the community mental health centres movement was emerging, a clear policy emphasis was placed upon rehabilitation:

> . . . the objective of modern treatment of persons with major mental illness is to enable the patient to maintain himself in the community in a normal manner. To do so, it is necessary (1) to save the patient from the debilitating effects of institutionalization as much as possible, (2) if the patient requires hospitalization to return him to home and community life as soon as possible, and (3) thereafter to maintain him in the community as long as possible. (Joint Commission on Mental Illness and Health, 1961)

The fact that for many people subsequently discharged from mental hospital rehabilitation has proved unrealistic has often tended to obscure this aim, but as a goal it tends to be central to the rationale for providing community-based services within liberal regimes.

Conservative regimes

Conservative countries, as we described earlier, tend to be most concerned with the maintenance of the status quo. The implication of this is that the market economy, although a central and defining feature of the socio-economic system, does not occupy such a core ideological status as found in liberal countries. In turn, this implies less concern about the relationship of welfare dependants, such as people with mental health problems, to the market. Consequently, the expansion in numbers of people with mental health problems, new views about the nature of mental health problems and the development of new physical treatments had relatively little impact upon the mental health policies of conservative countries. Germany and France, for example, provide little evidence of a concern with decommodification. Demand for labour was very high in France and Germany in the 1960s (see Figure 3.4), but this did not create any pressure for deinstitutionalization as a means of increasing the available labour supply. Indeed, it was only in the mid-1970s, when demand for labour was lower, that deinstitutionalization commenced.

Conservative countries also tend to display a tendency towards placing greater emphasis upon the principle of subsidiarity; that state welfare should be developed only where private, family, charitable and voluntary provision is not already active in the provision of services. Conservative states such as Spain and Germany have tended to be reluctant to develop community-based service such as day centres and domiciliary support, because this would tend to overlap with and replace the role of others (particularly the family, but also the church and other charitable groups) in the provision of social care.

Thus, whereas in liberal countries the aim of community care policy as one of rehabilitation was defined relatively early and clearly in the postwar period, in conservative countries the aims of mental health policy have tended to be less distinct. Conservative regimes are, by definition, defined to some extent by their reactionary nature, and this reflects in the lack of clear and decisive shift towards community-based policies based on clear and agreed goals concerning the pace of de-institutionalization or reintegration of mental patients into the community. That said, we should of course note that Italy represents a key exception to this trend, but other countries such as Belgium, Germany and particularly Spain do illustrate these general themes.

Social democratic regimes

In Social democratic countries the status of the market economy as an allocative mechanism for material reward is also lower than in liberal countries. There is less concern with ensuring social stratification is a product of the market, or that groups marginal to the market are encouraged or forced wherever possible to participate in it. Instead, emphasis tends to be placed upon the rights of citizens to receive social benefits. As with conservative countries, therefore, less emphasis has arisen upon the administrative recommodification of those within the mental health system. And like conservative countries, the high demand for labour in the 1950s had no apparent impact upon mental hospital bed space.

Since the latter part of the 1970s, the critique of institutions and arguments presented for the normalization of the social conditions of disadvantaged groups has had increasing influence upon the social policies of social democratic countries. In Sweden, in the 1950s and 1960s, the high number of beds per capita reflected a concern with ensuring mental hospital care was available to all who needed it. As views on the nature of institutional care became increasingly negative, and conversely views on community care became more positive, a policy shift came increasingly to be seen as the means by which the social rights of people with mental health problems could best be addressed.

Since the early 1980s the process of deinstitutionalization and the development of alternative services within social democratic countries has been rapid. Acknowledgement of the social rights of people with mental health problems to receive financial aid and other support, together with services allowing informal carers the choice of how much and what support to offer, has provided the underlying impetus towards the development of community care policy in social democratic countries.

Summary

Irrespective of why there has been policy change, both the orthodox and radical accounts of postwar mental health policy change tend to assume that what needs explaining is the shift in emphasis from institutional to community-based patterns of care and treatment. Generally, what we are being asked to consider are the reasons why 'For the past 25 years, the direction of public mental health policy has been to transfer the care of patients from state mental hospitals to settings in communities' (Bulger et al., 1993, 255).

To describe postwar mental health policy development in terms of a shift from institutional to community-based forms of care certainly reveals a significant part of the process which has occurred. Many writers, however, as we reviewed earlier, take from this the analytical question, 'why has this occurred?', when in fact a number of processes have occurred. Bennett and Morris, for example, capture the complexity of this situation in their comment that 'the current community-care movement [has] confused the separate aims of social reform and the pursuit of more effective methods of treatment' (1983, 13). On the one hand, we have an ideology of community treatment and care, while, on the other, we have a separation of treatment and care; the state increasingly focusing its resources on the provision of treatment to ever greater numbers of people, while at the same time devolving and delegating responsibility of care to the private sector, voluntary and charitable groups and, by no means least, the family.

Overall, there has of course been a shift in the second half of the twentieth century from an institutional to a community-based system of mental health service provision. But this, we have argued, represents little more than the administrative façade for the more substantial aspects of this process: an increase in accessibility of treatment facilities in order to address the newly defined and expanded range of mental health problems, and specialization of service provision as a means of shifting resources from the problems of psychiatric service users to a more specific focus upon the problem of mental illness.

The result of these trends has been the skewing of mental health expenditure. As demonstrated by the figures reviewed above on state mental health expenditure, it is not the case that the major postwar change in policy has been a shift from institutional to community treatment and care. As such the analytical question 'why has this occurred?' addresses only part of recent policy change. We need also to consider why new distinct and common patterns of skewing in governments' expenditure have emerged. One answer to this is provided by Aviram:

> Governments are usually reluctant to invest in the lengthy process of care of the disabled mentally ill unless it is persuaded that the social order is being undermined and that there is good potential for restabilizing the social system. All too often the lack of either one of these conditions explains why so many of the long term mentally ill are not under the care of the mental health system or fall between the cracks. (1990, 85)

Such a viewpoint may perhaps be overly conspiratorial. It would certainly be difficult for any government to accurately assess the impact upon the stability of the social system of any one area of expenditure. But it does highlight the concerns of governments: the concern with social stability and the threat to that posed by rising levels of mental illness that have occurred in the twentieth century. It is the concern with addressing this that has to a large extent resulted in the policy shifts that have occurred: a bifurcation of treatment and care services, the former being provided in increasingly specialized clinical locations, and the latter being provided in the community. Within this general policy shift we have identified three distinct patterns of mental health policy develop-

Table 5.3 *Regime-types and their relationship to the shift from institutional to community-based services*

	Onset	Pace	Style
Liberal	Early	Fast	Emphasis upon rehabilitation. Poor quality of long-term support services.
Conservative	Late	Slow	Emphasis upon maintaining the status quo. Minimum state provision based on the principle of subsidiarity.
Social democratic	Late	Fast	Emphasis upon social rights. Good-quality services.

ment, and the argument put has been that the nature of these patterns reflects the more general nature of the regime-type within which they are located. Table 5.3 summarizes the variations that have arisen within postwar mental health policy development.

PART 3: PROBLEMS AND ISSUES

Introduction

Central to the argument for deinstitutionalization and the development of community-based services is the contention that the prognosis of patients is likely to improve as a result of discharge from mental hospitals, and that people with mental health problems already in the community will benefit from remaining there rather than being institutionalized. In England, for example, the claim is made that

> ... the new style of service offers a much higher quality of life for people with a mental illness and a service more appreciated by their families than is possible in the traditional, large and often remote mental hospital. (Department of Health, 1989, para. 2.11)

Claims such as this made by policy makers have characterized the development of community care policy. At the same time, an increasing volume of evidence has grown to suggest that in practice the policy has proved less advantageous for many service users than such statements suggest is likely to be the case. Within the academic community it has in recent years often been asserted that while the principle of community care should be supported, its practice leaves much to be desired.

Rarely, if ever, are theory and practice quite so blatantly divorced, and the contention of this book is that the current problems of community care are a direct product of the central aims and objectives of policy makers that we have argued make up the reasons for the policy shift. We have argued that rather than being a policy intended to address first and foremost the interests of people with mental health problems, it addresses first the needs of governments and the requirements of the economic and social system more generally. Community care is not simply a good idea whose value came to be recognized by beneficent people. Rather, it arose as a policy response to changing circumstances; this concerning the changing nature and expansion of mental health problems in the twentieth century that we examined in Chapter 4. Perhaps not surprisingly, therefore, as we review in Chapter 6 and Chapter 7, a substantial range of problems and issues have arisen.

6
Problems and Issues in Community Care

There are, as numerous accounts have revealed, a range of problems and issues that have arisen as a result of the shift from institutional to community care, and in this chapter we review some of the more important of these.

Hospital and community support services

Transinstitutionalization

A consequence of the rundown and closure of the older mental hospitals has often been that the remaining patients who cannot be discharged have had to be moved from one institution to another. The impact of this on patients has rarely been studied, but what little evidence does exist suggests that there are some negative consequences. In England, Jones (1991) undertook a study of 24 patients who were moved from one mental hospital to another. A significant deterioration was found to occur in their behaviour patterns after one week, and significantly greater problems with social activity and speech skills than the patients had prior to the move continued to be found after six months. In the United States, Lentz & Ritchey (1971) similarly found that the functioning of mental patients transferred for administrative reasons tended to decline, although the deterioration in behaviour patterns was found to be temporary. In a study of the closure of a mental hospital in Sweden, Dencker & Långström (1991) found that over a five-year period 42 per cent of in-patients were discharged, for the most part into other institutions. Only eight patients were provided with alternative types of care. Overshadowing this, however, was the 68 per cent of all patients who died, for the most part before discharge (Dencker & Långström, 1993).

The movement of mental patients from one institution to another has not just involved mental hospitals. Over recent years an increasing amount of evidence has been collected indicating that for some patients discharge from a mental hospital is little more than a temporary interlude before their subsequent reincarceration within prisons. In England concerns about the increasing numbers of prisoners who displayed mental health problems were voiced within a decade of the policy of deinstitutionalization taking shape (Rollin, 1969; Tidmarsh & Wood,

1972). In the United States, in a review of national data over several decades of rates of deinstitutionalization and numbers being admitted and held in prisons, Palermo et al. (1991) found a significant negative relationship existed between mental health admissions and numbers held in jails. They conclude that a consequence of the policy of de-institutionalization for many mental patients is little more than trans-institutionalization, resulting in the overcrowding of prisons and the loss of psychiatric care for those people with mental health problems who are imprisoned. In Canada, too, there is growing concern with the high numbers of prisoners who exhibit mental health problems. There is some evidence that Canadian patients may be diverted from the criminal justice system less often than in the United States, but the problem remains substantial (Davis, 1992).

A two-tier service

In Chapter 5 we noted that one aspect of the process of specialization has been the growth in the number of psychiatric units within general hospitals, offering more intensive treatment for a shorter period than the old mental hospitals. Chronic patients have not been generally seen as suitable cases for admission to these units. The length of time they are likely to occupy a bed and their lack of responsiveness to treatment both make them unattractive to psychiatric units.

Increasingly, a two-tier mental health service is developing. With the focus of policy change being upon the provision of treatment to an increasing number of people, resources have tended to be focused upon those people who are most likely to respond. This reflects in the views expressed by a Royal Commission on the National Health Service in England, when it noted that 'The development of psychiatric units in District General Hospitals, in itself desirable, has had the effect of leaving to the large specialist mental hospitals the incurable, the behaviourally disturbed, the old and demented' (Merrison Commission, 1979, para. 6.44). In terms of finance, it reflected in the skewed pattern of expenditure (reviewed in Chapter 5) upon different service users. In a review of a number of studies of mental hospital service utilization in Western Europe and North America, Hansson and Sandlund (1992, 259) found that a small proportion of patients were receiving a relatively large proportion of resources. In Oslo, for example, it was found that 10 per cent of patients were in receipt of 75 per cent of resources, and in Connecticut 15 per cent of patients were in receipt of 70 per cent of resources.

In many countries the emergence of a two-tier service has come to be seen as increasingly problematic. In England the failure to discharge long-term residents was acknowledged by the Ministry of Health as early as the 1950s, when it noted a growing bifurcation in the resident population of mental hospitals between short- and long-term patients.

But this, it was argued, would be only a temporary problem that would be successfully overcome by modern methods of treatment (Ministry of Health, 1958, 28–29). This approach rapidly came to be recognized as being overly optimistic. By 1975 the government was compelled to recognize that mental health problems could not simply be treated like any other illness, and that a large number of chronically disabled people continued to exist and, unless provision was made for them, they would continue to occupy hospital beds (Department of Health and Social Security, 1975, para. 4.52).

In the Netherlands, it is recognized that certain groups are in receipt of preferential treatment: 'In general, patients in the psychiatric wards of hospitals are younger, female, with more years of schooling.' The disorders they displayed also tended to be less serious than those of patients in the old mental hospitals (Haveman, 1986, 460). In Canada, it is noted that 'Of particular concern is evidence of a two-tiered pattern of patient care, in which general hospital psychiatric units are disproportionately used by patients who are economically advantaged, less severely ill, supported by their families, and well linked to community practitioners' (Rochefort, 1992, 1086).

There is some evidence of a response being made to the problems being faced by long-term patients. In a survey of a number of European countries, Katschnig et al. (1993, 22) found that because of the loss of mental hospital bed space general hospital emergency rooms are increasingly used by chronic psychiatric patients, which in many cases has resulted in specific psychiatric emergency teams and units for short-term holding of patients being set up to deal with this demand. Overall, however, it remains the case that it is the long-term mentally ill who have tended to lose out in the shift from institutional to community care (Mangen, 1988). The irony of this of course is that is often claimed, particularly by supporters of the policy, that deinstitutionalization commenced in part as a result of concerns with the conditions experienced by long-term residents of the old mental hospitals:

> Now it is clear that this group, who were supposed to benefit most from the closure of the institutions, have in many cases fared worst. (Grove, 1994, 433)

The revolving door

Over the postwar period an increasing percentage of mental hospital admissions have tended to be of patients admitted previously. In Italy, from the late 1960s, there was a clear trend towards shorter and more frequent admissions, before a rapid decline in patient admissions occurred following the enactment of Law 180 (Donnelly, 1992, 89). In Spain readmissions as a percentage of all admissions rose in one hospital from 29 per cent in 1961 to 52 per cent in 1969 (Poveda, 1987, 182). In the Netherlands the number of people admitted to mental hospital who had two or more previous admissions rose by 120 per cent between 1970 and 1982 (Haveman, 1986, 462). In Denmark the number of patients admitted to mental hospital who had been previously admitted increased from 64 per cent to 77 per cent between 1970 and 1987 (Kastrup, 1987). In England in 1950 one-third of all admissions were first admissions, and by 1989 this had increased to more than two-thirds (Goodwin, 1993).

Just why the readmission rate has tended to rise is not clear. Firstly, the degree to which it has risen is subject to some confusion. Aside from any real increase in readmission rates it is suggested that better identification of previous patients, and a fall in the number of first-time admissions, may artificially tend to increase the apparent level of readmissions (Kastrup, 1987). Overall, however, the number of countries in which this trend is apparent, together with the long time period over which it has occurred, indicates a substantial change in the way in which hospital services are provided. People with mental health problems admitted to mental hospital are increasingly likely to experience a pattern of admission, discharge, relapse, readmission, discharge, and so on. The 'open door' policies introduced in the 1950s and 1960s have been replaced to some extent by the 'revolving door'.

This has increasingly come to be recognized as a problem in many countries. In Sweden, for example, it is recognized that, particularly for patients with schizophrenia, the cycle of admission and discharge is too frequent. It is suggested that patients are sometimes discharged inappropriately and that the support services available in the community are inadequate, both tending to result in the mental health of the patient deteriorating and consequently resulting in readmission (National Board of Health and Welfare, 1993).

A link between the lack of support in the community and the tendency of discharged mental patients to be readmitted is often made. However, the nature of that link is more difficult to specify. In a study of 12,737 patients who were admitted to Danish mental hospitals for the first time between April 1970 and March 1971, Kastrup (1987) found that in the following decade 2,073 were admitted three times or more. Males were found to be more likely (13 per cent) than females (9 per cent) to become revolving-door patients. In particular, young adult males (20.9 per cent) were most prone to frequent readmittance. But overall, the patterns of variance in the survey population, which might help predict likelihood of multiple readmission, were not found to be very strong (Kastrup, 1987). In a review of mental hospital readmissions in the United States, Rosenblatt and Mayer (1974) concluded that the only variable that consistently predicted readmission was the number of previous admissions. This, however, begs the question as to why the readmission rate first began to rise; something that almost certainly is related to the changing nature and style of mental health policy even if the specific nature of that link is difficult to specify.

The lack of community care facilities

In Chapter 5 we noted the skewed distribution of resources within mental health services, and the consequent dearth of money for the development of new community-based care services. A result of this has been growing levels of criticism of the inadequate level of support available to discharged patients or to service users who have never been admitted. Indeed, in all countries in Western Europe and North America, funding of community-based care is generally acknowledged to be inadequate (Benson, 1994, 121). In Italy community-based care services are recognized to be 'the weak link in the organization of Italian psychiatric care' (Crepet, 1990, 33). Reflecting this, in a survey of hospital administrators it was found that 83 per cent of admissions were thought to have been avoidable if adequate district-based support services had been in place (Crepet, 1990, 33). In the Netherlands 'many severely disturbed patients live in the community under marginal conditions and receive hardly any care except occasional crisis intervention' (Giel, 1987, 155). Even in a country such as Sweden it is recognized that the care and support needs of service users are inadequately addressed, with only half of those people in need receiving some form of day care provision, social activity or employment opportunity (National Board of Health and Welfare, 1993). As Table 6.1 demonstrates, many services have been insufficiently developed to meet existing levels of need. In particular, insufficient institutions for rehabilitation and not enough supported accommodation have been developed for discharged patients: 'there is mounting evidence that the daily life of many patients and their families in the 1990s is far from the visions outlined in the policy documents of the 1970s' (Garpenby, 1993, 298).

The poor quality of some community care facilities

The process of deinstitutionalization commenced, in part at least, as a means of returning people to more normal living arrangements. Under-lying this is a tendency to assume that simply by virtue of being located in the community, services will be of a better quality. There is, however, an increasing amount of evidence suggesting that for some service users the quality of care they receive in the community is not necessarily any better than they might have received in an institution, and may be worse. In England, as early as the 1960s, a study of local authority and voluntary provision of hostels found that the conditions they offered were as restrictive and in some cases even more so than the wards from which the residents had come (Apte, 1968).

More recently, the rapid growth of private residential and nursing homes offering accommodation to the more dependent mental patients has attracted attention. The terms and conditions of staff are often significantly worse than those in the public sector, and the quality of food and other services is sometimes poor. In Canada in 1989, the

Table 6.1 *Estimated absolute figures for different services psychiatric out-patients receive and services that other patients ought to have according to assessment by psychiatric staff (national survey two days in 1991 including 10,744 patients)*

Services	Ongoing	Missing
Social support in homes	15,440	5,180
Daily activity	31,930	26,010
Activities for befriending	26,470	22,400
Training to work	9,320	12,420
Basic school education	6,660	11,890
Sheltered job	6,180	12,830
Intervention from primary health care	28,100	3,870
Contact with patients' organizations	8,310	18,310

Source: Brink, 1994, 264

Vancouver city health department found that 18 of its 26 boarding homes for people with mental health problems fell 'significantly below the physical plant requirements for specialized residential care' (quoted in Rochefort, 1992, 1087). And in a study of private residential homes in Ontario, Hurl and Freiler concluded that:

> Market values of economy and efficiency underlying privatization have been given first priority and have superseded values of justice and equity. Consequently, service goals such as accessibility, comprehensiveness, responsiveness and flexibility have received less attention. The result is a service system which in many cases is fragmented, inefficient, inadequate and lacking in central direction. (quoted in Lightman, 1986, 27)

Similar concerns have been expressed in a number of other countries. In Germany, in a study comparing social conditions in a hospital, nursing homes and group homes, it was found that the nursing homes had the least stimulating social environments, and were at least as likely to foster the features of institutionalism as the state hospital (Kunze, 1985). More generally residential homes in Germany have been found to offer a lack of occupation during the day, and a relatively poor level of training amongst members of staff (Bennett, 1991, 633). Similarly in Italy, in many residential homes the standards of accommodation have been found to be of poor quality and levels of staffing have been found to be low (Pirella, 1987, 130). A study of the quality of life experienced by people with mental health problems in Sweden (Borga et al., 1992) found that to a large extent their basic needs for accommodation and income were met adequately. Their ability to participate more fully in society, however, was seriously curtailed by their mental health problems:

> The picture given is ... that of a group of individuals economically disadvantaged but still cared for by society to a reasonable extent, especially compared with some other countries. They are generally lonely: unmarried or divorced, living alone and gradually excluded from the labour market. (Borga et al., 1992, 470)

In the United States it has been found that the size of nursing homes has tended to increase. Increasingly, large corporations have taken over the private social care market and, as a means of achieving greater efficiency, have tended to build ever-larger residential facilities. In the 1980s more than 50 per cent of people placed in nursing homes were in facilities with more than 100 beds, and 15 per cent were in facilities with more than 200 beds (Scull, 1985, 548). United States corporations have begun to expand their operations internationally, and in the 1990s have been acquiring many private nursing and residential facilities in England. This trend towards larger homes clearly raises the question as to whether for many patients deinstitutionalization simply means the replacement of one institution with another.

The inadequate range of community care facilities

A further problem with community-based support services has been the limited range of services that have been made available. To achieve full participation in society, and not just existence at its margins, a fuller range of services to help people achieve an income, transport facilities and housing comparable to those around them would be required. The key to much of this is the availability of employment offering both a reasonable wage and the possibility of career development.

The lack of employment opportunities, and the lack of services to support people with mental health problems in finding and holding on to employment, is characteristic of most mental health services, and more generally reflects the limited vision of reintegration within community care policies. In England, Sayce notes that 'Capable people are routinely refused work solely because of a psychiatric history, with no legal redress' (1994, 11). A survey undertaken by the Royal College of Psychiatrists found that 28 per cent of employers would only occasionally employ someone who had previously suffered a mental health problem, and this figure rose to 50 per cent when considering those with existing problems (Mihill, 1995). In Sweden, despite the emphasis given to equality, Borga et al. (1992, 470) found in a survey of service users that 77 per cent of males and 61 per cent of females were unemployed. In Italy people with mental health problems have been found to be three to four times as likely as the general population to be unemployed (Crepet, 1990, 31). Moreover, for those people with mental health problems who do gain employment, the status, pay and conditions of the job are often poor (Link, 1982).

Some efforts to address these employment problems have been made. Since the late 1970s in a number of European countries, particularly Germany and Italy, there has been the development of cooperatives providing employment to people with mental health problems. These cooperatives are generally non-profit-making businesses which are subsidized from public funds. In Italy there are now over 2,000 such businesses, most often operating in the handicrafts and service sectors (Righetti, 1993). The aims of these cooperatives are to meet the economic goal of offering remunerative work just as any other commercial enterprise, while at the same time addressing the more social goal of promoting the health of members.

In the United States, the 'club-house' model has been developed as a means of providing occupation. These provide a social centre that people with mental health problems may attend, and where they are encouraged to participate in the running of the club, and in various programmes of vocational training. Emerging interest in this model is also being expressed in Europe, with nine club-houses having been established in England by 1995, and more being built. A further development in the United States in recent years is the Transitional Employment Programmes. These help people with mental health problems find employment with local employers, and at the same time guarantee the employer that any absences of the person employed will be immediately filled by another person participating in the scheme (Thornicroft & Bebbington, 1989, 746). These efforts have been reinforced to some extent by the passing of the Americans With Disabilities Act in 1990, which provides people with mental health problems basic rights, resulting in full access to community resources, especially the rights and privileges associated with the work role (Crist & Stoffel, 1992).

Overall, however, occupational services are relatively undeveloped in most countries. In a review of United States policy, Aviram notes that 'In view of the importance of employment, both for society as well as for the rehabilitation of the mentally ill, it is surprising that so little has been done in this area' (1990, 76). Equally, in many Western European countries there have been some attempts since the mid-1970s to provide employment rehabilitation services for psychiatric patients, but these have tended to be unimaginative and small-scale (Mangen, 1985).

The outcomes of community care

While criticism of conditions within the old mental hospitals has fuelled the shift towards deinstitutionalization, there has been a marked absence of evaluative studies that attempt to assess whether people with mental health problems do actually benefit from placement in the community: 'too few scientific studies on the effects of changing patterns of care have been conducted to allow generalization on the soundness of the concepts underlying the models of care now developing in Western Europe' (Breemer ter Stege & Gittelman, 1987, 8). Only in the 1990s has the World Health Organization begun to develop programmes to address this paucity of studies on the outcomes of the discharge process (Neelman & van Os, 1994, 1220).

In addition to this lack of information, there is also a lack of agreement over how to quantify or measure change in the state of a person's mental health. To the extent that the outcomes of community care policies have been measured, the results lack value partly because of considerable methodological problems of many of the studies: '[They] ... rarely employ a full range of social, clinical, economic and service usage outcome measures, and characteristically use small and heterogeneous samples, with imprecise, poorly validated and inconsistent measures' (Thornicroft & Bebbington, 1989, 739). We are left with a policy around which considerable support has grown based almost entirely upon support for its underlying principles rather than upon a knowledge of its outcomes. There is, however, a growing collection of evidence about the practice of community care that raises an increasing number of issues concerning the quality of life of discharged patients, and which to some extent at least raises questions over the often uncritical support which has helped sustain the policy.

The discharge process

The discharge process has sometimes been found to be poorly planned and implemented. Decisions over who is suitable and ready for discharge, for example, have often been found to proceed in an unsystematic manner (Kovess et al., 1995, 134). Moreover, the degree of planning undertaken for the discharge of selected patients is highly variable. Frequently, the treatment plan is far better organized than the social care needs of the patient being discharged (Thornicroft & Bebbington, 1989, 744). A study of a hospital in London found that patients were not consulted or involved in decisions about their discharge and received little if any advice about housing, day care, medication or social security entitlement (Kay & Legg, 1986).

The destination of discharged patients

Despite the fact that large numbers of patients have been discharged from mental hospitals over a long period of time, very little effort has been put into monitoring their quality of life or mental condition when living in the community (Kovess et al., 1995, 134). While community care policy tends to assume patients will go to live in the community, often with friends, family or relatives, the outcome of discharge has in practice been found to be highly variable. In the United States Leavin (1984) made estimates for the 55,000 patients who would have been in state hospital beds had deinstitutionalization not occurred in California. He estimated that 45 per cent were in residential homes, 22 per cent were living independently or with their families, 7 per cent were in locked facilities, 7 per cent in halfway houses and 9 per cent were in-patients. The remainder were untreated and mostly homeless. In a study of people with mental health problems in London, it was found that the majority of people either live with their families or live alone. Men were more likely than women to live in hostels or alone, while women were more likely than men to live with their families (Conning & Rowland, 1991).

In Toronto, Lightman (1986, 26) found that many discharged mental patients moved into the poorest areas, and occupied the worst housing. Discharged mental patients have tended to accumulate at the fringes of central business districts, where accommodation is relatively cheap, a fact that encourages welfare authorities to locate dependants and services there, which in turn leads to a process of 'dependant drift' where the more services are put into a district the more dependants drift to it and the more services it requires, and so on, in an ever-increasing cycle of service ghettoization (Dear & Wolch, 1987, 250).

In Italy, as in many other countries, there are no national data tracking the experiences of patients discharged from mental hospital. Some local studies have been conducted, however, which reveal a mixed outcome. Many patients return to live with their families, and many also move into alternative institutions such as group homes and elderly persons' homes (Donnelly, 1992, 89). A survey carried out in the Venice area found 60 per cent of discharged patients were living in a house, 34 per cent in a non-psychiatric institution, 13 per cent had a job, and 54 per cent were being followed by psychiatric or social service. In the Emilia Romagna region, of the patients discharged from psychiatric hospital wards between 1981 and 1985, 18.3 per cent were resettled with their families, 16.7 per cent were in a family home, 19.8 per cent were in a protected community, and 31.7 per cent were in an elderly persons' home (Crepet, 1990, 28).

On the basis of a study of ex-mental patients' readjustment within the community, Miller (1971) argues that there are four key measures that are likely to determine the quality of life for an ex-mental patient. These include sufficient material support, sufficient care and emotional support, a social network within which they were accepted, and a sense of control over their personal destiny. In over 1,000 case histories Miller found that where these factors were present, discharged mental patients had a good chance of successfully reintegrating into community life. In the majority of cases, however, these factors were absent, often resulting in a failure to reintegrate.

Subsequent studies have also tended to find that the social conditions of discharged patients are not conducive to the improvement of mental health. In Stockholm county, Sweden, Borga et al. (1992) found that of the survey population of discharged mental patients, 57 per cent were unmarried, 64 per cent lived alone, and 69 per cent were unemployed. The social conditions experienced by women, however, were found to be generally better than those experienced by men, concerning criteria such as the quality of their housing and the number of their social contacts. Women were more often married or divorced, while men were generally unmarried. Seventy-seven per cent of men were unemployed compared to 61 per cent of women (Borga et al., 1992).

Overall, the evidence of studies conducted in recent years reveals a heterogeneous pattern of outcomes for discharged patients. The assumption underlying the movement towards deinstitutionalization, that patients would receive support in the community and would thereby benefit from being discharged, has proved overly simplistic and sometimes erroneous. Two issues in particular have received considerable attention in recent years. Firstly, are families able or willing to adopt the role ascribed to them within community care policy? And secondly, to what extent has homelessness become the outcome of deinstitutionalization for people with mental health problems?

Family care

We examined in Chapter 2 the tension between the increased emphasis given to the role of informal carers within mental health policy in recent years, and the rather dubious assumptions that have supported this policy shift concerning the desire of families, friends and neighbours to want to care, and of people with mental health problems to want to be cared for by these people. The gap between the often-stated view that 'mental illness involves a burden on relatives, which is often dutifully or even cheerfully borne' (Bennett & Freeman, 1991), and the reality of caring that we identified has tended to result in considerable stress and strains within the caring process.

A point often noted by feminist writers is that the main burden of care falls upon women, but that this tends to be ignored by government (Smith, 1991). In 1989, 79 per cent of carers in receipt of Invalid Care Allowance in England were women. In Ireland in 1991, 2,538 women received the Carer's Allowance compared to 817 men. In France, the strain upon family carers has been found to have increased as a result of deinstitutionalization and this has particularly affected women (Therrien, 1990). Overall, there is evidence to suggest that the burden of caring falls disproportionately upon women in many countries (Ungerson, 1995, 45).

Informal care tends to be referred to amongst policy makers as a relatively uniform activity, involving a process of general support and tending. In reality, the range of needs presented by people with chronic mental and physical health problems are considerable. The personal hygiene needs of an elderly person with Alzheimer's, the need for acceptance of bizarre behaviour by a person with schizophrenia, and the need for understanding of the heightened state of emotion experienced by a person with a neurotic disorder all call upon a very different range of skills. While some informal carers may well demonstrate considerable aptitude in such circumstances, some may not. Ensuring paid staff are suitably qualified to undertake their particular professional roles is of course well established and generally accepted. Amongst informal carers such concerns have barely been acknowledged.

In addition to whether the skill base exists, substantial questions also exist over the extent to which informal carers have the time and energy to provide care. In a review of the capacity of the informal sector to provide care in European countries, Ungerson (1995, 40) argues that the ability of communities to provide care is decreasing. Demographic change, rising divorce levels, increased geographical mobility and increased female labour market participation are all tending to reduce the capacity of informal carers to provide care. For example, the number of women aged 50 to 69, who constitute a major source of informal care, will fall in the period to 2010 in Sweden and England, and will grow only a third as fast as the numbers in need of care in the Netherlands (Baldock & Evers, 1992, 293). Where parents are providing the care and support of their adult children, there will of course come the point where the availability of that care will decline and end. It is estimated that between 13,400 to 49,600 adults with severe and persistent mental illness who receive services from the public mental health system in New York state reside with one or both parents. Within this group, between 300 and 1,200 adults could have been expected to experience housing disruption due to parental death each year between 1990 and 1994. Additional housing with mental health supports and other programmes will be needed to accommodate the growing number of severely mentally ill adults whose housing may be disrupted because of the death of their parents (Grosser & Conley, 1995).

These issues concerning the available skill base, time and energy, and the gender of informal carers have contributed to increased concern over the scale of the burden of care they carry. The excessive burdens being placed upon some of the families of discharged patients have been the subject of study for some time (Grad & Sainsbury, 1968; Hoenig & Hamilton, 1969). Less attention, however, has been focused upon the gratifications of caring, or the relationship between levels of gratification and level of burden carried (Bulger et al., 1993, 255). And it is in this set of issues that we find a further set of problems.

An assumption to be found within community care policy is that once the level of symptoms has been reduced, a person with mental health problems is more easily discharged into the community. In fact, no simple correlation between the level of symptoms and the degree of burden experienced by carers has been found. In a study of carers in the United States, Thompson and Doll (1982) found that two-thirds of asymptomatic patients in their study were burdensome to care-givers. Moreover, of care-givers who reported no objective burden (concerning mainly measurable factors such as the level of hostility, and disruption of domestic life experienced by carers), 70 per cent reported severe subjective burden (concerning the emotional reactions of carers, such as worry, pleasure, anguish, and so on). Of care-givers who reported a high objective burden, only 50 per cent reported a high subjective burden.

A further assumption of community care policy is that support of the carer should help sustain the caring relationship. In fact, this is an area in which little research has been undertaken, and the few studies that have been done demonstrate little relationship between type and level of support offered and the level of burden experienced by carers. Moreover, it has been found that the subjective burden of care is not necessarily any less when the family member with mental health problems is being cared for in an institution (Bulger et al., 1993, 256).

Whether or not a person gains any satisfaction from providing care is one factor that has been found to be important in determining the quality of life of both those being cared for and the carer. In research on caregivers of family members with Alzheimer's disease, it has been found that the level of burden experienced by the carer was closely correlated to the quality of the relationship they had had prior to the caring relationship being established. Those with more positive memories experienced less burden, but they also were more likely to feel sad, frustrated and disappointed about the care-giving experience (Bulger et al., 1993, 257). Satisfaction levels with caring also appear to be related to socio-economic status of the carer. Bulger et al. (1993, 264), in a study of the experience of carers, found that those people who were relatively disadvantaged tended to report being happier with their care-giving role. This, they speculate, may be a result of their relatively low aspirations and consequently the perceived lower loss of opportunities that they might experience.

In total, very little thought has been given by governments to the increased burden upon families created by the policy of deinstitutionalization. The disparity between policy assumptions and the lived reality of people involved in informal care is increasingly wide, resulting in a range of pressures and problems for those concerned (Benson, 1994, 119). This appears to a common problem across most countries that have implemented community care. In Canada, for example, it is noted that:

> The family may be unwilling to assume responsibility for meeting the needs of its disadvantaged members. Responsibility, as remote decision-makers in government often do not seem to understand, may not simply be delegated to the family; it must also be taken up without undue reluctance. The individual may not want the family to assume responsibility for the meeting of his or her needs; the costs, in terms of control, for example, may simply be too great. Perhaps most importantly, the family may be unable to assume responsibility for its individual members because it lacks the necessary resources to do so. Responsibilities can be transferred without the means to carry them out, and, given the mood of the day, it is most unlikely that adequate resources will accompany any transfer of tasks. (Lightman, 1986, 26)

Reflecting these concerns, families have tended to become more organized. In the United States in 1979 a national family self-help group, the National Alliance for the Mentally Ill, was set up to lobby for better-quality services. Its membership now exceeds 140,000, and it has a full-time office in Washington, DC. It has had some success in lobbying for increased federal funds to be given to psychiatric research and some other concerns. The association also has over 1,000 local groups, which are active in providing education and support to family members involved in caring and in campaigning for improved state services for people with mental health problems (Benson, 1994). In England groups such as the National Schizophrenia Fellowship and the Carer's Association perform a similar function (Goodwin, 1993). In many other Western European countries also, associations of families of people with mental health problems have arisen and actively argued for better and more community-based facilities (Schene & van-Wijngaarden, 1995).

Homelessness

The characteristics of homeless people with mental health problems have been most extensively studied in the United States. In the 1980s, concern grew at the apparent increase in the number of people with mental health problems amongst the homeless. Estimates of the total number of homeless varied widely, from 250,000 to three million (Kiesler & Sibulkin, 1987, 200). Estimates of the prevalence of psychiatric disorders amongst the homeless varied between 20 per cent and 90 per cent, but clustered in the 40–60 per cent range. Estimates of number of homeless who have previously been hospitalized in a psychiatric facility clustered around one-third (Kiesler & Sibulkin, 1987, 200). As a consequence, the National Institute for Mental Health set about establishing 10 projects to examine the scale and nature of the problem.

Of all 10 studies, the proportion of homeless persons who had ever been a psychiatric in-patient ranged from 25 per cent to 40 per cent of the respondents (Tessler & Dennis, 1992, 32). It was found amongst four studies (in Baltimore, Los Angeles, Ohio and Boston), in which standardized assessment instruments to determine current psychiatric status were used, that between 28 per cent and 37 per cent were found to have a mental illness (Tessler & Dennis, 1992, 30). For every diagnostic category of mental illness, a higher prevalence was found amongst the homeless than among domiciled samples. This was found to be particularly so amongst the more severe and chronic conditions. Amongst the population of Los Angeles, for example, it was found that a homeless sample were 38 times more likely to be diagnosed with schizophrenia, 38 times more likely to have experienced a manic episode within the last six months, and five times as likely to have had a major depressive episode (Tessler & Dennis, 1992, 30).

Until the mid-1970s, the homeless population consisted primarily of older, white, alcoholic, poorly educated men. By the early 1990s the profile of the homeless population had altered considerably. The average age of homeless persons was estimated to be in the range of 30–40, over 50 per cent are from non-white ethnic groups, over 25 per cent are women, and between 33 per cent and 50 per cent have had a high-school education (Kiesler & Sibulkin, 1987, 200). Amongst the homeless population, some evidence was found that mental illness is more prevalent. In the New York City shelter study, 37 per cent of homeless women had indications of a mental disorder compared to 22 per cent of men. In other studies, in Ohio and St Louis no significant differences between the sexes in overall level of psychiatric symptoms were found (Tessler & Dennis, 1992, 3).

Similar problems have been found to exist in Canada. A recent study in Montreal found there to be around 15,000 homeless persons, of whom 44 per cent had a history of mental health problems (Rochefort, 1992, 1087). A study of the users of shelters for homeless persons in Vancouver revealed many had psychiatric problems (Acorn, 1993). Shelter users were predominantly young, male, single and mobile. About half reported a current physical health problem, 44 per cent reported use of non-prescribed drugs, and 69 per cent reported use of alcohol. Nineteen per cent reported a current mental or emotional problem, with schizophrenia and bipolar disorder the most common diagnoses reported. Depression, anxiety and tension were also found to be common problems. Overall, the number of individuals with mental illness in the population surveyed was found to be lower than that in similar populations in the United States, but the scale of the problem still appeared to be great.

These problems are by no means limited to North America. There is now a large body of evidence suggesting that homelessness amongst people with mental health problems is a growing dilemma in many Western European countries. A study of the extent of homelessness among 1,581 psychiatric patients in Copenhagen (Nordentoft et al., 1992) found that 342 patients (22 per cent) in contact with the psychiatric services had serious housing problems. A total of 112 (7 per cent) were long-stay patients without a home address, 134 (8 per cent) were in an unstable housing situation, and 96 (6 per cent) were actually homeless. The homeless among the psychiatric patients were characteristically single, on disability pension or general public assistance, most often under 45 years of age, often schizophrenic and, among the men, almost one-third were alcohol abusers. Approximately 20 per cent were estimated to need staff-supported housing, indicating that the number of places in psychiatric group homes or halfway houses needed to be increased.

Benjaminsen & Folen (1992) undertook a study of 94 of the 129 residents (73 per cent) in the institutions for homeless people in the county of Funen in Denmark. Eighty-nine per cent were men, 59 per cent were aged 30–49 years, 93 per cent were single, and source of incomes for 80 per cent were public assistance or disability pensions. More than half had been sentenced for crime at least once. The majority were found to be suffering from severe psychosocial strain. In 91 per cent a psychiatric diagnosis was established, the most frequent being alcoholism (73 per cent) and personality or character disorder (70 per cent).

In England it is estimated that between one and two million people are homeless, and the number is increasing rapidly (Scott, 1993, 315). Most homeless people are men, but about 10–25 per cent are women, of whom about half are accompanied by children (Scott, 1993). Recent studies suggest that as many as 50 per cent of the homeless population may have some form of mental disorder (Scott, 1993, 317). Twice as many homeless as domiciled people have psychiatric disorders, and these tend to be of a more severe nature. Single, middle-aged men still predominate, but there is evidence of a fall in the mean age. There is some evidence of overrepresentation of ethnic minorities in London, but there is insufficient evidence on this issue nationally (Scott, 1993, 316). In a review of the development of deinstitutionalization in Europe and the United States, Nordentoft (1990) argues that homelessness is becoming an increasingly severe problem.

> Compared to non-impaired homeless individuals, mentally disabled homeless persons are more likely to be homeless for longer periods of time, to have less contact with family and friends, to have more barriers to employment, poorer physical health, and more contact with the legal system. (Tessler & Dennis, 1992, 33)

There is some argument over the extent to which deinstitutionalization has been the cause of these problems. In the United States a reduction in the availability of unskilled work in the manufacturing sectors and a diminishing supply of low-cost housing in the cities are argued to have created at least some of the increased homeless problem (Tessler & Dennis, 1992, 6). Conversely, Bassuk & Edwards (1986) argue that problems in the implementation of deinstitutionalization, particularly the lack of commitment to the long-term care of chronically mentally ill persons, have contributed to the large numbers of severely mentally ill adults among the homeless. The lack of a full range of supervised and supported residences in the community, the serious shortage of affordable rental housing nationwide, and the federal government's 'crackdown on ineligibility' for Supplemental Income and Social Security Disability Insurance have also contributed to the increasing experience of homelessness among the chronically mentally ill.

In England it has been argued that most chronically mentally ill people are discharged to adequate accommodation (O'Neill, 1988). Amongst homeless people with mental health problems it has been found that there is an average interval of 30 months between hospital discharge and becoming homeless (Hepstinall, 1989). This, it is argued, tends to suggest that while the discharge of patients is most frequently an appropriate measure, there is a lack of resources within the community to provide adequate support. It is the inadequate implementation of deinstitutionalization, rather than the policy itself, which is argued to be at fault (Thornicroft & Bebbington, 1989).

Use of treatments

Side-effects of drug treatments

The use of drug treatments began in the early nineteenth century, with the discovery in 1826 of the sedative effect of bromide. In 1832 chloral hydrate was introduced, and use of the first barbituric acid began in 1903. By the mid-twentieth century drug treatments were in widespread use throughout Western Europe and North America. For example, in 1947 a total of 12.6 tons of barbiturates and 6 tons of bromide were distributed in Sweden. This amounted to 20 defined doses per 1,000 population being administered daily. In the second half of the twentieth century, however, there has been a dramatic rise in the quantity of psychotropic drugs being consumed; in Sweden, it is estimated that a three-fold increase in drug consumption has occurred since the end of World War II. Within this broad trend, the casual use of daytime sedatives has decreased, while maintenance therapy with anti-depressants and depot neuroleptics has increased (Allgulander, 1986, 473). A survey in 1981 found that 0.5 per cent of adults in Sweden reported daily use of tranquillizers or sedatives for at least a year, compared to 1.8 per cent in the United States and 5.8 per cent in Belgium.

There is some evidence to suggest a more cautious attitude towards prescribing drug treatments has taken effect in recent years. The use of benzodiazepines, for example, peaked in the late 1960s to early 1970s. In the United States there was a 34 per cent reduction in benzodiazepine prescriptions between 1973 and 1983, and a 15 per cent reduction in Sweden between 1972 and 1984 (Borga et al., 1991, 30). There is no evidence, however, of any such fall in the use of major tranquillizers, which continue to be the main form of treatment for more severely disturbed people with mental health problems. For example, in a study of a small Swedish town Rydin (1989) found that amongst 300 patients diagnosed as being schizophrenic, 95 per cent were receiving long-term treatment with a neuroleptic drug, and only three were on no medication.

The employment of drug treatments in psychiatric practice has for the most part come to be accepted as an appropriate and beneficial means of managing people with mental health problems: 'The benefits to the individual and to society of these drugs are widely recognized' (Allgulander, 1986, 473). There is, however, considerable and long-standing evidence to suggest that currently used drug treatments can be physically damaging. Schonecker (1957) was the first person to identify and describe tardive dyskinesia, an iatrogenic disorder that is associated with the use of neuroleptic drugs and is characterized by abnormal and involuntary bodily movements. These most frequently include facial movements but can include the movement of the limbs and trunk in varying degrees of severity. In 1973, Keegan and Rajput coined the term 'tardive dystonia' to describe another manifestation of neuroleptic-induced movement disorders. In recent years a number of variants have also been proposed, these including tardive akathisia and tardive psychosis, although the criteria used to diagnose these are less clear than those used for tardive dyskinesia.

Estimates of the prevalence of tardive dyskinesia in patients who have received neuroleptics on a long-term basis vary between 1 per cent and 50 per cent, with the majority of recent studies tending to show an average prevalence of 30 per cent (Muscettola et al., 1993, 29). In a review of the literature, Brown (1985, 153) concludes that as many as 62 per cent of in-patients in United States mental hospitals may have tardive dyskinesia.

Predicting who might be adversely affected by neuroleptic treatments has proved difficult. Cohen et al. (1991), for example, found that the length of neuroleptic treatment and current neuroleptic dose were not significantly associated with tardive dyskinesia. Female sex, schizophrenic diagnosis and increasing age, however, were associated with the condition, although the reasons why were not apparent. Other factors that have been associated with an increased susceptibility to tardive dyskinesia include organic brain abnormalities, altered dopaminergic function and a history of treatment with anti-parkinsonian medication (Muscettola et al., 1993, 29).

The only treatment available for this condition is the reduction of dosage or discontinuation of treatment with neuroleptics, although even this is frequently ineffective (Yassa et al., 1986). As a result of such evidence, it is now increasingly accepted that maintenance therapy doses should be far lower than those used in the acute phase (Borga et al., 1991, 224). In practice, however, it has been found that the longer a person is an in-patient in a psychiatric institution, the more likely they are to receive higher doses of neuroleptic medication. This is contrary to psychopharmacological principles, but, as Borga et al. bluntly note, 'psychopharmacological practice seems to be lax and not at all in pace with pharmacological research' (1991, 231).

A further problem arising with drug treatments is the potential that exists for their misuse. In part, this relates to the tendency sometimes apparent within psychiatry to experiment with treatments without sufficient knowledge of or regard to potentially harmful side-effects. The prescription of LSD provides a potent example of this. This drug was first used in the treatment of alcoholics in the United States and was subsequently used in a number of other countries. In England it is estimated that around 4,500 patients, mostly suffering from depression, were given LSD in the 1950s and 1960s. Patients treated with LSD have reported long-lasting side-effects, including flashbacks, paranoia and psychoses. Patients were sometimes administered the drug without being informed of its content or purpose. In England in 1995, a legal case was started by ex-patients in an attempt to gain compensation for the mental health problems they sustained as a result of being given LSD (Dyer, 1995).

Polypharmacy is a further area of experimentation sometimes undertaken by the psychiatric profession. This concerns the prescription of two or more drugs in combination for the treatment of mental disorders. While some such practices are well established and accepted, in a number of cases there has been a tendency towards administering high doses of a variety of drugs, the effects of whose interaction is not fully understood or known. In England, the mental health charity MIND estimates that several deaths a year result from such practices. Moreover, black people have been overrepresented in these incidents.

Compulsory treatment in the community

As increasing numbers of people with serious mental health problems are either being discharged from mental hospital, or not being admitted at all, there has been growing concern about the potential threat this may pose to the public, and to the welfare of the individuals concerned. Reflecting this, the American Psychiatric Association in 1982 argued that many people with mental health problems living in the community are in need of treatment, and that they are likely to deteriorate if they do not receive psychiatric services. Many of these people, however, have objected to receiving treatment, hence what was required was the introduction of involuntary out-patient treatment (Lamb, 1984). Similarly in England in 1987, the Royal College of Psychiatrists produced a discussion paper in which it set forward proposals for the introduction of a compulsory community treatment order.

In England, the Mental Health Act 1983 allowed for the appointment of a guardian, who has powers to compel a person with mental health problems to live in a certain place, and to attend at certain times for treatment, education or training (although they cannot enforce treatment upon the mental patient). It has, however, been little used, with only around 200 cases a year, mainly because of its lack of powers to deal with non-compliance (Pilgrim & Rogers, 1993, 155). To address this problem, the Mental Health (Patients in the Community) Act 1995 provides for the legal supervision of patients discharged into the community who are still under compulsory care orders of the 1983 Mental Health Act. The new Act enables patients to be discharged into the community, where they can be ordered to attend for treatment, attend education or training establishments, and reside at a specified place. A nominated supervisor has the role of ensuring the specified plan is followed by the patient. If it is not followed, then the patient may be 'taken and conveyed' to a hospital or clinic for treatment or to any other place for work, education or training.

In the United States by the early 1990s some 35 states had passed legislation allowing for involuntary out-patient civil commitment as a means of ensuring compliance with treatment, although only in 12 of these is this measure commonly used (Torrey & Kaplan, 1995). The penalties applied to patients for non-compliance vary considerably, but can involve automatic readmission (Maloy, 1992). Moreover, in some states it is not just discharged patients, as in England, but all people with mental health problems receiving treatment who may be subject to the constraints of out-patient commitment. An example of this is to found in California, where 'conservatorship' is a legal mechanism that has been introduced that allows an individual or agency to act on behalf of a person with mental health problems to determine what arrangements are necessary to provide adequate food, clothing, shelter and treatment, including hospitalization. The conservator may be a family member or other informal carer who, within the context of support by professional agencies, can undertake legal control of the conservatee (Lamb & Weinberger, 1993).

The developing use of involuntary treatment in the community has tended to be presented as a progressive development. In the United States the impetus towards the use of compulsion in the community has come from the repressive and stark conditions to be found in the mental hospital. Treatment in the community has successfully been presented as the least restrictive and least repressive milieu within which to provide necessary treatment:

> By giving up some of their freedom, many conservatees who would ordinarily need to be hospitalized for long periods are able to retain most of their independence and their community status. (Lamb & Weinberger, 1993, 909)

In England it has been argued that such a measure would help speed up discharge from hospital, and ensure that patients receive the benefits of a treatment programme that because of their mental health problem they might otherwise refuse. By intervening in this way the patient would be offered an alternative to hospital admission, and thereby achieve treatment within least restrictive circumstances.

In opposition to this, civil rights groups have argued that the implementation of such an order has implications for civil rights that are not met in other areas of legal compulsion. The application of compulsory treatment is based on the prediction of harm occurring either to the person with a mental health problem, or to those with whom they come into contact (Cockerham, 1992, 313). Whereas detention and compulsory treatment for those committing criminal acts is applied after the action, for those with mental health problems it can and is applied to those who are deemed to demonstrate a tendency in that direction; those who are deemed dangerous. They need not have committed any criminal offence, and the time for which they are detained can be indeterminate at the time of admission.

As we discussed earlier, psychiatric treatments are not necessarily therapeutic in their effect and can have damaging physical and mental consequences. As such, the development of new legislative powers allowing the use of involuntary treatment has resulted in threats to the basic human rights of people with mental health problems. Reflecting these concerns, Campbell and Heginbotham (1991) argue that people with mental health problems should be subject to the same legal processes as anybody else, and that the only law specifically concerned with mental health problems should be anti-discriminatory legislation.

There are also considerable practical problems with involuntary treatment. Deciding who should be subject to compulsory treatment orders, for how long they should be under such an order, and what criteria might be employed to release them are all contentious issues. Central to this is the assessment of the level of danger posed by the individual subjected to such as order, either to themselves or to others. Recent research evidence from the United States found that people who are experiencing psychotic symptoms may pose a slightly increased risk to the public. But more generally, experience of mental health problems in the past was not found to be predictive of a greater tendency to violence:

> None of the data give any support to the sensationalized caricature of the mentally disordered served up by the media. ... Compared with the magnitude of risk associated with the combination of male gender, young age, and lower socioeconomic status for example the risk of violence presented by mental disorder is modest. Compared with the magnitude of risk associated with alcoholism and other drug abuse, the risk associated with major mental disorders such as schizophrenia and affective disorder is modest indeed. Clearly, mental health status makes at best a trivial contribution to the overall level of violence in society. (Monahan, 1992, 253)

Just what actions or signs might be taken to indicate dangerousness is difficult to determine. Overall, the ability of the psychiatric profession to assess and predict the potential of an individual patient has been found to be very limited (Cockerham, 1992, 146). A further practical problem that arises concerns just what sort of person is to be considered an appropriate candidate for involuntary community treatment. For such an order to be required or to be effective it would require somebody who is capable enough to survive in the community, strong enough to confront authority and refuse treatment, and yet disturbed enough to warrant forced intervention. Bean and Mounser (1994, 100) argue that rather than people with mental health problems, it is the prison population who most closely fit such a description, and to whom control in the community is most likely to be extended.

The physical and mental health of service users

We noted earlier that the underlying rationale for the shift towards community care has been that it should result in an improvement in the prognosis of those served by it. For some people discharged from mental hospital, this undoubtedly will have been the case. However, there is

some evidence to suggest that for some service users deinstitutionalization has not had such an effect. A number of studies have found that the
physical health of service users living in the community is significantly
worse than average. This is particularly so amongst homeless persons
with mental health problems. For example, in England it was found
that:

> The homeless often show particular patterns of morbidity that require greater
> than average care. . . . Those attending casualty departments report a dis-
> proportionate prevalence of traumatic injuries (14–33 per cent), infections
> (with 5–15 per cent having active tuberculosis), scabies and lice (20 per cent),
> and cellulitis. . . . Those living on the streets have high rates (10–23 per cent) of
> peripheral vascular disease, leg ulcers and frost-bite. . . . Up to 10 per cent of
> London hospital beds are occupied by adults or children living in temporary
> accommodation. (Scott, 1993, 320)

Similarly in the United States, it was found in a study of Detroit that only
28 per cent of homeless persons who needed glasses had them, and 63
per cent had 'noticeable' dental problems. Some 30 per cent of this
sample had been hospitalized with a physical illness or injury at some
point in the previous year (Tessler & Dennis, 1992, 27).

While the problems of the homeless are perhaps extreme, the overall
physical health of all people with mental health problems living in the
community has been found to be worse than average. In a study of
30,000 sets of twins in Sweden, Allgulander et al. (1990) found that a
strongly positive relationship existed between the occurrence of mental
and physical health problems. A Danish study found that the dental
condition of the survey population was considerably worse than that of
the local community. Twenty per cent did not brush their teeth regularly
and a similar number had not visited the dentist on a regular basis
for the last three years. Forty-five per cent of the participants had
periodontal pockets deeper than 5 millimetres. Twelve per cent were in
need of fillings of more than 15 surfaces and 45 per cent were in need of
scaling or advanced periodontal treatment. Overall, 63 per cent of the
survey population were in great need of dental treatment (Hede, 1990).

Mortensen and Juel (1990) undertook a study of more than 6,000
people diagnosed as having schizophrenia in Denmark who were followed up from 1957 to 1986. They found that the overall health of the
survey group was significantly worse than the host population, and that
mortality from a number of causes that could be associated with side-
effects from neuroleptics was also increased. In a clinical assessment of
145 long-term users of psychiatric services in England, Brugha et al.
(1989) found that their overall level of physical health was poor. Forty-
nine per cent were overweight, 25 per cent smoked more than 20
cigarettes a day, and 28 per cent had dental or gum disease. Overall, 41
per cent were found to have medical problems. In addition to experiencing poor physical health when living in the community, it has also been
found that the mental health of discharged patients can deteriorate. A

recent study of patients with schizophrenia in England investigated clinical differences between a group with long stays in hospital and a group living in the community. Patients were matched for age, gender and diagnosis. It was found that those living in the community had a significantly higher incidence of depression and anxiety. They also received higher doses of neuroleptic drugs and were found to experience a higher incidence and severity of associated side-effects (Soni et al., 1992).

In a study of the closure of Friern and Claybury hospitals in England, the extent of crime, vagrancy, death and readmission in a prospective cohort of long-term mentally ill patients was measured during their first year out of hospital. Of 278 long-stay psychiatric patients discharged during the first three years (1985–8), 6 per cent were readmitted and remained in hospital for a year or more, but overall the majority were successfully resettled, and there was no apparent increase in the mortality rate of discharged patients. This relative success, however, relied heavily upon careful planning and a financial 'dowry' for each discharged patient being passed from health to social services. Moreover, patients who had yet to leave had more problems of social behaviour and were therefore likely to be more difficult to resettle (Dayson, 1993).

Similarly, in a follow-up study of a number of schizophrenic patients discharged from mental hospital in France, it was found that successful reintegration into the community was possible provided adequate care and support were made available to the patient (Singer & Danion, 1991). And conversely, in a review of attempts to reintegrate discharged patients into the community in Germany it was found that a lack of available services was closely correlated to a failure to reintegrate (Mitzlaff, 1990). A study of service provision in Paris came to similar conclusions: 'the lack of such structures, and the difficult socio-economic context condemn these patients to drifting aimlessly, locked out of any institution, which worsens their pathological state' (George, 1992, 259).

The prognosis discharged patients have depends to a large extent upon the type of community and quality of service provision they experience. The availability of family care improves prognosis, as does the availability of a range of support services (Davies, 1989). These findings may not be considered particularly surprising. They indicate, however, that given the general lack of development of an adequate amount, quality or range of community support services that we reviewed earlier in this chapter, the prognosis of many people with mental health problems may not have been improved by the shift to community care, and may in fact be worse: 'Uncertainty remains, not only about the fate of a substantial cohort of discharged psychiatric patients and their relatives but also whether the alternative innovations really are superior to mental hospitals' (Neelman & van Os, 1994, 1220).

Summary

The range and scale of problems affecting the community care policies of all countries in Western Europe and North America are considerable. A lack of resources devoted to the development of adequate alternatives to institutional care, together with a lack of concern for the quality of life of informal carers or of service users, has tended to characterize the development of community care policy. For some service users this has resulted in a deterioration rather than an improvement in their condition. Below is a letter written by a paid carer. Its tale of the experiences and life of herself and the three people with mental health problems within her care illustrates the poverty of everyday existence endured by many as a result of the failures of community care policy.

I run a home for three long-term patients with schizophrenia. Medicine is taken regularly under my distant supervision and they go out to the village and sustain some encouraging contacts. However, they only have £13.35 to spend per week, which means that smoking must be cut to 15 cigarettes a day and they are left with £4 for clothing, coffee/tea, sweets, transport and a pint of beer at Christmas . . . if ever.

Where can three men find free entertainment? They were brought up in a rural environment and would like an occasional connection with the farming community but they do not know the locals, as frequenting the pub is financially impossible.

I cook three meals a day, see to their cleanliness, watch over their physical welfare, sort their anxieties, wash their clothes, their bedding, mend what can be mended, iron, make tea, coffee, shop six miles away, take them to the doctor, help them with forms to fill, organise dentists, find their favourite programmes on TV, chat about things when possible . . . but have practically no time to enrich their social life. I too suffer from a shortage of funds. The money I am paid by Social Services is just adequate to cover everyday needs.

It is obvious that I cost far less than the psychiatric hospital, which is closing. I entered the deal with open eyes and I love the job. But is it fair that so little is spent on them? No day-centre, no outside support to give them a sense of worth, of being wanted, to enhance their very great need to be useful. Who cares about their pride, their contact with their 'community', and how they see their role in it? (printed in the *Guardian*, 3 October 1995).

7

Service Development Issues

In Chapter 6 we examined a number of issues that have arisen concerning the quality of the experience of service users and their carers within the framework of community care policy. A further set of issues that has arisen concerns the way in which service provision has developed. While support for the principle of community care has been almost universal, the administrative and organizational processes involved in its implementation have proved far more complex and controversial.

Community care as a 'boundary breaking' system

When mental health service provision was based primarily upon institutional care, the care, custody and treatment of patients were provided on one site: the mental hospital. Consequently, it was relatively easy to coordinate service provision amongst staff who worked together and who to a large extent shared a common work culture. As the shift towards community-based methods of treatment and care has progressed, however, the working relationships of staff groups have been dramatically altered. As Benson notes, in a review of mental health policy in the United States:

> Within the traditional state hospital system, patient services were, at least, minimally coordinated. With deinstitutionalization, however, patient care was radically decentralized, often leading to a chaotic patchwork of programs, entitlements, and services spread across a host of agencies and levels of government. (Benson, 1994, 121)

Increasingly, medical and social care staff have had to work in collaboration with each other, and the range of environments within which they work has greatly increased. The importance of the mental hospital within mental health services has tended to diminish while the general hospital, primary care clinics, community mental health centres, social service departments and a range of other organizations have become increasingly important. New staff groups such as community psychiatric nurses, social workers and community support workers, have become increasingly involved in the management and care of people with mental health problems.

There is, of course, no guarantee that these varied agencies and professional groups will work harmoniously. Different agencies may have different priorities; mental hospitals, for example, as we discussed in Chapter 2, may be concerned primarily with maintaining there own income and status. Equally, voluntary societies are often concerned with maintenance of their own finances, and not with the development of policy that might threaten their own position (Mangen, 1987, 81).

Professional rivalry

A result of these changes in mental health services has therefore been an increase in the level of conflict and rivalry between different agencies and professional groups. In particular, the psychiatric profession has seen its position threatened. As the status and size of its traditional power base, the mental hospital, have been eroded, psychiatrists have increasingly found themselves in a position where they have had to work within multidisciplinary teams in community settings. The concerns and priorities of the various staff members of these teams have tended to conflict. Medical and social models of psychiatric care have been juxtaposed, and the hierarchical organizational structures of the institutions have been replaced by a more egalitarian ethos in the community.

> A hospital-centred, medicalized system is typically governed by professional/ client relations characterized by treatment and care on the one side, and passivity and dependence on the other. In contrast, a community-centred and participative system is ideally characterized by democratic and egalitarian relations in an environment that is ostensibly experienced as natural and supportive. Its governing principle is to empower resource users: helpers are seen to be at the service of users, and the latter define their own needs. (White & Mercier, 1991, 21)

Many examples of this tendency towards professional rivalry can be found. In Alberta, Canada, in 1973, Bill 83 established the concept of 'Registered Therapist'. This title could be held by a range of staff such as social workers and nurses, and gave them a legal role in the compulsory admission of mental patients. To a large extent, however, the implementation of this was stymied by opposition from the psychiatric profession, which was unwilling to share power or acknowledge the expertise of other professional groups (Williams & Luterbach, 1976). In the United States there has been considerable opposition by many within the psychiatric profession to community mental health centres. Criticism was made of what they saw as an overemphasis upon achieving social reform rather than providing clinical treatment, as well as a tendency to emphasize the provision of social support rather than medical services. A general tendency towards deprofessionalization within the community mental health centres has also been criticized by the medical profession (Thompson, 1994, 990).

In England the Audit Commission (1986, 56) noted that there is considerable 'professional fragmentation' amongst groups responsible for the treatment of mentally distressed people. Social workers are often perceived by psychiatrists as lacking relevant skills, and of failing to prioritize people with mental health problems in their work (House of Commons, 1985, 316). General practitioners, too, share this wariness of the role of social workers in the provision of treatment: 'Doctors often feel that social workers do not "back them up", particularly in obtaining compliance with medication, and are chary of co-operating with people who not only do not have a medical or nursing training, but may have had no formal training at all!' (Royal College of General Practitioners, 1985).

In 1992 in Sweden a review of psychiatric services by a government commission found that psychiatric professionals have tended to maintain their own interests to too great an extent, the result being that they unnecessarily retain patients in the mental hospitals (Garpenby, 1993). In France, the relationships between general practitioners, private psychiatrists and the sector teams have also proved to be tense (Barres, 1987, 142). In Belgium office psychiatrists have resisted the development of out-patient services, and in Germany to establish an out-patient department outside a state hospital it has first to be demonstrated that there is a shortage of private practitioners in the locality (Bennett, 1991, 632).

These conflicts have tended to stymie the process of developing new services. Indeed, in a review of the European situation in the 1980s, Freeman et al. came to the conclusion that 'Conflicts between different professional groups no doubt still represent major constraints to the development of community-based mental health care' (1985, 91). In the 1980s and 1990s, as the resource base for health and social services has become more restricted, the only way to develop community care policies has been through the redistribution of existing budgets. Necessarily, therefore, any shifts towards community care involve a threat to existing power bases and the likelihood of conflict. Thus, as Sartorius notes in a review of developments in psychiatric services, 'The list of interprofessional tensions in the field of mental health is long and the battle fierce, and there are no signs that it will abate' (1987, 153).

Problems of coordination

One of the main results of these conflicts is a lack of coordination between services. In Canada, for example, there is a lack of coordination between provincial psychiatric hospitals, psychiatric units in general hospitals, and community mental health centres. This is recognized to be a major impediment to service planning and delivery:

> Psychiatric hospitals remain separate from other health care facilities and programs and from the communities they serve, both programmatically and often physically. General hospital psychiatric units function autonomously and, although there has been some increase in numbers of difficult-to-manage patients, they continue to be selective in the patients they admit and community mental health programs tend to be relatively small, possessing little influence or presence within the health care system and overburdened by demands for service. (Rochefort, 1992, 7)

Similar problems have arisen in Europe. In Sweden, a government commission, reporting in 1992, found there was a lack of coordination between health and social care provision (Garpenby, 1993, 298). In Italy, coordination and cooperation between hospital- and community-based services is often left to the initiative of individual practitioners (Crepet, 1990, 34). This, however, has proved a fragile basis upon which to operate. In Italy only half of the district mental health services have at least occasional contact with in-patient facilities, while 8 per cent have none at all (Donnelly, 1992, 93). In France there is little continuity of care or coordination between hospital and community services (Bennett, 1991, 6), and in Spain problems with the coordination of services and a lack of finance have slowed the development of new community care services (Comelles & Hernáez, 1994, 290). In Germany, too, it is widely recognized that there is a lack of coordination between services. The consequences of this, it is argued, are higher readmission rates and a lack of continuity of care (Rössler, 1992; Neelman & van Os, 1994).

In countries such as the Netherlands where there is little central control and where voluntary and private agencies play a major role, problems of coordination can be enormous. Hospital- and community-based services have tended to be in conflict over budgetary allocations and responsibility for patients (Van Der Veen, 1988, 29). The effects of this competition have included duplication of the types of care provided, insufficient collaboration and a lack of continuity of care (Dekker & Langenberg, 1994). Even in countries such as England where community care policy is under central direction, there have been substantial problems with coordinating services. Overall, the lack of coordination between services involved in the development of community care has proved to be a substantial problem in many countries (Grove, 1994, 433).

Measures to improve coordination

These problems are widely recognized, and a variety of solutions have been attempted. In France in 1972 local coordination councils were established (Kovess et al., 1995, 132), and in England, Joint Consultative Committees were established in 1975 (Goodwin, 1993). In the Netherlands in the 1980s, a strategy of regionalization was introduced in an attempt to improve coordination in service delivery. In each of several catchment areas created by the government, services were required to work together to offer a comprehensive network of care in which traditional hospital-based services would be increasingly superseded by community-based care (Dekker & Langenberg, 1994).

The creation of single authorities, with responsibility for the whole range of medical and social needs of service users in a certain area, represents a further method by which problems of coordination might be addressed. This has been attempted in a number of states in America, where local mental health authorities have been created and given responsibility to manage all publicly financed services. The mental health authority holds administrative, fiscal and clinical authority for managing the treatment and care of service users. Similar measures have been taken in the Canadian provinces of Alberta and Manitoba, where the health ministries have recently consolidated institutional and community-based mental health branches (Macnaughton, 1992). There is, however, little evidence that the merging of organizations responsible for service provision will result in improved service delivery (Bertsch, 1992, 1109). In particular, the problems associated with gaining control over an entire service area from a range of other agencies have proved considerable, making it unlikely that such authorities will become more widespread in North America (Benson, 1994, 122).

With the creation in the 1990s of internal markets within health and social service provision in a number of European countries, such as England and Sweden, some new opportunities for the merging of responsibility for the purchasing of services have developed. In England in 1996 the authorities responsible for the purchase of hospital and primary care services have been merged, and these agencies have become far more involved with the purchasing agents of social services in the planning of overall service delivery. As yet it is too early to establish the likely or actual impact of this upon the coordination of services and the effect this might have upon the quality of service provision.

A more radical solution to the problem of coordination is to introduce a voucher system, whereby the service user is provided the purchasing power with which to buy in the services they deem necessary. One such scheme was introduced in New York state in 1989. Each recipient of vouchers was engaged in an individual service plan, within which the service user could agree what services to purchase. Case managers were assigned to manage the programme, and retained some control over the process by countersigning any voucher expenditure a service user wished to make. It was found that service users were able to exercise greater choice over the services they received as service providers became more responsive to the stated wishes of their customers (Bertsch, 1992).

Case management

Perhaps the most important measure currently being implemented to overcome problems of organizational fragmentation is that of case management. Its aim is to improve continuity of care, and improve accessibility, accountability and efficiency. This is to be achieved through assessment of client need, the development of a service plan for each client, arrangement of service delivery, monitoring and assessing the service provided, and evaluation of service effect upon the client (Holloway, 1991, 2). People most likely to receive case management are those being discharged from mental hospital, who have prolonged and recent in-patient experience, and who are diagnosed as being psychotic (Holloway, 1991, 3).

Case management was first introduced in the 1980s in the United States, and has since been adopted or is being adopted to some extent in a number of European countries. In England in 1991 the Care Programme Approach was introduced to provide individual care plans for patients being discharged from mental hospital. A key worker is allocated to each discharged patient, with responsibility for ensuring the coordination of the services they receive. In 1993 Care Management was introduced, involving the appointment of care managers (normally social workers) with responsibility to assess patients' needs. This will normally involve a social worker acting as a case manager, responsible for commissioning and organizing health and social services from both public and private sources, to deliver a 'package of care' sufficiently well integrated as to appear to the service user as a 'seamless web'.

There is a growing belief in the effectiveness of case management services for people with mental health problems. This enthusiasm amongst service agencies is not, however, matched by those who have researched its effectiveness. In a review of recent outcome studies of case management in the United States, Rubin (1992) found it tended to be conceptualized and implemented in a variety of ways. For example, great variation has been found within the process of deciding what needs should be assessed, some placing emphasis upon intra-psychic needs, and others focusing more upon behavioural problems. It also faces its own set of organizational problems and issues that may reduce the effectiveness of the services. For example, it assumes that case managers, often because they control financial resources, will have sufficient powers to ensure their aims are responded to. In practice, it has often been found that it is the case manager's personal standing and the strength of their working relationships which prove to be more important in shaping the care provided to their client (Kanter, 1989). Belcher (1993), too, found considerable tension within the role of the case manager. They frequently find themselves working within tight financial constraints, and consequently the high costs of providing the intensive support some clients required was often found to result in trade-offs being made between remaining within budget and the quality of care offered.

Reflecting these problems, in the United States Rubin (1992) could find no consistent pattern of improved functioning of people with mental health problems as a consequence of case management. Similar conclusions have been reached elsewhere. A study undertaken in Germany to assess the effect of case management on the hospitalization rate followed the progress of 162 patients discharged from psychiatric hospitals over a two-and-a-half-year period. For each of these patients a matched control patient was identified, each identical in diagnosis, sex, age, living conditions and number of previous in-patient episodes. The study found no significant effects of case management on the rate of rehospitalization, nor on the length of time in hospital in case of a rehospitalization (Rössler, 1992).

There is evidence that where case management is focused specifically upon attempting to reduce hospital utilization, admission rates can be significantly reduced. A parallel effect, however, appears to be an increase in the rate of suicide and other serious incidents amongst those kept out of hospital (Holloway, 1991, 3). Equally, the savings achieved by reducing hospital admission tend to be offset to some extent by increased use of residential care (Jerrell & Hu, 1989). Overall, therefore, studies of the introduction of case management reveal an as yet unclear picture as to whether the effectiveness or efficiency of service provision is improved.

What future for the mental hospital?

In the 1960s and 1970s it was widely assumed amongst countries pursuing a policy of deinstitutionalization that the process of moving patients from hospital to community settings was relatively straight-forward. But, as a review of mental health policy in England clearly notes, this was not to prove to be the case.

> Earlier community care policies were embarked on in the apparent belief that
> ... modern medical or psychological techniques would lead to a massive
> reduction in the need for long-term care. There are now only vestiges of such
> a blithely over-optimistic attitude. (House of Commons, 1985, para. 26)

There is, as we reviewed in Chapter 6, growing disquiet over the quality of care experienced by people discharged from mental hospital, and of those people with mental health problems who are now managed entirely in the community. Reflecting this, there has in recent years emerged a debate over the extent to which deinstitutionalization is possible or desirable. Significantly, this debate has arisen in those countries where deinstitutionalization has been pursued with the greatest rigour. In England, particularly in the inner cities, it is increasingly recognized that the rundown of mental hospitals has resulted in over-crowding of the remaining bed space and as a result patients are sometimes discharged too early, or have to sleep in corridors and admission wards rather than being given their own beds (Mental Health Act Commission, 1993). By 1995 some mental hospitals were reporting occupancy rates of 130 per cent, meaning that three in ten beds were used by two patients every day (Mental Health Act Commission, 1995). In California, it is argued that the result of deinstitutionalization has been a raising of the admission criteria to the point where only the most disturbed are found a hospital bed, while others who might previously have been admitted to a hospital bed are referred on to other services (Lamb & Shaner, 1993, 975).

In a review of community care policy in the United States, Wolch & Evans (1988) maintain that deinstitutionalization has failed to meet expectations, concerning a lack of facilities in the community, and witnessed by problems such as the growing numbers of mentally disturbed homeless people. Reflecting these concerns, in recent years there has, to some extent, been a shift in opinion towards supporting a return to institutional care for at least some mental patients:

> The emphasis on provision of shelters as an expedient response to the burgeoning problem of the homeless mentally disabled; growing concern about upgrading or expanding institutions such as jails and state mental hospitals; and the increasing number of mental health professionals who are aligning themselves with the 'new asylum movement' all point towards growing support for reinstitutionalizing the mentally disabled. (Wolch & Evans, 1988, 264)

The dangers of institutionalization revisited

In the United States, Lafond and Durham consider that the most telling question now facing mental health policy makers is 'Why did such universally supported strategies fail so miserably?' (1992, 152). They argue that the policy has failed partly as a result of lack of resources, but also because of other non-economic factors. These include the overly optimistic claims of liberal reformers for the likelihood of success in rehabilitating ex-mental patients, and also the lack of resources given over to the chronically mentally ill. Consequently, there has been disappointment in the results and a loss of support for the principles of community care. Reflecting these concerns, Lamb (1992, 669) argues that a moratorium on further reductions in mental hospital bed space be put in place until and unless more adequate community facilities are developed, and a more accurate assessment of the need for hospital care is made.

In New York City a policy was introduced in the late 1980s to hospitalize some of its homeless mentally ill persons (Aviram, 1990, 83). This consists of the development of residential centres of up to 250 beds, sometimes using existing state hospital buildings. As Aviram comments, 'For all practical purposes, this plan embodies a return to a state hospital custodial care approach' (1990, 84). Moreover, several states have recently broadened their involuntary civil commitment laws to make it easier to hospitalize mentally ill people against their will. The concern underlying these laws has been about the lack of effective treatment being given to people with mental health problems living in the community, and for whom a more custodial environment is deemed necessary (Durham, 1989, 128).

In England, similar concerns have also been expressed. Wing (1990) argues that by offering asylum, mental hospitals offer an important function that should be retained. He maintains that community care will come to deserve the odium now attached to the worst practices of former times if the tradition of asylum practised in the best of the large hospitals is not acknowledged, and given high priority in service planning. These concerns have had some influence in the 1990s in England. The National Schizophrenia Fellowship, a charity representing service users and their families, supports a suspension of further deinstitutionalization until greater resources and a more adequate organization of services within the community can be created.

Since New Year's Eve, 1992, when Ben Silcock climbed into the lions' cage at London Zoo, the attention given to the plight of discharged mental patients and also to those people they have attacked has increased dramatically. The killing of Jonathan Zito by Christopher Clunis, of Jonathan Newby by John Rous, and a number of other cases have helped generate a moral panic over the continued running down of the mental hospitals. Reflecting these concerns, in 1996 the government announced plans for the building of 5,000 beds in new residential units to accommodate mental patients who have failed to cope in the community.

In Italy in recent years there is some evidence of increasing pressure for and need of institutional facilities. The rate at which the hospital population has declined has lessened, and the reasons for the continued decline is increasingly due to the death rather than the discharge of in-patients. In some regions in Italy readmissions are allowed and there is some evidence of increasing use of mental hospital bed space. This, it is argued, is the result of a lack of community care facilities, the severe problems of a certain proportion of people with mental health problems, and the lack of family support for some people with mental health problems (Crepet, 1990, 28).

In addition to these particular concerns in certain countries, the future role of the mental hospital generally has been a concern among feminist writers. A distinguishing feature of their argument is that it is not just service users but also female informal carers who have suffered as a result of the lack of development of adequate services. Finch (1984) argues that social and cultural assumptions about the family, and within the social security system and other welfare institutions, result in few possibilities for developing equal opportunities for women while main-taining the current emphasis upon community care policy. Consequently, she argues, what is required is a reversal of policy direction: community care should in part be replaced by a return to institutional care.

It is not simply with hindsight that these arguments have gained force. Warnings about the consequences of inadequate funding and coordina-tion of community care facilities abound within the social care literature over the last 30 years:

> Developments in the next few years may show that the present proposals with regard to the mental hospital are retrogressive rather than progressive, and that we shall have to think again. (Jones, 1964, 71)

Obviously severe problems will arise if the NHS attempts to reduce psychiatric hospital care and turn patients out into a community where mental health facilities are inadequate. (Maynard, 1975)

Equally, the shift towards viewing institutional care more positively does little more than resurrect nineteenth-century mainstream opinion. At its outset, the asylum movement was a progressive and reformist force. The provision of a place of sanctuary was regarded as an essential part of the treatment process:

To remove the patient from the midst of those circumstances under which insanity has been produced must be the first aim of treatment. There is always extreme difficulty in treating satisfactorily an insane person in his own house amongst his own kindred. An entire change in the surroundings will sometimes of itself lead to his recovery. (Henry Maudsley, 1876, cited in Skultans, 1979, 132)

The lost positive functions of institutional care

Any discussion of the future role of the mental hospital necessarily involves a set of assumptions over the existing and possible functions it may have. Bachrach (1976) distinguished between the manifest and latent functions of the mental hospital. Manifest functions are those that are recognized, intended or anticipated by policy makers, and latent functions are those that are not. The former might include secure provision for potentially dangerous patients, a site for intensive treatment, asylum, and so on. The latter might include economies of scale gained from the centralization of activities, job security for staff, and the segregation from society of those seen as deviant.

It is the loss of these latent functions that has become the subject of increased attention (Gralnick, 1985; Wasow, 1986). It is noted, for example, that 'For those who seek some stability in chaos, the adoption of the patient role and presence in the ambience of safe care can be restorative' (Segal & Baumohl, 1988, 251). More generally,

It is often assumed that mental patients chafe at the bit while waiting for release from hospital, and that once released they return to communities and residencies they regarded as home. In fact, large numbers of chronic patients have no home, except insofar as the mental hospital has served as one. (Segal & Baumohl, 1988, 250)

The overplaying of negative functions of institutional care

In the past, and perhaps to some extent still, it is undoubtedly the case that the organization and administration of institutional care have left much to be desired. The development of the anti-institutional critique in the 1960s and 1970s, which we examined in Chapter 2, undoubtedly exposed practices that should be considered unacceptable in any modern system of treatment and care. In a diary of everyday life in the ward of a large mental handicap hospital, Thomas chronicles in a graphic fashion just what this could amount to in the daily life of an institution:

> Tea mixed with milk and sugar to save time mess and trouble. How many lumps, say when with the milk? You must be joking. (1980, 35)

> Bad habit I picked up from the other nurses. Fitting out someone for his trip to the workshop and muttering 'That'll do', as if the guy's appearance meant nothing to him, just a neat reproduction of my own preferences or lack of them. Not asking the guy if he was all right. Whether it'll do. If a person is not allowed a say in what he looks like, then what is the point? (1980, 38)

> Haircuts en masse – short back and sides, no one is allowed to refuse. Choice of raincoat from a communal pile, communal underwear and socks. Communal combs and brushes. One tube of toothpaste and a couple of tooth mugs for twenty-five patients. (1980, 43)

Within this somewhat pessimistic view of the nature of institutions, however, is an assumption that the very process of long-term incarceration within mental hospital necessarily tends to create its own form of mental health problem. Goren and Orion (1994) argue that the problems of institutionalization are to a large extent associated with the traditional nineteenth-century model of the mental hospital, with its emphasis upon the incarceration of social undesirables and its consequent 'madness-maintaining' character. This model is, however, by no means the only one available. They argue that twentieth-century institutional architecture based on the Dutch concept of 'dwelling', and designed to promote normalcy, if more widely adopted, would tend to promote the mental health of in-patients.

It has also been argued that institutional care need not be as regimented as many studies have found them to be. In mental hospitals where efforts have been made to place greater emphasis upon personal autonomy, significant improvements in alertness, active participation and general sense of well-being have been found to occur (Segal & Baumohl, 1988, 252). Moreover, it has been found that an important part of the experience of hospitalization for patients is the degree to which they are kept informed. The greater the level of information given them about the reasons for their admission and treatment, the more satisfied patients proved to be (Gregoiro, 1990).

The suggestion of some writers in recent years is that in part the critique of institutional care has itself contributed to problems within the mental hospital. The steep decline in status and scale of mental hospital provision in the United States has resulted in the role of the state hospital becoming uncertain, making it difficult to attract and keep qualified professional staff (Munetz & Gellner, 1993). Some of the problems that exist with institutional care have arisen as a result of community care policies. In particular, with the rundown of mental health services and the increases in throughput of patients, hospital life has become more transient. As a result, the formation and maintenance of personal relationships are made more difficult (Segal & Baumohl, 1988, 252).

Can community care substitute for institutional care?

Deinstitutionalization and the development of community care have been generally seen by policy makers as complementary developments; as one declines, the other takes over. This model, where it is assumed that new services provide an adequate substitute for old, is, however, increasingly being questioned. The assumption that a continuing process of deinstitutionalization and rehabilitation would be possible has consistently run up against the problem that for many in-patients a relatively high level of support and care is required.

In England tension between the goal of deinstitutionalization and addressing the needs of in-patients has been a constant theme. As early as the late 1950s the Chief Medical Officer found it impossible to support the Minister of Health's enthusiasm for immediate and rapid de institutionalization. He noted that with an ageing population, the lack of success in rehabilitating the 'hard core of organically deteriorated patients', and the possible future rejection by the community of 'eccentrics', institutional provision should in fact retain an important role in mental health service provision (Chief Medical Officer, 1959, 131). Since then it has come to be recognized that many in-patients could not be discharged. In a review of studies of the success of rehabilitation, Wing found that for many patients it was not effective. He concludes that 'These results suggested that there would be an accumulation of long-stay patients even when everything was done, within the limits of current knowledge, to avoid this' (1981, 144).

The difficulties associated with large-scale hospital closure are illustrated by a study in Sweden of the characteristics of patients in long-term care facing relocation into the community (Dencker & Långström, 1991). It was found that of the long-stay population, 91 per cent of the patients were 65 years old or more and that more than half of them were organically demented. Thirty-nine per cent were severely impaired in their ability to organize daily living functions, and needed nursing care around the clock. It was found that all remaining long-stay residents would require long-term care and support.

Similarly in the United States, an attempt to discharge all 368 patients at Northampton State Hospital (Massachusetts) over a 10-year period met with limited success. While 75 per cent were discharged to community settings, and over 50 per cent of the patients were never re-hospitalized, many others proved to need continual and highly intensive support (Geller, 1990). In Canada, a study carried out in a psychiatric hospital in the Montreal region revealed that in spite of deinstitutionalization, long-term stay remained an important factor in the use of beds. For some patients, the hospital remained a permanent home, either from their first admission or from the time they were institutionalized after multiple admissions (Mercier, 1986).

A number of studies have been undertaken to establish the extent to which community-based services are able to substitute for institutional care. In Stockholm county between 1982 and 1988 the reduction in the number of patients admitted to psychiatric hospitals with schizophrenia was similar to the increase in number admitted to psychiatric clinics at general hospitals. While the degree to which the same patients were involved in each case could not be established exactly, it was strongly suspected that the overlap was high (Borga et al., 1991, 225). A study conducted in Belgium found that the development of mental health centres did not have the effect of reducing mental hospital admissions (Verhaegey, 1987, 50). A number of surveys conducted in the Netherlands also found no relationship between the level of development of community support services and the level of demand for hospital admission (Giel, 1987, 160). Similarly, in Lombardy and Veneto in Italy the number of mental hospital admissions is relatively high (277 and 247 admissions per 100,000 inhabitants, respectively, in 1986 and 1987) despite the development of a district-based service. In areas where there are few district services, such as Sicily, the rate is much lower (123.4) (Crepet, 1990, 33).

Overall, in a review of the European evidence, Katschnig et al. (1993, 3) come to the conclusion that little evidence exists to support the proposition that rates of psychiatric hospitalization can be reduced by the development of community psychiatric services, and indeed there is some evidence to suggest that the hospitalization rate even increases where community psychiatric services are set up.

In the United States there is a growing body of evidence suggesting that the needs of chronic and more seriously disturbed patients who have been discharged have proved particularly difficult to meet in the community. In California, where the number of non-forensic state mental hospital beds has decreased to 8.3 per 100,000, it has been found that the new generation of chronically and severely mentally ill persons who have reached adulthood since deinstitutionalization have been the most severely affected by the lack of in-patient facilities. Many turn to drug abuse and become homeless or incarcerated in jail. It is estimated that there are at least 15 patients per 100,000 population who are too aggressive, too disturbed or too damaged to survive in surroundings that are anything less controlled than those offered in a mental hospital (Lamb & Shaner, 1993). The problems that result from this situation are clearly reflected in the views of two professors of psychiatry:

> We all wish that intermediate and long-term 24-hour, highly structured care would not be necessary, especially with modern antipsychotic medications and our broad array of psychosocial treatments and rehabilitation. We may even wish that all the vast numbers of persons who populated our state hospitals in the past did not need acute long-term care but were simply victims of the poor system of mental health care at the time, of the lack of modern treatment, and of the nature of the hospitals themselves. Unfortu-

nately, our clinical experience does not allow us such an easy explanation. (Lamb & Shaner, 1993, 973)

While it is clear that the relatively simplistic policy assumption concerning the substitutability of institutional care with community care is misplaced, there is evidence to suggest some relationship between the two types of service. In a German study a cohort of patients with schizophrenia was investigated concerning the impact of out-patient psychiatric treatment on the length of stay in hospital and the length of stay in the community (Hafner et al., 1989). They found a difference in the median survival time in the community of around 160 days between those patients who received low levels of out-patient treatment and those who received an average amount. Once readmitted, however, there was little relationship between length of stay and levels of previous out-patient treatment. On a number of other variables, such as the range and severity of symptoms, a correlation was also found between that quantity of out-patient treatment and the apparent effectiveness of treatment programmes. The effectiveness of out-patient treatment was, however, far greater with those living in sheltered accommodation than for those living alone or with their families.

In the United States, an enhanced programme of community treatment was introduced in one hospital catchment area for a period of three years. Over this time it was found the length of time that people were admitted to mental hospital from this area was reduced by 28 per cent, compared with an increase of 15 per cent among persons in the hospital's other catchment areas. In the year after the programme was implemented, participants were hospitalized for a mean of 27.7 days, compared with a mean of 80 days in the year before the programme. Overall, it was found that the community treatment programme significantly reduced use of in-patient days and improved continuity of care (Dincin et al., 1993).

To date, the evidence available concerning the ability of community-based services to replace institutional care is ambiguous. A comparative study of psychiatric services by ten Horn et al. (1988, 278) captures this well. They found that in Mannheim, Germany, there was some evidence of new community-based services having the effect of reducing hospital admission rates, but in Groningen in the Netherlands there was not. Moreover, the significance of the available evidence is open to varied interpretation. In many countries, the number of admissions to mental hospitals continued to rise following the introduction of community-based psychiatric services (Rössler et al., 1992, 445). This is frequently taken to demonstrate the fact that community services cannot be used as a replacement for institutional care, but that they represent an additional service often providing care to people who might otherwise not come into contact with psychiatric services. However, Test & Kapp (1985) argue that a substantial time lag exists between the setting up of services and any impact they may have upon hospital admission rates, length of stay and other measures. As a result, use of hospital admission rates as a criterion by which to measure the effectiveness of community-based programmes is highly problematic.

One way in which we might seek to resolve this debate is to compare public and private mental hospital bed space trends. For while the public sector is responsive to policy dictates, private services provide, to some extent, a measure of how the public perceive the relative role and merits of institutional and community care. In general, what we find is that the pace at which private hospital bed space has been reduced has been slower. In Italy, for example, the decrease in private mental hospital beds was 25.6 per cent between 1978 and 1987 (Crepet, 1990, 28), and the admission rate has remained stable (De Salvia & Barbato, 1993). This contrasts with the public mental health system, where the number of mental hospital beds has, as reviewed earlier, been dramatically reduced. In the United States the number of private psychiatric hospitals has actually grown rapidly in recent years, from 150 in 1970 to 444 in 1988. Over the same period the number of beds contained in these hospitals increased from 14,294 to 42,225 (Manderscheid & Sonnenschein, 1993). For people who can pay, it seems clear that the community is often perceived as an inadequate substitute for institutional care.

Another way in which we might seek some resolution of the debate is by considering the extent to which institutional care and community care are, in reality, policy alternatives. For example, in New York state in 1965 there were 85,000 psychiatric in-patients. By 1981 39,500 of these residents had died within the hospital and 31,200 had been discharged. Most of this latter group consisted of patients who had been admitted for less than a year. Twenty-five thousand residents remained who had been there in 1965 (Bennett & Freeman, 1991, 20). The decline of the mental hospital population has to a large extent been a result of patients dying and not being replaced by new long-stay admissions. While certainly many mental patients now live in the community where previously they might have been provided long-term institutional care, the reverse is far less common.

The role of institutions in the care of people with mental health problems

It is often noted that the issues people with mental health problems face in the community are a product of an intolerant and prejudicial society, rather than problems of the policy itself. To give in to this would represent a defeat that in the long term would tend to result in greater levels of marginalization and oppression. A return to institutional care would be a retrograde step; community care should continue to be supported on the basis that desegregation, in the long run at least, is possible (Pilgrim & Rogers, 1993). Mossman and Perlin (1992) contend that any movement towards reinstitutionalization would infringe civil liberties of service users, further stigmatize them, and probably not help them. They argue that psychiatrists can help the homeless mentally ill by championing their rights, and by focusing public discourse on the broad national need for improved access to medical and psychiatric care.

Moreover, the focus of many accounts upon the problems of community care tends to undervalue the successful outcomes often achieved. Reflecting this, Barham (1993, 143) acknowledges that community care is beset by a number of problems, but that this should not lead us to support a return to institutional care. While images of homelessness and vagrancy sometimes dominate the picture presented of the results of community care, he argues that some examples of good practice do exist and that these should be built upon. Offering a more pessimistic view, Oliver (1990) maintains that the exclusion of people with disabilities is associated with the emphasis given to individualism, achievement and independence in capitalist societies, and as such the scope for reintegration is limited.

Overall, however, this argument over the appropriate role of the mental hospital tends all too readily to become polarized between those in support of institutional and those in support of community care. Policy assumptions concerning the negative impact and consequences of institutional living, and conversely the positive effect of discharge and community living, are clearly too simplistic. What research is increasingly revealing is that for some people at least the mental hospital continues to serve an important function. For some it might be avoided, others regard it as a temporary oasis, and still others regard it as home (Segal & Baumhohl, 1988, 250). Policy assumptions concerning what people with mental health problems either want or need have been overly simplistic. As with any group of people, there will be varied aims and interests concerning desired living arrangements.

Most if not all contributors to this debate fully recognize that the needs of people with mental health problems are diverse and as such facilities ranging from secure accommodation to support in daily living are required (Wasow, 1993). What is at issue, however, is the scale and type of needs that exist, and whether or not service provision mirrors this. What is also at issue is whether the reintegration of most people with mental health problems is achievable, and if so how this might best be achieved. And finally, we might also reflect upon who should make these judgements. The role of people with mental health problems in the making of mental health policy has been minimal, and the extent to which we should expect service users to be the foot-soldiers of a conflict in which their views and their experiences are deemed secondary to a set of ideals propounded by others is a matter of considerable moral difficulty.

Community tolerance and the experience of discharged patients

The role of public education

A long-standing concern with the development of community care (which we examined in Chapter 2) has been that the somewhat rosy assumptions made about the goodwill and tolerance of the community is misplaced. A common response to the problems of community rejection of people with mental health problems has been to call for improved public education, in an attempt to reduce ignorance and therefore fear of mental illness. It is frequently noted that 'The provision of services may have developed in advance of the public education necessary for these services to function effectively' (Thornicroft & Bebbington, 1989, 747), and that 'Only concerted and continuous efforts at public education can hope to turn or at least check the tide of fear and hostility towards real integration' (Grove, 1994, 433).

In many countries attempts have been made to encourage more positive attitudes by the development of educational materials. In England, the Ministry of Health engaged in 'public enlightenment' campaigns as early as the mid-1950s, and since then has repeatedly brought out information designed to increase the public's understanding of the nature of mental health problems and to encourage greater community acceptance (Goodwin, 1993). In Italy the reduction of stigmatized attitudes towards mental health problems has been a key part of the strategy to return patients to the community.

While emphasis on public education has been a long-standing and consistent theme in relation to community care policy, very little effort has been made to assess its impact. In a review of North American public education campaigns, Taylor (1988, 236) notes that there has been a distinct lack of evaluation of their effectiveness. In Italy, despite the importance attached to combating the marginalization of people with mental health problems, there is little evidence that public opinion has become any more tolerant or accepting (Papeschi, 1985). In a survey of attitudes towards people with mental health problems in England, Sayce found little evidence to support the view that public education was likely to be effective. Only half the survey group felt that more public education on the nature of mental health problems was required, and most indicated support for community care policy but were concerned about the potential danger discharged patients posed when left unsupervised, and with the lack of adequate funding for community care: 'A public information drive might work on its own if people opposed the idea of community care, but in general they do not, they just oppose the practice' (Sayce, 1994, 11).

Discrimination against people with mental health problems also needs to be placed within the context of more widespread patterns of inequality within societies. Given such a context, Sayce claims, it is highly unlikely that the public will discard long-held and often negative images of mental health problems. Overall, 'there are problems with believing the public can be educated out of its opposition to aspects of community mental health care policy' (Sayce, 1994, 11). In a comparative study of community response to people with physical disabilities, Hanks and Hanks (1948) found that social integration is greater in societies in which per capita income is high and more equally distributed, where competitiveness in individual and group achievement is minimized, and where emphasis on hierarchy and rank order is supplanted by an emphasis on individual capacity. It has also been found that public support for community-based programmes is strongest in communities that are racially homogeneous (Wade, 1993, 539). In this context, the capacity of governments to shift community attitudes through measures such as public education campaigns might be considered minimal.

There has in fact been very little theoretical work undertaken that examines the basis upon which attitudes towards people with mental health problems are established and altered. The particular characteristics of community mental health facilities and their users, and the physical and social structure of the host neighbourhood have been identified as key factors, but the relationship between them remains obscure (Taylor, 1988, 230–233). In Scotland, research undertaken by the Glasgow Media Group (Philo et al., 1993) found that the public's attitudes towards people with mental health problems are more influenced by images and stories presented on the media, than they are by their own experiences. These images are often of a very negative kind, involving stories of the activities of particular disturbed individuals, and tend therefore to have a damaging effect on the level of community tolerance.

Furthermore, the aim of increased tolerance has tended to be poorly specified within programmes of public education. What degree of tolerance is required and what proportion of the public would be required to show tolerance remains a matter of conjecture. Also unclear is what specific bearing upon the quality of life of people with mental health problems greater tolerance would generate. Greater acceptance may not amount to greater interaction, and for some service users increased interaction may not be desired.

Citizenship rights and service users

Given the lack of success in changing public attitudes, an approach based not on public concern and sympathy but upon the citizenship rights of all has in recent years found increasing favour. Reflecting this, in a number of countries there has been a growing movement towards the development of patient organizations since the early 1970s. The size and activities of these groups vary considerably. Some are more active in advocacy and campaigning, and participation in the policy-making process, while others focus more upon self-help. In the United States, for example, as part of a state initiative begun in 1989, the Pennsylvania Office of Mental Health funded the development of nine consumer-operated drop-in centres (Kaufmann et al., 1993). In Canada it is increasingly recognized that service users and their families should be consulted and involved in the policy-making process. Consumer participation on planning boards has been implemented in a number of provinces over the last few years (Macnaughton, 1992).

In England, similar emphasis has been placed upon incorporating service users and their informal carers in service planning and development in the 1990s. In Sweden, users' associations and family associations have traditionally been met with suspicion. In recent years, however, it has been argued that a more positive attitude has been taken by professional staff to such groups, and measures have been taken to provide them with financial support (Brink, 1994, 266). In the Netherlands, the Clients' Union was formed in 1973, and since then some shift towards acknowledgement of the rights of service users has taken place. A Patients' Council and patients' advocates have been installed in every hospital, and service users have also gained some participation in policy making (Van Hoorn, 1992). In many areas of Italy, largely as a result of the influence of the Psichiatria Democratica movement, patient views are given considerable regard by professional workers.

Service users have also tended to become more organized and demanding in their attitude towards service provision. In England, groups such as 'Survivors Speak Out' and the 'Campaign against Psychiatric Oppression' both lobby for change in the way in which treatment and care services are delivered. In Sweden and a number of other countries, advocacy services have been developed in order to present service users' views more effectively (Bean, 1988, 27). Overall, there is some evidence to support the view that people on the receiving end of mental health services are having an increasingly important role to play in the development of mental health services. Whether this influence will grow, however, is open to debate (Van Hoorn, 1992). The basic interests of the state, and of other groups such as psychiatrists and the pharmaceutical industry, as we argued earlier, are in the maintenance of a medically dominated, curative approach to the problem of mental illness. This suggests that the likely impact of increased user involvement in service development is likely to be marginal.

Citizenship rights and informal carers

It is not just service users who occupy a marginal position within the community, but also their carers. Feminist writers have been particularly concerned about the scale of demands upon women carers. Lister (1990) argues that women lack full social and political citizenship, and that this can be overcome only through radical changes in the organization of domestic and personal life, of paid employment, and of state welfare provision. While the scale and difficulty of such a project are large, it remains feasible: 'It will require the opportunistic seizing of initiative as and when occasions arise for radically new collectivist – and most importantly – feminist policies to become accepted' (Dalley, 1988, 150).

Baldwin and Twigg (1991) are less optimistic about the possibilities for generating ideological change, but do maintain that some development is possible. They argue that feminists have paid insufficient attention to people being cared for, including, for example, the different needs and wishes of a disabled teenager and an elderly person. Equally, the relationship between the carer and person being cared for requires further investigation and greater emphasis, concerning, for example, how different forms of care might be developed that best suit their needs. 'The debate', Baldwin and Twigg argue, 'now centres on the boundaries between individual, "family" and collective responsibility for meeting needs arising from disability or old age' (1991, 130).

These proposals would rely upon acceptance of collective responsibility, and upon the rights of individuals to choice and self-determination. This would include an emphasis upon minimizing dependency via the development of better opportunities in housing, health, employment and social security, together with the creation of frameworks to enable women to exercise real choice through, for example, the support for people opting to care. Baldwin and Twigg maintain that such an approach has some chance of success: 'It seems to us quite possible to envisage a tactical approach that would improve the current situation of carers without jeopardizing the longer-term strategic aim of eradicating sexual divisions in caring' (1991, 131).

Summary

In this chapter we have reviewed some of the attempts made to overcome the organizational problems of community-based mental health policies, and considered some of the main debates concerning appropriate measures for the future. In the community, problems associated with the coordination of service provision have been a major factor hindering the provision of good-quality services. In the institution, problems with defining its role for the future have become increasingly pressing.

The old asylum model allowed for two paths down which people might go: either cure, where the mental patient improved and was discharged, or chronicity, where their condition remained the same or deteriorated and they became a long-term patient. This model, Barham (1993) argues, has tended to be replicated in community settings. The problem with this is that the focus is upon what treatment, if any, is likely to improve the mental health of the patient. Instead, attention should be given to developing services that might improve the quality of a person's life irrespective of whether their mental condition is improving or worsening. A clearer focus on identifying the needs of people with mental health problems for employment, good-quality housing, transport facilities, and so on, could be developed irrespective of whether they happen to reside in institutional or community settings.

Segal and Baumohl make a simple and telling point: that people with mental health problems are not a monolithic group defined simply by their mental disorder. Rather, they display a variety of needs, interests and desires. As such, the policy implications are straightforward:

> Quite simply, what we advocate is diversity. If chronic patients are ever to be at home anywhere, they must find environments consistent with their varying tastes. (Segal & Baumohl, 1988, 261)

8

Conclusion: Which Way Forward? Mental Health Services for the New Millennium

Whether or not the development of community-based systems of care has been to the advantage of people with mental health problems is disputed. Those from a medical and treatment-orientated perspective tend to be more positive in their appraisal:

> ... there is a slow-moving but nonetheless visible improvement in mental health care throughout Western Europe. The inpatient facilities are, on average, smaller; more professionals and other personnel are involved in day-to-day care; and compulsory admissions are on the decline. (Breemer ter Stege & Gittelman, 1987, 19)

While those whose focus is more upon the social consequences of mental health policy for service users tend to reach more negative conclusions:

> ... for many mentally ill persons, treatment in the community has neither improved their clinical condition nor their overall quality of life. (Benson, 1994, 120)

These differences of view between commentators on the impact of community-based services reflect the division between treatment and care services that has arisen in the postwar period. Competition for resources and authority over policy development between advocates of the medical and social models has characterized much of the debate:

> The real dispute is ... between those who want to improve the social prospects of people with long-term mental illness, to reclaim them not for mental patienthood but for citizenship, and those who settle for a highly restricted vision of the 'place' of people with mental illness in social life. (Barham, 1993, 149–151)

This dispute continues. Advocates of a treatment-orientated approach maintain that advances in understanding of the brain's functioning together with the development of new treatments will, in time, overcome the problem of mental illness to a large extent. Critics of this model maintain that psychiatric research has largely failed to reveal a biological basis for behaviour and that it is not mental illness but the problems faced by people with mental health problems that should command our attention.

These arguments about the relationship of the medical and social model underlie much of the debate about future developments in mental health policy that we have reviewed in Part 3. While these discussions about the desirability of various future policy options have their place, they need to be located within an understanding of how and why mental health policy has evolved: whose interests it addresses, and what purposes it serves. In our review of these issues in Part 2 we argued that rather than being a policy designed first and foremost to address the needs, wishes or interests of people with mental health problems, its primary purpose was to reconcile the various and often conflicting pressures upon governments. In part, this does simply concern a humanitarian process of addressing the welfare needs of a particular group of people. It also concerns the process of defining this need in certain ways, and of specifying appropriate responses to it which reflect the imperatives of the prevailing socio-economic system.

For the twenty-first century these imperatives are likely to make themselves increasingly evident. As national market economies are broken down and replaced by the global economy, countries find themselves facing increasingly common and fierce competitive pressures. These changes are having substantial effect upon the ability of states to determine their own national social policies (Pierson, 1991, 188). While various forces continue to determine welfare state development, the ability of countries to sustain policies such as a commitment to full employment and to principles such as universalism in welfare provision is declining because of the increased competitive pressures being faced. Moreover, in Western Europe the movement towards economic and political union is placing pressures upon member states to gain greater control of public expenditures, and this, too, is tending towards reducing the ability of governments to independently determine welfare arrangements of their respective countries.

Concurrent with the development of these economic and political pressures has been a rapid growth in most of the countries of Western Europe and North America in the number of people reliant upon welfare transfers. It is estimated that in most European countries anywhere between 25 per cent and 33 per cent of the working age population are excluded from employment, either permanently or for long periods of time. Added to this is the increasing number of elderly people. By 2030, it is estimated that in Switzerland 27 per cent of the population will be aged 65 and over, in Germany 26 per cent, the Netherlands 23 per cent, Italy and France 22 per cent, and England 19 per cent (Rickford, 1995). Alzheimer's disease, which constitutes one of the main disabling diseases associated with advancing years, the others being strokes and arthritis, is therefore likely to become increasingly prevalent (Rickford, 1995).

Elderly people account for just over 41 per cent of health expenditure, but because of the increasing numbers of elderly in the population, by 2015 this may increase to as high as 58 per cent (International Labour Organization, 1989). In England, it is estimated that the formal costs of looking after dependent people will triple, from £12 billion in 1995 to £34.5 billion in 2031. This estimate itself assumes a scale of informal care with a value of some £20.3 billion (Brindle, 1995). The resulting demands upon public spending have been, and will be, considerable:

> The sheer numbers of people relying on public help is putting a lot of pressure on public finances – a pressure to which governments have felt obliged to react with cutbacks and restrictions, but also with reexamination and modification of existing social policy. (Abrahamson, 1991, 255)

The eventual outcome of these pressures upon policy making is difficult to determine. Abrahamson (1991, 262) argue that because of the globalization of the world economy there is a general movement towards liberal and corporate welfare arrangements. The implication of this is that the social policies of different nation states will tend to converge around a relatively low base, where individuals are increasingly responsible for the quality and quantity of their own welfare arrangements.

This analysis is perhaps of use when considering some general movements in the organization of welfare, such as the development of a more mixed economy of care. In a review of recent developments in Western European welfare policies, Ungerson (1995, 40) found that increased emphasis was being given to the containment of public expenditure. This is reflected in a number of policy shifts, including a shift towards the development of domiciliary rather than residential support, an emphasis upon the role of informal carers, and an emphasis upon the development of private sources of welfare provision. Similarly, in a study of Sweden, the Netherlands and the United Kingdom, Baldock & Evers (1992) found a general shift away from state domination of welfare provision towards more pluralistic patterns of service delivery.

A common mental health policy for the twenty-first century?

In Chapter 5 we argued that the postwar period provides evidence of three patterns of mental health policy development. Over time we are tending to see the individual policies of different nations converge around the common themes of deinstitutionalization, and the development of community-based services focused upon the treatment rather than the care of people with mental health problems. But within each of the three regime-types certain tendencies concerning the timing, pace and style of policy development have been apparent.

Over the last few years, however, we can also find examples of policy developments within each regime-type that are indicative of movement away from its characteristic form. In liberal regimes the emphasis given to a rapid reduction in mental hospital bed space and the rehabilitation of patients is being reviewed. In Chapter 7 we noted some movement towards reinstitutionalization in the United States and England, this being a policy development that tends to reverse the previously dominant themes characteristic of the regime-type. A model of care based upon almost no long-term mental hospital bed space is being replaced by a vision of (what is being phrased in England as) a spectrum of care.

In conservative regimes emphasis has tended to be placed upon status maintenance. In Chapter 6 we noted the recent introduction in Germany of a statutory long-term care insurance scheme. By increasing the available state support, the conservative principle of subsidiarity is in small measure eroded. Social democratic regimes are having to face the fact that to successfully compete in the global market the social rights of their citizens may have to be compromised. Reflecting this, an emphasis upon returning service users to the labour market, together with growing problems in improving or maintaining quality of community-based care services, is apparent. In Chapter 1, for example, we noted the introduction in Sweden of the Law on Support and Service to People with Lowered Level of Functioning 1994. This has promoted a shift towards focusing resources upon rehabilitation, a theme we identified as being characteristic of liberal regimes.

Nineteenth-century mental health policies were characterized by an increasing level of uniformity; compulsory admission to an asylum became the main option available to people with mental health problems throughout Western Europe and North America. The twentieth century has been characterized by far greater variety. Deinstitutionalization has occurred at different times and at different rates, and the development of new community-based services has allowed for wide variations in style of provision. For the early twenty-first century it may be that we are moving once again towards uniformity. It is possible that what we are now seeing emerge is a model of mental health service provision that synthesizes the policy routes that have so far been characteristic of each of the three regime-types.

Governments within conservative regimes may well tend to be more proactive in organizing the administration and delivery of services. Social democratic regimes may face curtailment of the quality of social care services, together with a refocusing of service provision upon returning people to their place in the labour market. Liberal regimes may well face a reversal of policy development. The dramatic reduction in bed space, together with a focus upon rehabilitation of most if not all patients, may tend to give way to an acknowledgement that many people with mental health problems are unable to cope with life in the community, and others require far more support if they are to lead reasonably secure and untroubled lives.

Within the emerging market economies of Western Europe and North America people with mental health problems were amongst the first groups to be recognized to require state intervention. Their inability to support themselves through the normal wage–labour relationship and their potential for social disruption have guaranteed constant state supervision of their activity. The development of community care in the postwar period represents the latest means by which governments have sought to intervene, and the convergence of their policies in recent years reflects an emerging consensus over the appropriateness of this as a means of responding to mental health problems within a modern market economy.

This arrangement allows for increased numbers of people to be treated without a commensurate increase in cost, a result of the process of specialization and increased accessibility that we examined in Chapter 5. For people with mental health problems its rationale is less obvious. The loss of asylum and the lack of development of social care services has left some in a very vulnerable position. Others, however, have been more successfully reintegrated into the community. For informal carers community care policy has resulted in a greatly increased burden of care, but to some extent families do express a desire to provide care. In the community, reaction to the disturbing behaviour of some discharged patients has led to the introduction of compulsory supervision and treatment in the community. But equally, some support for the reintegration of people with mental health problems into the community is expressed.

Overall, community care policy has offered to governments the least bad means of managing people with mental health problems and, as we enter the twenty-first century, there is little sign that this will change. Thus, across the whole of Western Europe and North America a range of in-patient treatment services are being developed, including secure hospital provision, psychiatric units in general hospitals, community mental health centres and a number of smaller initiatives. Treatment is also being made available in day hospitals, out-patient clinics, general practitioner clinics and other dispensaries, and by private office psychiatrists. Developments in services to provide care and support have included the development of accommodation schemes, financial support, day centres and other social centres, and a range of other schemes. How long this arrangement will continue to suit government interests, or how long it will prove acceptable to professional groups, the community or indeed people with mental health problems, is as yet unclear.

References

Abrahamson, D. (1991) Welfare and poverty in Europe of the 1990s: social progress or social dumping?, *International Journal of Health Services*, 21, 2, 237–264.

Abrahamson, D. & Johnson, W. (1982) Do long-stay patients want to leave hospital?, *Health Trends*, 14, 14.

Acorn, S. (1993) Mental and physical health of homeless persons who use emergency shelters in Vancouver, *Hospital and Community Psychiatry*, 44, 9, 854–857.

Alber, J. (1988) Is there a crisis of the welfare state? Cross-national evidence from Europe, North America and Japan, *European Sociological Review*, 4, 3, 181–207.

Allgulander, C. (1986) History and current status of sedatives: hypnotic drug use and abuse, *Acta Psychiatrica Scandinavica*, 73, 465–478.

Allgulander, C., Nowack, J. & Rice, J. (1990) Psychopathology and treatment of 30,344 twins in Sweden. I. The appropriateness of psychoactive treatment, *Acta Psychiatrica Scandinavica*, 80, 325–334.

Anderson, E., Rogers, A. & Peacock, B. (1984) A family impact analysis: the de-institutionalization of the mentally ill, *Family Relations*, 33, 1, 41–46.

Apte, R. (1968) *Halfway Houses: A New Dilemma in Institutional Care*, London, Bell.

Armer, F. (1957) The magnitude and cost of mental illness in the community, *The Lancet*, i, 1029–1037.

Ashford, D. (1986) *The Emergence of the Welfare States*, Oxford, Blackwell.

Audit Commission (1986) *Making a Reality out of Community Care*, London, HMSO.

Aviram, U. (1990) Community care of the seriously mentally ill: continuing problems and current issues, *Community Mental Health Journal*, 26, 69–88.

Bachrach, L. (1976) *Deinstitutionalization: An Analytical Review and Sociological Perspective*, Department of Health, Education and Welfare, National Institute of Mental Health.

Baldock J. & Evers, A. (1992) Innovations and care of the elderly: the cutting-edge of change for social welfare systems. Examples from Sweden, the Netherlands and the UK, *Ageing and Society*, 12, 289–312.

Baldwin, S. & Twigg, J. (1991) Women and community care: reflections on a debate, in M. Maclean & D. Groves (eds), *Women's Issues in Social Policy*, London, Routledge.

Barham, P. (1993) *Closing the Asylum: The Mental Patient in Modern Society*, London, Penguin.

Barres, M. (1987) Sectorization and overcapacity in France, *The International Journal of Social Psychiatry*, 33, 140–143.

Barton, R. (1959) *Institutional Neurosis*, Bristol, Wright.

Bassuk, E. & Edwards, K. (1986) Homelessness and the implementation of deinstitutionalization, *New Directions for Mental Health Services*, 30, 7–14.

Bean, P. (1988) Mental health care in Europe: some recent trends, in C.J. Smith & J. Giggs (eds), *Location and Stigma*, London, Unwin Hyman.

Bean, P. & Mounser, P. (1994) The community treatment order: proposals and prospects, *Journal of Social Policy*, 23, 1, 71–80.

Belcher, J. (1993) The trade-offs of developing a case management model for chronically mentally ill people, *Health and Social Work*, 18, 1, 20–31.

Benjaminsen, S. & Folen, M. (1992) Psykiatriske lidelser blandt hjemlose i Fyns Amt [Psychiatric diseases among the homeless in Funen county], *Ugeskrift Laeger*, 154, 18, 1264–1270.

Bennett, D.H. (1991) The international perspective, in D.H. Bennett & H.L. Freeman (eds), *Community Psychiatry: The Principles*, Edinburgh/London, Churchill Livingstone.

Bennett, D.H. & Freeman, H. (eds) (1991) *Community Psychiatry: The Principles*, Edinburgh/London, Churchill Livingstone.

Bennett, D.H. & Morris, I. (1983) Deinstitutionalization in the UK, *International Journal of Mental Health*, 2, 336–348.

Benson, P. (1994) Deinstitutionalization and family caretaking of the seriously mentally ill: the policy context, *International Journal of Law and Psychiatry*, 17, 2, 119–138.

Bertsch, E. (1992) A voucher system that enables persons with severe mental illness to purchase community support services, *Hospital and Community Psychiatry*, 43, 11, 1109–1113.

Bigelow, D. & McFarland, B. (1994) Financing Canada's mental health services, *New Directions for Mental Health*, 61, 63–72.

Bock, T. (1994) Long-term mental illness in Germany, *International Journal of Social Psychiatry*, 40, 4, 276–282.

Borga, P., Widerlov, B., Cullberg, J. & Stefansson, C. (1991) Patterns of care among people with long-term functional psychosis in three different areas of Stockholm county, *Acta Psychiatrica Scandinavica*, 83, 223–233.

Borga, P., Widerlov, B., Cullberg, J. & Stefansson, C. (1992) Social conditions in a total population with long-term functional psychosis in three different areas of Stockholm county, *Acta Psychiatrica Scandinavica*, 85, 465–473.

Bourdon, K., Peters, W., Smith, T. & Albar, N. (1992) Estimating the prevalence of mental disorders in U.S. adults from the Epidemiologic Catchment Area Survey, *Public Health Report*, 107, 6, 663–668.

Braun, P., Braun, R. & Larson, B. (1981) Overview: deinstitutionalization of psychiatric patients, a critical review of outcome studies, *American Journal of Psychiatry*, 138, 736–749.

Breemer ter Stege, C. (1992) Mental health care in Eastern Europe, *International Journal of Mental Health*, 4, 3–9.

Breemer ter Stege, C. & Gittelman, M. (1987) The direction of change in Western European mental health care, *International Journal of Mental Health*, 16, 6–20.

Brenner, M. (1973) *Mental Illness and the Economy*, Cambridge, MA, Harvard University Press.

Brill, H. & Patton, E. (1959) Analysis of population reductions in New York state mental hospitals during the first four years of large-scale use of tranquillizing drugs, *American Journal of Psychiatry*, 116, 495–508.

Brindle, D. (1995) Battle to rescue care from chaos, *The Guardian*, 20 September, 32.

Brink, U. (1994) Psychiatric care and social support for people with long-term mental illness in Sweden, *International Journal of Social Psychiatry*, 40, 4, 258–268.

Broverman, I. & Kline, D. (1970) Sex-role stereotypes and clinical judgments of mental health, *Journal of Consulting and Clinical Psychology*, 34, 1–7.

Brown, M. (1985) *Introduction to Social Administration*, 6th edition, London, Hutchinson.

Brown, P. (1985) *The Transfer of Care: Psychiatric Deinstitutionalization and its Aftermath*, London, Routledge & Kegan Paul.

Bruce, M. (1991) Poverty and psychiatric status, *Archives of General Psychiatry*, 48, 470–474.

Brugha, T., Wing, J. & Smith, B. (1989) Physical health of the long-term mentally ill in the community: is there unmet need?, *British Journal of Psychiatry*, 155, 777–781.

Bulger, M., Wandersman, A. & Goldman, C. (1993) Burdens and gratifications of caregiving: appraisal of parental care of adults with schizophrenia, *American Journal of Orthopsychiatry*, 63, 2, 255–265.

Burnett, R. (1953) The treatment of mental illness, *The Lancet*, i, 101–105.

Burns, T. & Raftery, J. (1991) Cost of schizophrenia in a randomized trial of home-based treatment, *Schizophrenia Bulletin*, 17, 3, 407–410.

Campbell, T. & Heginbotham, C. (1991) *Mental Illness: Prejudice, Discrimination and the Law*, Dartmouth, Aldershot.

Caplan, R., Andrews, F. & Conway, T. (1985) The social effects of diazepam use: a longitudinal field study, *Social Science and Medicine*, 21, 8, 887.

Carrol, E. (1993) Swedish austerity: benefits at risk, *International Journal of Health Services*, 23, 3, 249–258.

Carter, J. (1986) Deinstitutionalization of Black patients: an apocalypse now, *Hospital and Community Psychiatry*, 37, 1, 78–79.

Castel, F., Castel, R. & Lovell, A. (1979) *La Société psychiatrique avancée*, Paris, Éditions Grasset. English translation (1982) *The Psychiatric Society*, New York, Columbia University Press.

Castles, F. (ed.) (1989) *The Comparative History of Public Policy*, Cambridge, Polity Press.

Charatan, P. (1954) An evaluation of chlorpromazine, largactil, in psychiatry, *Journal of Mental Science*, 100, 882–893.

Chief Medical Officer, *Annual Reports*, London, HMSO.

Cochrane, A. & Clarke, J. (1993) *Comparing Welfare States: Britain in International Context*, Milton Keynes, Open University.

Cockburn, C. (1977) *The Local State: Management of Cities and People*, London, Pluto Press.

Cockerham, W. (1990) A test of the relationship between race, socio-economic status, and psychological distress, *Social Science and Medicine*, 31, 1321–1326.

Cockerham, W. (1992) *Sociology of Mental Disorder*, London, Prentice Hall.

Cockerham, W., William, C., Kunz, G. & Lueschen, G. (1988) Psychological distress, perceived health status, and physician utilization in West Germany, *Social Science and Medicine*, 26, 829–838.

Cohen, S., Khan, A. & Zheng, Y. (1991) Tardive dyskinesia in the mentally retarded: comparison of prevalence, risk factors and topography within a schizophrenic population, *Acta Psychiatrica Scandinavica*, 83, 234–237.

Comelles, J. & Hernáez, M. (1994) The dilemmas of chronicity: the transition of care policies from the authoritarian state to the welfare state in Spain, *International Journal of Social Psychiatry*, 40, 4, 283–295.

Conning, A. & Rowland, L. (1991) Where do people with long-term mental health problems live? A comparison of the sexes, *British Journal of Psychiatry*, Supplement, 10, 80–84.

Conrad, P. & Schneider, J.W. (1980) *Deviance and Medicalization: From Badness to Sickness*, St Louis, MO, Mosby.

Cooper, B. & Bauer, M. (1987) Developments in mental health care and services in the Federal Republic of Germany, *International Journal of Mental Health*, 16, 78–93.

Corrigan, P. (1990) Consumer satisfaction with institutional and community care, *Community Mental Health Journal*, 26, 2, 151–165.

Crepet, P. (1990) A transition period in psychiatric care in Italy ten years after the reform, *British Journal of Psychiatry*, 156, 27–36.

Crist, P. & Stoffel, V. (1992) The Americans With Disabilities Act of 1990 and employees with mental impairments: personal efficacy and the environment, *American Journal of Occupational Therapy*, 46, 5, 434–443.

Cumming, E. & Cumming, J. (1957) *Closed Ranks: An Experiment in Mental Health Education*, Cambridge, MA, Harvard University Press.

Dalley, G. (1988) *Ideologies of Caring*, London, Macmillan.

David, P. (1966) Establishing mental health priorities, *The Lancet*, i, 3–6.

Davies, M. (1989) Community adjustment of chronic schizophrenic patients in urban and rural settings, *Hospital and Community Psychiatry*, 8, 824–830.

Davis, S. (1992) Assessing the criminalization of the mentally ill in Canada, *Canadian Journal of Psychiatry*, 37, 8, 532–538.

Dayson, D. (1993) The TAPS Project (12): crime, vagrancy, death and readmission of the long-term mentally ill during their first year of local reprovision, *British Journal of Psychiatry*, Supplement, 19, 40–44.

De Salvia, D. & Barbato, A. (1993) Recent trends in mental health services in Italy, *Canadian Journal of Psychiatry*, 38, April, 195–202.

Deacon, B. (ed.) (1992) *The New Eastern Europe: Social Policy Past, Present and Future*, London, Sage.

Dear, M. & Wolch, J. (1987) *Landscapes of Despair: From Deinstitutionalization to Homelessness*, Oxford, Polity Press.

Dear, M., et. al. (1979) Economic cycles and mental health care: an examination of the macro-context for social service planning, *Social Science and Medicine*, 13C, 43–53.

Dekker, J. & Langenberg, S. (1994) Trends in mental health care in Amsterdam, *Hospital and Community Psychiatry*, 45, 5, 494–496.

Demay, J. (1987) The past and the future of French psychiatry, *International Journal of Mental Health*, 16, 69–77.

Dencker, K. & Långström, G. (1991) The closure of a mental hospital in Sweden: characteristics of patients in long-term care facing relocation into the community, *European Archives of Psychiatry and Clinical Neuroscience*, 240, 6, 325–330.

Dencker, K. & Långström, G. (1993) The closure of a mental hospital in Sweden: 5 years of transition to district-based long-term care, *European Archives of Psychiatry and Clinical Neurology*, 243, 2, 109–123.

Dennerstein, L. & Astbury, C. (1995) *Psychosocial and Mental Health Aspects of Women's Health*, Geneva, World Health Organization.

Department of Health and Social Security (1975) *Better Services for the Mentally Ill*, Cmnd 6233, London, HMSO.

Department of Health and Social Security (1976) *Priorities for Health and Personal Social Services in England*, London, HMSO.

Department of Health and Social Security (1981) *Care in the community: A consultative document on moving resources for care in England*, London, HMSO.

Department of Health and Social Security (1986) *Annual Report of the Health Service in England 1985–6*, London, HMSO.

Department of Health and Social Security (1987) *Annual Report of the Health Service in England 1986–7*, London, HMSO.

Department of Health (1989) *Caring for People: Community Care in the Next Decade and Beyond*, London, HMSO.

Department of Health (1991) *Health and Personal Social Service Statistics for England*, London, HMSO.

Department of Health (1995) *Annual Report of the Health Service in England 1994–5*, London, HMSO.

Department of Health and Welfare (1988) *Mental Health for Canadians: Striking a Balance*, Health and Welfare, Canada.

Department of Health and Welfare (1990) *Mental Health Services in Canada*, Health and Welfare, Canada.

Dincin, J., Wasmer, D. & Witheridge, T. (1993) Impact of assertive community treatment on the use of state hospital inpatient bed-days, *Hospital and Community Psychiatry*, 44, 9, 833–838.

Donnelly M. (1992) *The Politics of Mental Health in Italy*, London, Routledge.

Donnison, D. (1979) Social policy since Titmuss, *Journal of Social Policy*, 8, 2, 145–156.

Durham, M. (1989) The impact of deinstitutionalization on the current treatment of the mentally ill, *International Journal of Law and Psychiatry*, 12, 2 & 3, 117–131.

Dyer, C. (1995) Legal aid for patients given LSD, The *Guardian*, 11 October.

Esping-Anderson, G. (1990) *The Three Worlds of Welfare Capitalism*, Cambridge, Polity Press.

Falop, J. (1955) Psychiatric illness, absenteeism and employment, *The Lancet*, i, 856–859.

Faris, R. & Dunham, H. (1939) *Mental Disorders in Urban Areas*, Chicago, University of Chicago Press.

Fenton, W. & McGlashan, T. (1987) Sustained remission in drug-free schizophrenics, *American Journal of Psychiatry*, 144, 1306–1309.

Finch, J. (1984) Community care: developing non-sexist alternatives, *Critical Social Policy*, 9, 6–18.

Flora, P. (ed.) (1986) *Growth to Limits: The Western European Welfare States since World War II*, Berlin, De Gruyter.

Foucault, M. (1973) *Madness and Civilization: A History of Insanity in the Age of Reason*, New York, Vintage Books.

Fox, T. (1954) Notes and news, *The Lancet*, i, 1087.

Franks, D.D. (1987) The high cost of caring: economic contribution of families to the care of the mentally ill, Unpublished PhD dissertation, Brandeis University.

Freeman, H., Fryers, T. & Henderson, J. (1985) *Mental Health Services in Europe: 10 Years On*, Copenhagen, World Health Organization.

Friedson, E. (1975) *Profession of Medicine – A Study of the Sociology of Applied Knowledge*, New York, Dodd, Mead.

Garpenby, P. (1993) From ideology to reality: mental health in Sweden, *European Journal of Public Health*, 3, 4, 296–298.

Geller, P. (1990) Self-concept and the institutionalization of mental patients: an overview and critique, *Journal of Health and Social Behavior*, 17, 263–271.

George, M. (1992) Changing patterns of mental health care, *Hospital and Community Psychiatry*, 43, 7, 256–268.

Giel, R. (1987) The jigsaw puzzle of Dutch mental health care, *International Journal of Mental Health*, 16, 152–163.

Ginsburg, N. (1992) *Divisions of Welfare*, London, Sage.

Ginzberg, E. (1987) Mental health policies and programs for the twenty-first century, *Integrative Psychiatry*, 5, 156–158.

Godt, H. & Blinkenberg, S. (1992) Trends in psychiatric hospitalization and changes in admission patterns in two counties in Denmark from 1977 to 1989, *Social Psychiatry and Psychiatric Epidemiology*, 27, 263–269.

Goffman, E. (1961) *Asylums: Essays on the Social Situation of Mental Patients and other Inmates*, London, Penguin.

Goldberg, D. (1986) The assault on psychiatry, *The Lancet*, 125, i, 667–669.

Goldberg, D. (1991) Cost-effectiveness studies in the treatment of schizophrenia: a review, *Schizophrenia Bulletin*, 17, 3, 453–459.

Goleman, D. (1994) Half of US population suffers from mental disorder, The *Guardian*, 15 January.

Goodwin, S. (1989) Community care for the mentally ill in England and Wales: myths, assumptions and reality, *Journal of Social Policy*, 18: 27–53.

Goodwin, S. (1993) *Community Care and the Future of Mental Health Service Provision*, 2nd edition, Aldershot, Avebury.

Goren, S. & Orion, R. (1994) Space and sanity, *Archives of Psychiatric Nursing*, 8, 4, 237–244.

Gough, I. (1979) *The Political Economy of the Welfare State*, London, Macmillan.

Gove, W. & Fain, T. (1973) The stigma of mental hospitalization: an attempt to evaluate its consequences, *Archives of General Psychiatry*, 28, 494–500.

Grad, J. & Sainsbury, P. (1968) The effects patients have on their families in a community care and a control psychiatric service: A two year follow-up, *British Journal of Psychiatry*, 114, 285–296.

Graf von der Schulenburg, J. (1994) Forming and reforming the market for third-party purchasing of health care: a German perspective, *Social Science and Medicine*, 39, 10, 1473–1481.

Gralnick, A. (1985) Build a better state hospital: deinstitutionalization has failed, *Hospital and Community Psychiatry*, 36, 738–741.

Graziani, M. (1989) Reinserimento socio-familiare del malato mentale: aspetti psicologici delle difficoltà ad esso connesse [Socio-familial reinsertion of the mental patient: psychological aspects of related difficulties], *Psichiatria*, 30, 4, 299–302.

Gregoiro, P. (1990) The phenomenology of psychiatric hospitalization: the patient's experience and expectations, *Acta Psychiatrica Scandinavica*, 82, 210–212.

Griffin, L., O'Connel, P. & McCommon, H. (1989) National variations in the context of struggle: post-war conflict and market distribution in the capitalist democracies, *Canadian Review of Sociology and Anthropology,* Spring, 149–163.

Grinten, T. (1985) Mental health care in the Netherlands, in S. Mangen (ed.), *Mental Health Care in the European Community,* London, Croom Helm.

Grob, G. (1991) *From Asylum to Community: Mental Health Policy in Modern America,* Princeton, Princeton University Press.

Gronfein, W. (1985) Psychotropic drugs and the origins of deinstitutionalization, *Social Problems,* 32, 437–454.

Grosser, R. & Conley, E. (1995) Projections of housing disruption among adults with mental illness who live with aging parents, *Psychiatric Services,* 46, 4, 390–394.

Grove, B. (1994) Reform of mental health care in Europe, *British Journal of Psychiatry,* 165, 431–433.

Gustafsson, R. (1989) Origins of authority: the organization of medical care in Sweden, *International Journal of Health Services,* 19, 1, 121–133.

Haerlin, C. (1987) Community care in West Germany: concept and reality, *The International Journal of Social Psychiatry,* 33, 2, 105–110.

Hafner, H., et al. (1989) The evaluation of mental health care systems, *British Journal of Psychiatry,* 155, 7 12.

Halpern, D. (1993) Minorities and mental health, *Social Science and Medicine,* 36, 5, 597–607.

Hanks, J. & Hanks, L. (1948) The physically handicapped in certain non-Western societies, *Journal of Social Issues,* 4, 11–19.

Hansson, L. & Sandlund, M. (1992) Utilization and patterns of care in comprehensive psychiatric organizations, *Acta Psychiatrica Scandinavica,* 86, 255–261.

Harrison, G. (1988) A prospective study of severe mental disorder in Afro-Caribbean patients, *Psychological Medicine,* 18, 643–657.

Haveman, M. (1986) Dehospitalization of psychiatric care in the Netherlands, *Acta Psychiatrica Scandinavica,* 73, 456–463.

Haveman, M (1989) Trends in der intramuralen Versorgung von psychiatrischen Patienten in den Niederlanden: Ein quantitativer Rückblick [Trends in in-patient care in Dutch mental hospitals: A retrospective view], *Nervenarzt,* 60, 4, 236–242.

Hede, B. (1990) Tandforholdene hos hjemmeboende kroniske psykiatriske patienter [Dental health among homebound mental (psychiatric) patients], *Tandlaegebladet,* 94, 8, 309–313.

Heidenheimer, A., Helco, C. & Adams, H. (1990) *Comparative Public Policy: The Politics of Social Choice in America, Europe and Japan,* London, Macmillan.

Hepstinall, D. (1989) Glimmer of psychiatric hope for homeless men in London, *Social Work Today,* 23 February, 16–77.

Hicks, A. (1988) Social democratic corporatism and economic growth, *The Journal of Politics,* 50, 677–704.

Hoenig, J. & Hamilton, M. (1969) *The De-Segregation of the Mentally Ill,* London, Routledge & Kegan Paul.

Hollingshead, A. & Redlich, F. (1958) Social stratification and psychiatric disorders, *American Sociological Review,* 18, 163–169.

Hollingsworth, J. (1992) Falling through the cracks: care of the chronically mentally ill in the United States, Germany, and the United Kingdom, *Journal of Health, Politics, Policy and Law,* 17, 4, 899–928.

Holloway, F. (1991) Case management for the mentally ill: looking at the evidence, *The International Journal of Social Psychiatry,* 37, 12, 2–13.

Hordern A. & Hamilton, N. (1963) Drugs and moral treatment, *British Journal of Psychiatry,* 109, 687–690.

Hoult, J. (1986) Community care for the acutely mentally ill, *British Journal of Psychiatry,* 149, 137–144.

House of Commons (1985) *Second Report from the Social Services Committee: Community Care with Special Reference to Adult Mentally Ill and Mentally Handicapped People,* London, HMSO.

Huffine, C. & Clausen, J. (1979) Madness and work: short- and long-term effects on occupational careers, *Social Forces*, 57, 1049–62.

Ingleby, D. (1983) Mental health and social order, in S. Cohen & A. Scull (eds), *Social Control and the State*, London, Heinemann.

International Labour Organization (1989) *From Pyramid to Pillar – Population Change and Social Security in Europe*, London, ILO.

Jaques, M. & Davies, P. (1970) Cultural attitudes towards disability: Denmark, Greece and the United States, *International Journal of Social Psychiatry*, 16, 54–62.

Jerrell, J. & Hu, T. (1989) Cost effectiveness of intensive clinical case management compared with an existing system of care, *Inquiry*, 26, 224–234.

Jessop, B. (1994) The transition to post-Fordism and the Schumpeterian workfare state, in R. Burrows & B. Loader (eds), *Towards a Post-Fordist Welfare State?* London, Routledge.

Joint Commission on Mental Illness and Health (1961) *Action for Mental Health*, New York, Basic Books.

Jones, E. (1991) Interhospital relocation of long-stay psychiatric patients: a prospective study, *Acta Psychiatrica Scandinavica*, 83, 214–216.

Jones, K. (1964) Revolution or reform in the mental health services, in J. Farndale (ed.), *Trends in the National Health Service*, London, Pergamon Press.

Jones, K. (1972) *A History of the Mental Health Services*, London, Routledge & Kegan Paul.

Jones, K. (1983) *Issues in Social Policy*, London, Routledge.

Jones, K. (1988) *Experience in Mental Health*, London, Sage.

Jones, K. (1993) *Asylums and After*, London, Athlone Press.

Kanter, J. (1989) Clinical case management: definition, principles, components, *Hospital and Community Psychiatry*, 40, 361–368.

Kastrup, M. (1987) Who became revolving door patients? *Acta Psychiatrica Scandinavica*, 76, 80–88.

Katschnig, H., Konieczna, T. & Cooper, J. (1993) *Emergency Psychiatric and Crisis Intervention Services in Europe*, Copenhagen, World Health Organization.

Kaufmann, C., Farmer, J. & Ward-Colasante, C. (1993) Development and evaluation of drop-in centers operated by mental health consumers, *Hospital and Community Psychiatry*, 44, 7, 675–678.

Kay, A. & Legg, C. (1986) *Discharged to the Community: A Review of Housing and Support for People Leaving Psychiatric Care*, London Housing Research Group, City University.

Keegan, D. & Rajput, A. (1973) Drug-induced dystonia tarda: treatment with L-dopa, *Disorders of the Nervous System*, 38, 167–169.

Kelstrup, A., Lund, K., Lauritsen, B. & Bech, P. (1993) Satisfaction with care reported by psychiatric inpatients, *Acta Psychiatrica Scandinavica*, 87, 374–379.

Kessler, R. & Neighbors, H. (1986) A new perspective on the relationship among race, class and psychological distress, *Journal of Health and Social Behaviour*, 27, 107–115.

Kiesler, C. (1992) U.S. mental health policy: doomed to fail, *American Psychologist*, 47, 9, 1077–1082.

Kiesler, C. & Sibulkin, A. (1987) *Mental Hospitalization: Myths and Facts about a National Crisis*, London, Sage.

King, D. (1987) *The New Right: Politics, Markets and Citizenship*, London, Macmillan.

Klein, R. (1983) *The Politics of the NHS*, Harlow, Longman.

Knowles, C. (1991) Afro-Caribbeans and schizophrenia: How does psychiatry deal with issues of race, culture and ethnicity?, *Journal of Social Policy*, 20, 2, 173–190.

Koizumi, K. & Harris P. (1992) Mental health care in Japan, *Hospital and Community Psychiatry*, 43, 1100–1103.

Kovess, V., Boisguérin, B., Antoine, D. & Reynauld, M. (1995) Has the sectorization of psychiatric services in France really been effective?, *Social Psychiatry and Psychiatric Epidemiology*, 30, 132–138.

Kringlen, E. (1993) Psychiatry towards the year 2000, *Acta Psychiatrica Scandinavica*, 87, 297–301.

Kunze, H. (1985) Institutionalization in community care in West Germany, *British Journal of Psychiatry*, 147, 261–264.

Lafond, J. & Durham, M. (1992) *Back to the Asylum*, Oxford, Oxford University Press.

Laing, R.D. (1960) *The Divided Self*, London, Tavistock.

Lamb, H.R. (ed.) (1984) *The Homeless Mentally Ill*, Washington, DC, American Psychiatric Association.

Lamb, H.R. (1992) Is it time for a moratorium on deinstitutionalization?, *Hospital and Community Psychiatry*, 43, 7, 669.

Lamb, H. & Shaner, R. (1993) When there are almost no state hospital beds left, *Hospital and Community Psychiatry*, 44, 10, 973–976.

Lamb, H. & Weinberger, L. (1993) Therapeutic use of conservatorship in the treatment of gravely disabled psychiatric patients, *Hospital and Community Psychiatry*, 44, 2, 147–150.

Lasch, C. (1977) *Haven in a Heartless World: The Family Besieged*, New York, Basic Books.

Lassenius, B., Veroff, J. & Douvan, E. (1973) Prognosis in schizophrenia: The need for institutionalized care, *Acta Psychiatrica Scandinavica*, 49, 294–305.

Leavin, A. (1984) *The Impact of Deinstitutionalization on Ten San Francisco Bay Area Counties*, San Francisco, Department of Public Health, City and County of San Francisco.

Lelliott, P. & Wing, J. (1994) A national audit of new long-stay psychiatric patients. I: Method and description of the cohort, *British Journal of Psychiatry*, 165, 160–169.

Lentz, R. & Ritchey, J. (1971) 'Routine' vs. 'therapeutic' transfer of chronic mental patients, *Archives of General Psychiatry*, 25, 187–191.

Levy, A. (1992) New Israeli psychiatric legislation, *Medical Law*, 11, 3–4, 281–296.

Lewis, G., Croft-Jeffreys, C. & David, A. (1990) Are British psychiatrists racist?, *British Journal of Psychiatry*, 157, 410 415.

Licht, R., Gouliaev, G. & Lund, J. (1991) Trends in long-stay hospitalization in Denmark: a descriptive register study, 1972–1987, *Acta Psychiatrica Scandinavica*, 83, 314–318.

Lightman, E. (1986) The impact of government economic restraint on mental health services in Canada, *Canada's Mental Health*, 34, 1, 24–28.

Link, B. (1982) Mental patients' status, work, and income: an examination of the effects of a psychiatric label, *American Sociological Review*, 47, 202–215.

Lister, R. (1990) Women, economic dependency and citizenship, *Journal of Social Policy*, 19, 4, 445–467.

Littlewood, M. (1980) Ethnic minorities and psychiatric services, *Sociology of Health and Illness*, 2, 194–201.

Littlewood, R. & Lipsedge, M. (1988) Psychiatric illness among British Afro-Caribbeans, *British Medical Journal*, 296, 950–951.

Lurie, S. (1992) Mental health policy and expenditure analysis, *Canada's Mental Health*, 40, 1, 11–14.

Lyons, M. & Hayes, R. (1993) Student perceptions of persons with psychiatric and other disorders, *American Journal of Occupational Therapy*, 47, 6, 541–548.

MacGilp, D. (1991) A quality of life study of discharged long-term psychiatric patients, *Journal of Advanced Nursing*, 16, 10, 1206–1215.

McGlashan, T. (1989) A selective review of recent North American long-term follow-up studies of schizophrenia, *Schizophrenia Bulletin*, 14, 515–542.

McGovern, D. & Cope, R. (1987) The compulsory detention of males of different ethnic groups, with special reference to offender patients, *British Journal of Psychiatry*, 150, 505–511.

McGuire, T. (1991) Measuring the economic costs of schizophrenia, *Schizophrenia Bulletin*, 17, 3, 375–388.

Macnaughton, E. (1992) Canadian mental health policy, *Canada's Mental Health*, 40, 1, 3–10.

Maddison, A. (1984) Origins and impact of the welfare state, 1883–1993, *Banca Nazionale del Lavoro Quarterly Review*, 148, 55–87.

Madianos, M. (1994) Recent advances in community psychiatry and psychosocial rehabilitation in Greece and the other southern European countries, *The International Journal of Social Psychiatry,* 40, 3, 157–164.

Maloy, K. (1992) *Critiquing the Empirical Evidence: Does Involuntary Outpatient Commitment Work?,* Washington, DC, Mental Health Policy Center.

Manderscheid, R. & Sonnenschein, M. (eds) (1993) *Mental Health, United States, 1992,* Washington, DC, US Department of Health and Human Services.

Mangen, S. (ed.) (1985) *Mental Health Care in the European Community,* London, Croom Helm.

Mangen, S. (1987) Mental health policies in Europe: An analysis of priorities and problems, *The International Journal of Social Psychiatry,* 33, 76–82.

Mangen, S. (1988) Implementing community care: an international assessment, in A. Lavender & F. Holloway (eds), *Community Care in Practice,* New York, Wiley.

Mangen, S. (1994) Continuing care: an emerging issue in European health policy, *International Journal of Social Psychiatry,* 40, 4, 235–245.

Marmor, T. & Gill, K. (1989) The political and economic context of mental health care in the United States, *Journal of Health, Politics, Policy and Law,* 14, 3, 459–475.

Marshall, P. (1992) The mental health HMO: capitation funding for the chronically mentally ill. Why an HMO?, *Community Mental Health Journal,* 28, 2, 111–120.

Martin, F.M. (1984) *Between the Acts: Community Mental Health Services 1959–1983,* London, Nuffield Provincial Hospitals Trust.

Martin, S. (1984) *Hospitals in Trouble,* Oxford, Blackwell.

Matthews, R. (1987) Decarceration and social control: fantasies and realities, in J. Lowman, R. Menzies & T. Palys (eds), *Transcarceration: Essays in the Sociology of Social Control,* Aldershot, Gower.

Maynard, A. (1975) *Health Care in the European Community,* London, Croom Helm.

Means, R. & Smith, R. (1994) *Community Care: Policy and Practice,* London, Macmillan.

Mechanic, D. (1968) *Medical Sociology: A Selective View,* New York, Columbia University Press.

Mechanic, D. (1980) *Mental Health and Social Policy,* Englewood Cliffs, NJ, Prentice Hall.

Mechanic, D. & Rochefort, D. (1990) Deinstitutionalization: an appraisal of reform, *Annual Review of Sociology,* 16, 301–327.

Mental Health Act Commission (1993) *Fifth Biennial Report,* London, HMSO.

Mental Health Act Commission (1995) *Sixth Biennial Report,* London, HMSO.

Mental Health Foundation (1993) *The Fundamental Facts,* London, Mental Health Foundation.

Mental Health Foundation (1995) *Annual Report,* London, Mental Health Foundation.

Mercier, C. (1986) L'hôpital psychiatrique: d'hier à demain [The psychiatric hospital: past and future], *Canadian Journal of Psychiatry,* 31, 1, 35–43.

Merrison Commission (1979) *Royal Commission on the National Health Service,* Cmnd 7615, London, HMSO.

Mihill, C. (1995) Jobs denied to the mentally ill, The *Guardian,* 30 August.

Miller, D.H. (1971) Words that fail, in S. Wallace (ed.), *Total Institutions,* Chicago, Aldine.

Mills, C.W. (1959) *The Sociological Imagination,* New York, Oxford University Press.

Ministry of Health, *Annual Reports,* London, HMSO.

Mishra, M. (1990) *The Welfare State in Capitalist Society,* Hemel Hempstead, Harvester Wheatsheaf.

Mitzlaff, S. (1990) Psychiatrisch–psychosoziale Tätigkeit in der BRD: das alte und die neuen Aufgaben [Psychiatric–psychosocial activity in the FRG: old and new responsibilities], *Psychiatry, Neurology and Medical Psychology,* 42, 6, 348–355. `

Monahan, J. (1992) Mental disorder and violent behaviour: perceptions and evidence, *American Psychologist,* 47, 4, 511–521.

Mortensen, P. & Juel, K. (1990) Mortality and causes of deaths in schizophrenic patients in Denmark, *Acta Psychiatrica Scandinavica,* 81, 332–337.

Mossman, D. & Perlin, M. (1992) Psychiatry and the homeless mentally ill: a reply to Dr. Lamb, *American Journal of Psychiatry*, 149, 7, 951–957.

Munetz, M. & Gellner, J. (1993) The least restrictive alternative in the postinstitutional era, *Hospital and Community Psychiatry*, 44, 10, 967–973.

Munk-Jorgensen, P. & Jensen, J. (1992) Trends in psychiatric hospitalization in Denmark: a 10-year register-based investigation, *Acta Psychiatrica Scandinavica*, 86, 79–83.

Muscettola, G., Pampallona, S. & Barbato, G. (1993) Persistent tardive dyskinesia: demographic and pharmacological risk factors, *Acta Psychiatrica Scandinavica*, 87, 29–36.

National Board of Health and Welfare (1993) *Psychiatric Care and Social Support for the Long-term Mentally Disturbed in Sweden*, Stockholm, National Board of Health and Welfare.

Neelman, J. & van Os, J. (1994) Caring for mentally ill people, *British Medical Journal*, 309, 1218–1221.

Neighbors, H., Calver, R. & Pine, W. (1992) Ethnic minority mental health service delivery: A review of the literature, *Research in Community and Mental Health*, 7, 55–71.

Nordentoft, M. (1990) Afinstitutionalisering og hjemloshed blandt psykisk syge: i historisk perspektiv [Deinstitutionalization and homelessness among the mentally ill: a historical review], *Nordisk Psykiatrisk Tidsskrift*, 44, 5, 435–441.

Nordentoft, M., Knudsen, H. & Schulsinger, F. (1992) Housing conditions and residential needs of psychiatric patients in Copenhagen, *Acta Psychiatrica Scandinavica*, 85, 5, 385–389.

Novack, L. (1992) A normality for us without confinement for them, *International Journal of Social Psychiatry*, 38, 62–70.

OECD (1985) *The Role of the Public Sector: Causes and Consequences of the Growth of Government*, OECD Economic Studies Special Issue No. 4, Paris, OECD.

OECD (1990) *Economic Outlook Historical Statistics*, Paris, OECD.

Offe, C. (1984) *Contradictions of the Welfare State*, London, Hutchinson.

Okin, R. (1992) California's new State–Local Program Realignment Act: an experiment in financing care, *Hospital and Community Psychiatry*, 43, 11, 1140–1145.

Oliver, M. (1990) *The Politics of Disablement*, London, Macmillan.

O'Neill, M. (1988) Tunnel vision, *Insight*, September, 12–15.

Overholser, W. (1958) Has chlorpromazine inaugurated a new era in mental hospitals?, in G. Hirsch (ed.), *The New Chemotherapy in Mental Illness*, New York, Philosophical Library.

Palermo, G., Liska, F. & Smith, M. (1991) Jails versus mental hospitals: a social dilemma, *International Journal of Offender Therapy and Comparative Criminology*, 35, 2, 97–106.

Papeschi, R. (1985) Denial of the institution: a critical review of Franco Basaglia's writings, *British Journal of Psychiatry*, 146, 247–254.

Percy Commission (1957) *Report of the Royal Commission on Mental Illness and Mental Deficiency*, Cmnd 169, London, HMSO.

Perris, C. (1987) The development of psychiatric care in Sweden (with particular reference to one of the northern counties), *International Journal of Mental Health*, 16, 198–224.

Phillipson, C. (1989) Developing a political economy of drugs and older people, *Ageing and Society*, 9, 431–440.

Philo, G., Grierson, P. & Taylor, S. (1993) *Media Representations of Mental Health/Illness*, Glasgow, University Media Group.

Pierson, C. (1991) *Beyond the Welfare State?*, Cambridge, Polity Press.

Pilgrim, D. & Rogers, A. (1993) *A Sociology of Mental Health and Illness*, Milton Keynes, Open University Press.

Pinkney, A., Gerber, G. & Lafavre, H. (1991) Quality of life after psychiatric rehabilitation: the clients' perspective, *Acta Psychiatrica Scandinavica*, 83, 86–91.

Pipe, R., Baht, A. & Matthews, B. (1991) Section 136 and African/Afro-Caribbean minorities, *International Journal of Social Psychiatry*, 37, 1, 14–23.

Pirella, A. (1987) Institutional psychiatry between transformation and rationalization: the case of Italy, *International Journal of Mental Health*, 16, 118–141.

Poullier, J. & Sandier, S. (1991) *Health Data*, Paris, OECD.

Poveda, J. (1987) Mental health care in Spain, 1960–1985, *International Journal of Mental Health*, 16, 182–197.

Prior, L. (1993) *The Social Organization of Mental Illness*, London, Sage.

Rafferty, J. (1992) Mental health services in transition: the United States and the United Kingdom, *British Journal of Psychiatry*, 161, 589–593.

Redick, R. (1990) Patient care episodes in mental health organizations, United States: selected years between 1955 and 1986, *Mental Health Statistical Note*, 192, 1–11.

Rees, L. (1966) Mental illness: its causes and consequences, *The Lancet*, i, 18–19.

Rehin, G. & Martin, F. (1968) *Patterns of Performance in Community Care*, Oxford, Oxford University Press.

Rice, D. & Jones, N. (1990) *The Economic Costs of Alcohol and Drug Abuse and Mental Illness: 1985*, Rockville, MD, National Institute of Mental Health, DHHS Publication 90–1694.

Richman, A. & Britton, B. (1992) Level of care for deinstitutionalized psychiatric patients, *Health Report*, 4, 3, 269–275.

Rickford, M. (1995) Finding the means for a dignified end, The *Guardian*, 21 June.

Riecher-Rössler, A. & Rössler, W. (1993) Compulsory admission of psychiatric patients – an international comparison, *Acta Psychiatrica Scandinavica*, 87, 231–236.

Righetti, M. (1993) Cooperatives as a social enterprise in Italy: a place for social integration and rehabilitation, *Acta Psychiatrica Scandinavica*, 88, 238–242.

Ritchie, J. & Jacobs, T. (1989) *Keeping in Touch with the Talking*, Birmingham Community Care Special Action Report, Birmingham City Council.

Rochefort, D. (1992) More lessons of a different kind: Canadian mental health policy in comparative perspective, *Hospital and Community Psychiatry*, 43, 11, 1083–1090.

Rollin, H. (1969) *The Mentally Abnormal Offender and the Law*, Oxford, Pergamon Press.

Room, G. (1979) *The Sociology of Welfare*, Oxford, Basil Blackwell and Mott.

Rose, N. (1986) Psychiatry: the discipline of mental health, in P. Millar & N. Rose (eds), *The Power of Psychiatry*, Cambridge, Polity Press.

Rosenblatt, A. & Mayer, J. (1974) The recidivism of mental patients: A review of past studies, *American Journal of Orthopsychiatry*, 44, 697–706.

Rössler, W. (1992) Wilhelm Griesinger and community care, *Nervenarzt*, 63, 5, 257–261.

Rössler, W., Löffler, B. & Fätkenheuer, B. (1992) Does case management reduce the rehospitalization rate?, *Acta Psychiatrica Scandinavica*, 86, 445–449.

Rothman, D. (1971) *The Discovery of the Asylum: Social Order and Disorder in the New Republic*, Boston, Little, Brown and Co.

Royal College of General Practitioners (1985) *Memorandum Submitted to the House of Commons Social Services Committee*, London, HMSO.

Rubin, A. (1992) Is case management effective for people with serious mental illness? A research review, *Health and Social Work*, 17, 2, 138–150.

Rydin, D. (1989) *Schizofreniinventering*, Varnamo, Varnan sjukhus.

Salleh, M. (1993) Decentralization of psychiatric services in Malaysia: what is the prospect?, *Singapore Medical Journal*, 34, 2, 139–141.

Sartorius, N. (1987) Mental health policies and programs for the twenty-first century: a personal view, *Integrative Psychiatry*, 5, 3, 151–154.

Sayce, L. (1994) Power to the people, *Community Care*, 10 March, 11–12.

Scheff, T. (1966) *Being Mentally Ill: A Sociological Theory*, New York, Aldine.

Schene, A. & van-Wijngaarden, B. (1995) A survey of an organization for families of patients with serious mental illness in the Netherlands, *Psychiatric Services*, 46, 8, 807–813.

Schnabel, P. (1992) Down and out: social marginality and homelessness, *The International Journal of Social Psychiatry*, 38, 59–67.

Schonecker, M. (1957) Ein eigentümliches Syndrom in oralen Bereich Megaphen Applikation, *Nervenartz*, 28, 35.

Scott, J. (1993) Homelessness and mental illness, *British Journal of Psychiatry*, 162, 314–324.

Scull, A. (1979) *Museums of Madness: The Social Organization of Insanity in Nineteenth-Century England*, London, Penguin.

Scull, A. (1984) *Decarceration: Community Treatment and the Deviant – A Radical View*, 2nd edition, Cambridge, Polity Press.

Scull, A. (1985) Deinstitutionalization and public policy, *Social Science and Medicine*, 20, 5, 545–552.

Scull, A. (1987) Decarceration reconsidered, in J. Lowman, R. Menzies & T. Palys (eds), *Transcarceration: Essays in the Sociology of Social Control*, Aldershot, Gower.

Sedgwick, P. (1982) *PsychoPolitics*, London, Pluto Press.

Segal P. & Baumohl J. (1988) No place like home: reflections on sheltering a diverse population, in C.J. Smith & J. Giggs (eds), *Location and Stigma*, London, Unwin Hyman.

Shepherd, M. & Tester, D. (1989) *Psychological Medicine – The Natural History of Schizophrenia*, Cambridge, Cambridge University Press.

Singer, T. & Danion, A. (1991) Psychiatric and physical illness, socio-demographic characteristics, and the use of psychotropic drugs in the community, *Journal of Clinical Epidemiology*, 44, 303–311.

Skultans, V. (1979) *English Madness: Ideas on Insanity 1580–1890*, London, Routledge & Kegan Paul.

Smith, H. (1991) Caring for everyone? The implications for women of the changes in community care services, *Feminism and Psychology*, 1, 2, 279–292.

Soni, S., Mallik, A. & Reed, P. (1992) Differences between chronic schizophrenic patients in the hospital and in the community, *Hospital and Community Psychiatry*, 43, 12, 1233–1238.

Spanjer, M. (1992) *Care in the Netherlands*, Rijswijk, Ministry of Welfare, Health and Cultural Affairs.

Star, S. (1955) The public's idea about mental illness, Paper presented at the National Association for Mental Health meetings, Chicago, November.

Stockman, D.A. (1986) *The Triumph of Politics*, London, The Bodley Head.

Strauss, E. (1957) Medical staff of mental hospitals, The *Lancet*, i, 930.

Szasz, T. (1961) *The Myth of Mental Illness: Foundations of a Theory of Personal Conduct*, New York, Hoeber-Harper.

Taylor, S. (1988) Community reactions to deinstitutionalization, in C.J. Smith & J. Giggs (eds), *Location and Stigma*, London, Unwin Hyman.

ten Horn, G., Moschel, G. & Giel, R. (1988) Patterns of mental health care in two European areas: Mannheim, Federal Republic of Germany; and Groningen, The Netherlands, *Acta Psychiatrica Scandinavica*, 77, 271–281.

Tessler, R. & Dennis, D. (1992) Mental illness among homeless adults, *Research in Community and Mental Health*, 7, 3–53.

Test, M.A. & Kapp, F. (1985) The long-term treatment of young schizophrenics in a community support program, *New Directory of Mental Health Services*, June, 26, 17–27.

Tester, S. (1996) *Community Care for Older People: A Comparative Perspective*, Basingstoke, Macmillan.

Therrien, R. (1990) La désinstitutionnalisation, les malades, les familles et les femmes: des intérêts à concilier [Deinstitutionalization, the patients, the families and women: interests to reconcile], *Santé Mentale au Québec*, 15, 1, 100–119.

Thomas, F. (1980) Everyday life on the ward, in J. Ryan & F. Thomas, *The Politics of Mental Handicap*, Harmondsworth, Penguin.

Thompson, E. & Doll, W. (1982) The burden of families coping with the mentally ill: an invisible crisis, *Family Relations*, 31, 379–388.

Thompson, J. (1994) Trends in the development of psychiatric services, *Hospital and Community Psychiatry*, 45, 987–992.

Thornicroft, G. & Bebbington, P. (1989) Deinstitutionalisation: from hospital closure to service development, *British Journal of Psychiatry*, 155, 739–753.

Tidmarsh, D. & Wood, S. (1972) Psychiatric aspects of destitution: a study of the Camberwell Reception Centre, in J.K. Wing & A.H. Haily (eds), *Evaluating a Community Psychiatric Service*, London, Oxford University Press.

Torrey, E. & Kaplan, R. (1995) A national survey of the use of outpatient commitment, *Psychiatric Services*, 46, 8, 778–784.

Uffing, H., Ceha, M. & Saenger, H. (1992) The development of deinstitutionalization in Europe, *Psychiatric Quarterly*, 63, 3, 265–278.

Ungerson, C. (1995) Gender, cash and informal care, *Journal of Social Policy*, 24, 1, 31–52.

Van Der Veen, H. (1988) Rehabilitation in Dutch mental health care, *International Journal of Mental Health*, 17, 24–32.

Van Hoorn, E. (1992) Changes? What changes? The views of the European patients' movement, *International Journal of Social Psychiatry*, 38, 30–35.

Verhaegey, L. (1987) The evolution of Belgian psychiatry, *International Journal of Mental Health*, 16, 42–57.

Vestergaard, J. (1994) The Danish Mental Health Act of 1989: Psychiatric discretion and the new legalism, *International Journal of Law and Psychiatry*, 17, 2, 191–210.

Wade, J. (1993) Institutional racism: an analysis of the mental health system, *American Journal of Orthopsychiatry*, October, 63, 4, 536–544.

Walker, A. (1989) Community care, in M. McCarthy (ed.), *The New Politics of Welfare: An Agenda for the 1990s*, Basingstoke, Macmillan.

Walsh, D. (1987) Recent trends in mental health care in Ireland, *International Journal of Mental Health*, 16, 108–117.

Warner, R. (1989) Deinstitutionalization: how did we get where we are?, *Journal of Social Issues*, 45, 17–30.

Wasow, R. (1986) The need for asylum for the chronically mentally ill, *Schizophrenia Bulletin*, 12, 162–167.

Wasow, M. (1993) The need for asylum revisited, *Hospital and Community Psychiatry*, 44, 3, 207–209.

Weiner, H. (1985) Schizophrenia: Etiology, in H. Kaplan & B. Sadock (eds), *Comprehensive Textbook of Psychiatry*, Volume 1, 4th edition, Baltimore, Williams and Wilkins.

Weinstein R. (1979) Patient attitudes towards mental hospitalization: a review of quantitative research, *Journal of Health and Social Behaviour*, 20, 237–258.

Westbrook, M., Legge, V. & Pennay, M. (1993) Attitudes towards disabilities in a multicultural society, *Social Science and Medicine*, 36, 5, 615–623.

White, D. & Mercier, C. (1991) Reorienting mental health systems: The dynamics of policy and planning, *International Journal of Mental Health*, 19, 4, 3–24.

Whiteford, H. (1993) Australia's national mental health policy, *Hospital and Community Psychiatry*, 44, 10, 963–966.

Williams, F. (1989) *Social Policy: A Critical Introduction: Issues of Race, Gender and Class*, Cambridge, Polity Press.

Williams, J. & Luterbach, E. (1976) The changing boundaries of psychiatry in Canada, *Social Science and Medicine*, 10, 15–22.

Wilmoth, G. & Burnett, B. (1987) Receptivity and planned change: Community attitudes and deinstitutionalization, *Journal of Applied Psychology*, 72, 1, 138–145.

Windgassen, K. (1992) Treatment with neuroleptics: the patient's perspective, *Acta Psychiatrica Scandinavica*, 86, 405–411.

Wing, J.K. (1981) From institutional to community care, *Psychiatric Quarterly*, 53, 2, 137–153.

Wing, J.K. (1990) The functions of asylum, *British Journal of Psychiatry*, 157, 822–827.

Wing, J.K. & Olsen, R. (1979) Principles of the new community care, in J.K. Wing & R. Olsen (eds), *Community Care for the Mentally Disabled*, Oxford, Oxford University Press.

Wolch, J. & Evans, T. (1988) To back wards? – prospects for reinstitutionalization of the mentally disabled, in C.J. Smith & J. Giggs (eds), *Location and Stigma*, London, Unwin Hyman.

World Health Organization (1951) *Technical Report Series*, No. 31, Geneva.

World Health Organization (1953) *Third Report of the Expert Committee on Mental Health*, Technical Report Series No. 73, Geneva.

World Health Organization (1955) *Hospitalization of Mental Patients*, Geneva.

World Health Organization (1970–4) *Statistics Annual* (issued Geneva, 1974), 1970.

Yassa, R., Nair, V. & Dimitry, R. (1986) Prevalence of tardive dystonia, *Acta Psychiatrica Scandinavica*, 72, 629–633.

Zola, I. (1975) Medicine as an institution of social control, in C. Cox & A. Mead (eds), *A Sociology of Medical Practice*, London, Collier Macmillan.

Subject index

Name index